COMMON FAITH

For my parents, teachers and family

Common Faith

Education, Spirituality and the State

KEVIN MOTT-THORNTON

Routledge
Taylor & Francis Group
LONDON AND NEW YORK

First published 1998 by Ashgate Publishing

Reissued 2018 by Routledge
2 Park Square, Milton Park, Abingdon, Oxon, OX14 4RN
711 Third Avenue, New York, NY 10017

Routledge is an imprint of the Taylor & Francis Group, an informa business

A Library of Congress record exists under LC control number: 97076935

ISBN 13: 978-1-138-61590-8 (hbk)
ISBN 13: 978-1-138-61591-5 (pbk)
ISBN 13: 978-0-429-46272-6 (ebk)

Contents

Preface

It is often argued that both governments and schools should take an active interest in the spiritual and moral development of young people. This book is an attempt to show that philosophical analysis has an important part to play in the process of educational policy making in this area. It is an exploration of educational and political ideals, designed to throw light upon the logical relations between them. There are two distinct but overlapping aspects of the discussion of spiritual development as an educational aim that follows.

First, there are questions connected with the meaning of spirituality itself and the appropriateness of using such terminology in the educational context. I argue for a procedural characterisation of 'common spirituality', applicable to all, and suggest that a clear distinction should be made between this and the idea of 'spiritual development', which is inevitably linked to some particular understanding of the good life.

Second, I explore the question of whether a suitable methodology can be established for the promotion of spiritual development in schools that is consistent with the particular political perspectives that currently inform our understanding of education. In particular, I question whether any *common* approach to spiritual development, based upon normative or descriptive ideas about the nature of the national culture, can be either educationally adequate or politically acceptable. Allied to this, is an exploration of the ways in which a programme of spiritual development might be organised on a national basis while avoiding these problems. There I challenge both the communitarian and popular liberal approaches to personal education, and argue in favour of one which nurtures, rather than promotes, pluralism.

This book is the fruit of my three years of part-time research with the University of London Institute of Education. I would like to acknowledge the help that I received from my doctoral supervisors, Graham Haydon and Michael Totterdell. Thanks are also due to Terry McLaughlin, of the University of Cambridge, and Andrew Wright, of Kings College, London, who examined the original thesis in May 1997.

Many others had the good grace to read and comment upon one or more of the seminar papers that I produced on the way to the completion of this work. Among those I am particularly grateful to the following for their interest, encouragement and criticism: David Carr, Paul Hirst, Stephen Mulhall, Mike Newby, John White and Patricia White.

I would also like to acknowledge the support of generations of colleagues and pupils at Mulberry School in Tower Hamlets, where I had the good fortune work for twelve years.

In addition, I would like to express my gratitude to the St.Gabriel's Trust and the Philosophy of Education Society of Great Britain for the financial support that was given to aid my research.

Without doubt the greatest thanks are due to my wife Diana and my daughter Eva for their continued support and tolerance of this venture.

1 Introduction

The notion of spiritual development has been an explicit and intrinsic part of the legislative framework of education in England and Wales since 1944. To my knowledge there have been three main attempts by governments or their national representatives to set out in some detail the meaning of the word 'spiritual' in the context of state education. Its use in the legislation implies the belief that there is a dimension or aspect of state education connected with personal development and the promotion of values but not exhaustively characterised by either. It is a term which is able to cover religious development without being exclusively associated with any particular religion or with religion as such.

The use of the word 'spiritual' in an educational setting has always had a political dimension, reflecting certain beliefs about what values the state can legitimately use its powers to promote through state schools, as well as embodying certain beliefs about the pluralist nature of modern Britain. The term has been recognised by as a way of establishing a professional and political consensus on the teaching of controversial matters against a background of cultural and religious diversity in post-war Britain. It is the semantic breadth of the word 'spiritual' that made it particularly suitable and preferable to the word 'religious' in the context of an educational consensus regarding the appropriateness of what might be called a 'liberal' approach to the promotion of values in state schools and in the face of growing cultural and religious diversity. In what follows I shall assume that the concept of spiritual development, as used in an educational context, was intended to have just this kind of political dimension. I have no space to defend this assumption but would refer the reader to a helpful discussion of these historical matters in an article by Jack Priestley. [1]

Given all of this, any adequate discussion of the attempt to introduce a policy on spiritual development as one of the aims of a particular school or of the education system as a whole will require consideration of at least three related sets of questions. Firstly, there are questions connected with the *meaning* of the word 'spiritual' and its appropriateness within an educational context. Secondly, there is the question of whether a suitable approach can be established for the *development* of spirituality that is consistent with the particular political perspectives which inform our understanding of state schooling in Britain. Following from that there will be the question of whether the political perspectives that currently inform the deliberations of educational policymakers are, in fact, suitable. It is my intention to explore all of these questions.

I am engaged in this book upon an exercise in the *practical* philosophy of education and consequently my aim will be to explore certain ideas and policy ideals, throwing light on the logical relations between them. It will hopefully offer an analysis that should be helpful to those responsible for guiding schools in the task of implementing school policies in the area of moral and spiritual development.[2] While particular reference will be made to the British context the implications of the analysis offered here could be applied to any school in any education system.

I will explore the prospects for a number of approaches to the development of spirituality and ask whether they could provide the basis for a common conception of educational development in line with that envisaged by John Dewey in his influential book 'A Common Faith'. The question of *how* the spiritual education should be organised nationally is also addressed, and questions about *who* precisely should be responsible for devising the exact nature of policies on personal development are linked with questions of a political nature. Here again I will be content to set out the logical parameters and to show that the assumptions which animate much thinking about the promotion of values in education are, at the very least, questionable.

In line with communitarian thinking, I argue that all education embodies the promotion of particular substantive values and that even those values thought wholly procedural by liberal educationalists (e.g. autonomy) are in fact substantive values that cannot be given a purely rational justification in the setting of a pluralist society. Any notion of spiritual development will, on this view, embody a substantive developmental ideal which in turn rests logically upon some notion of the human good which is exclusive and non-pluralist in its educational implications. Paradoxically this will even include developmental ideals that are *pluralist*, since they would self evidently rule out the development of personal characteristics based upon a particular conception of the good.

However, having taken the implications of pluralism thus far and to the very heart of the meaning of spiritual *development*, I do not agree with the view, held by some communitarians, that it is therefore *impossible* to characterise the meaning of 'spirituality', for educational purposes, in a way that is free of any *particular* substantive conception of spiritual development.[3] In the second main section of chapter two, I examine David Carr's attempt to use an analysis of the grammar of the word 'spiritual' to develop a distinctive and educationally authoritative conception of spiritual development. I question the assumption that common usage can be taken as authoritative, in this respect, *and* also show that the particular conception that he favours is not, *in any case*, supported by the logic of common usage.

Chapter three begins with an examination and criticism of John Dewey's attempt, in his book A Common Faith, to outline a concept of 'the religious' that can, in principle, be separated from the beliefs of traditional religion. It is argued that, while it provides a promising basis for the development of a non-evaluative account of spirituality, it is based, as it stands, upon scientism and fails to take account of the historical and traditional dimension of all human experience. In the central sections, several aspects of the accounts of human agency offered by MacIntyre and Taylor are also examined and rejected. It is argued that a conception of narrative unity is *not* an essential aspect of the logic of human action and that the ability to *articulate* one's conception of the good is also not a condition of agency. Taylor's view that socially constructed frameworks of evaluation are logically inescapable aspects of any attempt by individuals to orient themselves towards the good is examined and shown to be groundless. In the final part of that chapter the positive account of common spirituality which emerges from the preceding discussion and which will provide the basis for discussion of the educational issues, is outlined.

The claim that procedural values[4] utilised in the context of education do in fact have substantive implications for the personal development of children forms the basis of several critical communitarian discussions of the 'liberal' approach to education. The more sophisticated among such critiques of liberal education rest upon strong advocacy of the view that in the post modern setting the neutral rational underpinning that it requires is no longer available.[5] Even so, it might be argued that the state, in this particular cultural setting, has a duty either to promote liberal, democratic or pluralist values or that it is, at least, justified in discounting any substantive double effects of its educational policies. Ironically, such an inherently liberal or pluralist view could be based upon strongly communitarian arguments alluding to the fact that school children will have to live out their lives in a particular society saturated in these values and that schools have a duty to support them in this. This is precisely the kind of view which is explicit in the autonomy-promoting communitarian liberalism of Joseph Raz and the political liberalism of John Rawls. Their non-universalist liberal frameworks are quite capable of accommodating a moderate version of the post-modern perspective. It might be argued that liberalism and its culture of autonomy (Raz) or democracy (Rawls) form just one tradition among others and as such is unable to justify its superiority on *purely* rational grounds, but if it can be shown that liberalism is *the* particular tradition which informs a particular culture then there are historical and contingent grounds for a rational argument to the effect that its substantive values should be actively promoted. This 'perfectionist' liberal response to the communitarian challenge gives renewed relevance, in the British educational context, to the very interesting question of the nature of British society or of the British polity. Cultural analysis of this kind has been adopted, as a starting point, by a number of writers in order to support views about the kinds of values that ought to be promoted in state schools.

I take up these issues in chapter four which is something of an overture to all that follows since a number of the issues raised there are explored in full in the chapters that follow. Each of the writers featured in chapter four, John Haldane, Mike Newby, John White and Stephen Macedo, make recommendations for educational policy that rely significantly upon claims about national or political culture. In exploring their use of cultural references, I will identify the structural similarities in approach that appear to unite 'liberal' and 'communitarian' writers and which, arguably, dominate educational theorising in general. I link these similarities to a political perspective which I characterise in detail and dub 'social democratic liberalism'. All these writers have significant things to say about *religion* and, in discussing their views, I identify two versions of 'secularism', one based upon a commitment to impartiality and another which is hostile to some forms of religion when used uncritically to formulate educational policy.

In chapter five, after exposing, through a series of detailed arguments, the tensions that appear to exist between the justificatory apparatus of Rawls' political liberalism and the types of civic education that are alleged, by Rawls and others, to follow from it, I move on to examine the educational implications of a perfectionist liberalism,[6] built around a substantive commitment to the value of autonomy. In the final sections I attempt to outline some of the paradoxical educational implications of a commitment to the development of complex autonomy and its links with the concepts of transcendence and spirituality.

In the first part of chapter six, I attempt to show that any educational approach to spiritual development will have to involve some particular evaluative developmental ideal. This will involve some adherence to a specific notion of human well-being. In order to aid the process of policymaking, and to show the logical implications of taking up a range of policy positions, I put forward a framework for mapping developmental ideals. In the final section, I use the framework to discuss the prospects for two currently popular approaches to spiritual development. I show that, viewed from within a liberal political framework, the promise of these approaches is more apparent than real.

Chapter seven begins with a demonstration of the incompatibility between a commitment to common schooling and the development of autonomy, since the latter requires, as a primary educational aim, the formation of persons into a particular cultural tradition. Kekes' criticism of liberalism from a pluralist perspective is explored in the following section and his apparent commitment to an educational programme, having as its central aim the development of *pluralism*, is exposed as somewhat inconsistent. This discussion leads on to the proposal of three normative models of pluralism the third of which, 'civic pluralism', is then related to the approach of the conservative political tradition. In the final section an alternative model of the organisation of personal development within the state system is proposed, and linked to the conservative or civic pluralist political perspective. It involves significantly, the rejection of the ideal of common state schooling and is therefore compatible also with the liberal commitment to the development of autonomy.

The advocacy of pluralism, which emerges in chapter seven, reflects at base my adherence to anti-rationalism. Rationalism is a central aspect of the modernist and enlightenment projects[7] which have animated much thinking about public policy. It is an intellectual culture described most convincingly by Michael Oakeshott.[8] It is the view that it is *reason* which animates practice and that reason manifests itself in public policy by the universal application of a set of rationally defensible principles. It is rationalism which underpins the most popular form of liberalism, that of social democratic liberalism. This liberalism is progressive in that it regards the increasing rationalisation of public policy as an essential aspect of the *good society*. Such thinking will inevitably lead towards the centralisation of policy at a national level.[9]

If there is an underlying thesis to be found within these pages, it is brought out by the reference in my title to John Dewey's interesting and influential book 'A Common Faith'. That work embodies a vision fundamental to the educational programme of social democratic liberalism. It is based upon a commitment to a common conception of personal development and the acceptance of a particular set of values on a national basis. In this thesis I hope to have provided the conceptual apparatus that might enable that view, especially as applied to spiritual development, to be explored and questioned. My contention is that *any* common conception thus conceived would at best be inadequate and, at worst, compromise the deep political assumptions that made it look attractive in the first place.

This is a very wide ranging study which raises a number of issues that could form the basis of a future research agenda which might be outlined briefly as follows:

1. I have attempted here to suggest a connection between a liberal approach to education and a number of philosophical positions. The connections which I have put forward, for example between liberalism and critical

realism, require further examination. In addition this study raises important issues about the organisational implications of a commitment to the development of autonomy and raises questions about the nature of autonomy itself both of which might form the basis of future work. My discussion[10] raises important questions about the overall coherence of regarding autonomy itself as an *overriding* educational aim.

2. Clearly this study raises the key issue of the extent to which commonality of personal education is an essential prerequisite of social cohesion. The various organisational models set out here will provide the basis for further discussion of this crucial issue. At present it is largely *assumptions* about all of this which separate the main political perspectives that underpin rival approaches to educational policy. Comparative work might be carried out to investigate the workability of the organisational arrangements which I propose towards the end of my study and to throw some empirical light upon its advantages and disadvantages. In particular, it might be asked whether the minimalist and non-rationalist model of state involvement in this area of educational policy, is compatible with the safeguarding of the legitimate interests of children and society.

3. I propose a characterisation of common spirituality which I regard, on the basis of experience and speculation, as an essential aspect of future policy. There is scope for future investigation of the *adequacy and impartiality* of my particular characterisation[11] and for empirical work on the question of its usefulness and workability within particular educational institutions.

Notes

---

[1] Priestley (1985). See also Gilliat (1996) for further evidence of the centrality of the language of 'spirituality' to the formulation of education policy since 1944.

[2] It will also be relevant to those concerned with developing policies on personal and social development, even where no direct reference to spirituality is made. My reasons for saying this will become very clear in due course.

[3] While I accept the view expressed recently by David Carr (1996), that we should take a 'rival traditions' approach to spiritual education, I do not think that we are forced to adopt such an approach simply because we cannot extract the language of the spiritual from its place in any particular spiritual tradition. My preference for the rival traditions conception of spiritual education emanates from political considerations that will emerge later.

[4] Values to which all are compelled to agree in order that their own diverse preferred traditions of substantive value might be protected and practised. The democratic political culture that operates in most western societies might be defended in this way as a procedural political culture to which a diverse range of

people should agree since it protects their own treasured values from the influence of the most powerful in society.

5 A view now accepted even by former leading exponents of the foundationalist approach based upon rational deliberation. See Hirst (1993).

6 That is, one which advocates state intervention in order to promote or reflect the cultural values of a particular society. Anti-perfectionist liberals, on the other hand, say that it is a defining characteristic of the liberal state to remain scrupulously impartial with respect to substantive cultural values, in intention if not in outcome.

7 For a fuller characterisation see MacIntyre (1981), chapters 4 and 5.

8 See his essay 'Rationalism in Politics' in Oakeshott (1962).

9 Or at the highest possible level.

10 At the end of chapter five and the beginning of chapter seven.

11 Given at the end of chapter three.

2 Spirituality, Religion and Education

Summary

In the first section I discuss Terry McLaughlin's account of the political dimension to any account of personal development and the problems which are thrown up for the proponents of what he calls a 'liberal democratic' approach. I examine several assumptions which underlie his account and suggest that these raise further questions of a political nature that point beyond the two rival frameworks of liberal democracy and communitarianism that he considers.

In the second main section I examine David Carr's attempt to use common usage of the terminology of spirituality to develop a distinctive and educationally authoritative account of spiritual development. I question the assumption that common usage can be used as authoritative and show that the particular conception that he favours cannot, in any case, be supported by the language of spirituality in common use.

In the next section I look at John White's critique of recent guidance on spiritual development given by the agency responsible for the inspection schools in England and Wales. I argue that his account assumes too close a relationship between a liberal approach to policy and secular humanism and is characterised by an unsympathetic over interpretation of the text. In addition, I note that both he and David Carr share the view that where the language of transcendence is used it betrays a necessary commitment to a religious perspective.

Finally, I set out reasons for attempting to find a common, non-evaluative conception of spirituality to underpin any educational account of spiritual development.

2.1 The political dimension and the spiritual dimension

When attempting to give the notion of spirituality some specific meaning so that the question of its educational suitability can be explored, it is very easy to start to beg significant questions at the outset. It is this aspect of theorising about spiritual education that makes it a complex challenge. It is likely that only those with some sympathy for the philosophical approach will be able to tolerate the degree of critical uncertainty that a satisfactory and impartial discussion of the topic will require, especially in its early stages.

In particular, we will be faced early on with questions about the very nature and aims of education. Those questions, in turn, will inevitably be informed by particular views about the nature of the state and its relationship to the education system. That will bring in issues of political philosophy. And, adding an important dimension to this complex picture, are issues about whether one's assumptions in these areas are about what is *actually* the case or whether they embody an ideal view of how, according to some alternative conception, things *ought* to be. These empirical and prescriptive assumptions will themselves rest upon structures of supposed justification and *all* of that might have an indirect effect on the proposed conception of spiritual education.

It would, of course, be quite impossible to hold this entire picture in view at each stage. It is, however, very important that the presence of this bigger picture is clearly on the horizon when any particular aspect of the topic is being discussed. In this chapter, my aim will be to try to get some idea of what a suitable or appropriate spiritual education might be about, while flagging up a number of issues that will be explored in some depth at a later stage. I will do this by looking critically at recent philosophical discussions of the issue of spiritual development that have arisen in response to recent government initiatives in Britain and the publication of official guidance in this area.

In a recent discussion of spiritual education, Terry McLaughlin[1] takes up the fairly obvious and uncontroversial link that would appear to exist between talk of spiritual education and that of the education of the 'whole child'. Spiritual education will relate to those aspects of the curriculum which will touch upon and significantly influence the development of the child not just as a thinking being but also as a person. For McLaughlin this raises important issues about the very possibility of such a conception of education within the setting of what he calls the 'common school'.[2] In McLaughlin's view, these issues follow from a commitment to a set of political values which he describes as the 'liberal democratic perspective' and which underpin our educational attitudes. From this perspective any attempt by the common school to operate a programme of spiritual development along the lines of a particular substantive conception of the spiritual would run into problems of legitimacy, since the kinds of values offered by such schools, because of their constitution as 'common' is bound to be one that is based upon a society wide consensus and some collective notion of the common good. He goes on to claim that while such agreement *is possible* it will not produce anything substantial enough to adequately support the programme of active personal formation that a commitment to spiritual education would require. This is because our society contains a wide range of people holding widely differing views about what constitutes the good life. Spiritual education would require an holistic perspective and that is not something about which a consensus exists in our society. McLaughlin suggests that it is part of the liberal democratic perspective to assume that

> ...there is no objectively conclusive way of determining which,if any, of these 'holistic' views of life- or 'thick' theories of the good- is correct.. Therefore such thick views cannot be permitted to impose their particular vision on all citizens in the public domain [3]

Schools, on this view, are part of the 'public domain' and are therefore required to be suitably restrained in their imposition of particular values. The values which they can impart will have to be justified in terms of the *common* good[4] *or* they will have to be a requirement of *any* conception of personal education, as such. McLaughlin uses a legal illustration to make this point.

> For example, from the point of view of some 'thick' theories of the good, re-marriage after divorce is morally unacceptable, since, because marriage is morally indissoluble and divorce has only legal and not moral force, the couple in question are living in a state of permanent adultery .[5]

He goes on to say that such a view could not be imposed on all citizens, through the civil law on divorce, since such a view could not be objectively justified to the satisfaction of all. At least on

McLaughlin's account of the liberal democratic perspective, the notion of consensus and commonality about the objectivity of certain values is of paramount importance for the governance of life in the 'public' domain.

Certain important and pertinent assumptions are present in McLaughlin's account which are not, there at least, brought into focus. While throwing light on the assumptions *which follow* from the liberal democratic perspective, he presents it as a fairly homogeneous entity with clear educational implications. The first main assumption that is embodied in his comparison between the constraints on common schools and the constraints on the construction of civil law is that the state school is required to be a 'common school'. Just as the law must apply to all within its jurisdiction, so must the conception of educational provision be common to all who are educated by the state. This may well reflect the present understanding of the character of the state school and, as such, be in line with the status quo but a thorough going exploration of this area should reflect the fact that a different organisational perspective is at least possible, desirable and may even be necessary in order to accommodate the inclusion of spiritual development in state schools.

The second, and connected, presupposition is that the common school is primarily to be regard as part of the *public* domain but one over which certain parents may exert a moral right of veto. Elsewhere, he says

> Whilst..thick theories cannot form the basis of common schooling, they can underpin forms of distinctive schooling chosen by parents as part of the exercise of their moral rights over their children's upbringing and education [6]

At this point another very important issue lies just beneath the surface of discussion. Even if parents do have certain moral rights over the upbringing of their children as evidenced by the fact that some parents may choose an alternative education from that based on common or public values, is it necessary to claim that state schools *have* to be seen, even from the liberal democratic perspective, as part of the *public* domain and therefore as inevitably constrained in the ways that McLaughlin suggests? In view of the fact that he does recognise that parents may exercise their moral rights over their children's upbringing and education and this is not in violation of the liberal democratic perspective, it seems rather odd that this question is not raised. If the existence of state funded religious schools illustrates the fact that some state schools are not presently required to see themselves as part of the public domain but rather as somewhat publicly constrained extensions of the domain of family life, then one might expect some explanation as to why most state schools *have* to be regarded differently.[7] I will take this issue up in greater detail later on in the study and ask whether, even from the liberal perspective, it is necessary to regard schools as *primarily* part of the public domain and therefore constrained, by political or organisational considerations, to disavow thick theories of the good.[8]

Elsewhere in the same discussion, he briefly describes an alternative conception of the educational project known as 'communitarianism'. It is a conception of the character of the political process which embodies a picture of the state education system quite different to that of liberal democracy and one which is ostensibly much better able to accommodate the 'thick' theories of the good that might underpin any holistic conception of spiritual education. The communitarian views the separation of the domains of the 'public' and the 'private', a central aspect of liberalism, with suspicion. It is alleged that liberalism operates with an attenuated and individualistic view of human persons which fails to recognise the necessity of the strong public maintenance of a particular social fabric embodying some quite specific set of values. Traditionally, it is alleged, liberalism has both failed to see the historical and cultural contingency of its own assumptions and values. Its exponents have tended, for ideological rather than empirical reasons, to overplay the plurality and incommensurability of views within society and thereby to undermine the apparent prospect of producing rational grounds for the public promotion of substantive values. But, communitarians allege, this does not in fact prevent a very particular set of values from being promoted in the public domain in the name of liberal restraint and an important aspect of that value system is a subjectivist view of values and the promotion of a divisive individualism.[9]

From the communitarian perspective then the state has, in McLaughlin's words, a responsibility for the 'moral ecology' that exists within society and this has strong implications for spiritual education since it is but a short step from this to the idea that the state school should also take some responsibility for, and account of, the 'spiritual ecology' of society when formulating its educational programme. A programme conceived along these communitarian lines will embody a 'thick' theory of the good. And it is a part of the communitarian attack upon liberal education that it, on the one hand, is blind to its own assumptions and, on the other, that it promotes substantive values of a *liberal* kind. In attempting scrupulously to promote only procedural values, designed to promote the common good, liberal state schools are in fact, on the communitarian view, effectively promoting the values of a substantive or comprehensive liberalism without justification.

2.2 Distinctiveness, consensus and language

Just this kind of communitarian perspective is the evident backdrop to David Carr's recent discussion of spiritual education.[10] His communitarianism is wholly implicit in this particular paper, though he has set out explicitly his commitment to communitarianism in other papers bearing more directly on moral education. Firm evidence of his perspective is given by the fact that his discussion includes no reference to the kinds of worries about the prospect of developing pupils in accordance with particular substantive theories of the good that raise concerns for Terry McLaughlin, who operates from out of a liberal democratic political framework. The issues of legitimacy regarding the possibility of the common school taking responsibility for the substantive personal development of pupils, that figure large in liberal discussions, don't figure at all in Carr's discussion.

This is plainly evident in the following quotation from the concluding paragraph of his paper,

> ..if in the interests of discerning a distinctive and coherent conception of the enterprise in question, we construe spiritual education as primarily concerned with the pursuit of spiritual knowledge, the grasp of spiritual truths and the cultivation of spiritual dispositions, then this is a matter which can only be addressed adequately by those parts of the school curriculum which are directly concerned with the explication of such truths and dispositions and ...this must mean religion and the arts more than mathematics or home economics.[11]

As this suggests, the main burden of his discussion is to try to map out a coherent conception of spirituality distinct from other aspects of educational provision like, for example, the area of the moral. Carr's discussion of the meaning as well as delivery of spiritual education embodies certain methodological assumptions, quite apart from those mentioned above, arising from his communitarian perspective. I would like to spend some time exposing these assumptions and raising them rather to the status of issues for further discussion.

In the first part of his discussion he sets out his reasons for refusing to try to come up with an exact definition of spirituality but he does think that the subject requires a clearer characterisation as a prelude to effective implementation, going well beyond what he calls the 'scattershot' approach of the National Curriculum Council discussion paper, which also eschews an exact definition of the spiritual in favour of a very broad characterisation of the following kind,

> The term needs to be seen as applying to something fundamental in the human condition which is not necessarily experienced through the physical senses and/or expressed through everyday language. It has to do with relationships with other people and, for believers, with God. It has to do with the universal search for individual identity-with our responses to challenging experiences, such as death, suffering, beauty and encounters with good and evil. It is to do with the search for meaning and purpose in life and for values by which to live.

The following aspects of spiritual development are then listed:

-Beliefs
-A sense of awe, wonder and mystery
-Experiencing feelings of transcendence
-Search for meaning and purpose
-Self-knowledge
-Relationships
-Creativity
-Feelings and emotions [12]

It is worth speculating that those who constructed this broad characterisation of the domain of the spiritual took themselves to be working under just those political constraints that McLaughlin called the liberal democratic perspective. Feeling that it would be wrong for the state to attempt to impose upon schools a particular thick theory of the good, they attempted to come up with something which might be capable of incorporating the full range of views on such issues, including both the religious and non-religious. It is likely that those who constructed this characterisation wished to avoid anything *distinctive* since such distinctiveness would generate unwanted controversy. Carr, looking at the situation from the communitarian perspective, feels that distinctiveness is unavoidable and that scope exists for developing a characterisation of the spiritual which is legitimised by the *language* of the 'spiritual' as it is found in common usage. He is inclined to look for a tighter characterisation of the logic of the spiritual based on authoritative sources of meaning embodied within our common language.

While Carr sees a distinctive conception of the spiritual as essential, he feels that an attempt to provide a *definition* would be '*..an extremely unpromising strategy to adopt*'. This interesting assumption demonstrates that he regards educational policy making in this area as, in part, dependent upon the search for the authoritative sources of *meaning*, which for him, lie within the logic of the common usage of the terminology. But this is an assumption that betrays a communitarian strategy for circumventing just the same kinds of problems which led those who constructed the NCC characterisation to go for a scattershot approach.[13] For, it might be thought, if we can extract a distinctive and partial account of the 'spiritual' from language itself through deft logical analysis of common usage, then we might hope that our account has the authority over all in society enjoyed by language itself. This may give rise to an account of the spiritual that displeases some people but which has greater authority than that even of political or educational policy makers, but of society itself. The distinctive account that might be produced by this method would arguably be appropriate to the common school, not because it is impartial but because it is a by product of our *common* social engagement. Further on I will examine the legitimacy of this strategy and the validity of Carr's analysis of the logic of the term 'spiritual'.

Carr is quite correct to suggest that attempts to *define* key concepts linked to traditional philosophical discussions have become unfashionable with the onset of functionalist theories of meaning, and particularly that of the later Wittgenstein. One could also agree that it is unwise to search for the definitive account of spirituality, particularly given the multiplicity of often incompatible uses of the word. It would be unwise to tie oneself down in this way were one merely engaged in a philosophical exploration of the word. One can agree with this overall policy in general philosophical disputes, like those, for example, about the nature of knowledge and of spirituality in that context. That does not, however, mean that one is thereby required to subscribe to the view that a definition of spirituality would be unwise in this particular *educational* context. To assume this much from the outset requires additional justification beyond a reference to currently fashionable philosophical wisdom. I will take up this issue in more detail later but, in order to show that there is some justification for keeping a more open mind on this issue, it is worth considering the contrast between the traditional philosophical disputes to which Carr refers and the educational context which presents itself in discussions of spiritual *education*, where philosophers are in the business of offering advice to policy makers who may have little or no interest in how well the characterisation which they put in place lines up with common usage and may wish for a characterisation which can be used to *determine* usage within the education system rather than to *reflect* the variety of usage outside it.

If we reject Carr's assumption that policy makers should defer, on communitarian grounds, to common usage when attempting to develop a distinctive account of spirituality, and if it can be shown that some measure of *stipulation* by policy makers is inevitable in this area, then it may be unwise to somehow undermine the practical and theoretical benefits of seeking a definition at the outset as Carr suggests. As long as such a procedure does not purport to have produced a definition which is somehow *definitive* for *all* contexts of use, then I can't see how such a particularistic definition could contravene even the anti-univeralism of current philosophical wisdom. And the view that it is unwise *in all contexts* to set out to produce a definition looks very much like the kind of *universal* claim that current philosophical wisdom would require us to avoid.

The sources of common meaning, embodied in the logic of common usage, provide the basis upon which Carr can assert in the last paragraph of his paper that '*..spiritual education has a special, indeed intrinsic, connection with some realms of knowledge more than others*'[14] As we have already seen, from one perspective at least it just will not do at all, within the context of the state education system, to make what McLaughlin calls a particular 'thick' theory of the good one's exclusive source for a conception of spiritual education. But even from within the kind of communitarian perspective that Carr himself adopts, it is possible and, one would think, advisable to offer some justification for the sources which one uses in order to characterise what spiritual development might mean within state schools. In particular, it would seem to be obligatory, given the particularistic and historically contingent nature of the communitarian perspective to give some indication of the constituency over which their favoured substantive conception of the good is to range. Is it, for example, intended to range over the national community or over a particular school community? In addition, one would expect some explicit justification of the origins of the sources which feed their educational thinking. And it has to be said that in the course of an otherwise able, coherent and most helpful exposition, Carr doesn't make explicit reference to any of this. One can only *assume* that his discussion is intended to range over the whole of the education system rather than to one particular constituency within it since he begins his discussion by offering some comments on the statements on spirituality offered by the *National* Curriculum Council.

In setting out his favoured conception, Carr uses a number of quite specific sources which include, from within the tradition of Western philosophy, Plato and Aristotle. One could ask, for example, why a much more recent and perhaps more culturally influential account by Hegel[15] was omitted from the analysis. He also refers explicitly and extensively to the Christian religion in order to discern the logic of spirituality and to reach his particular conclusions about the delivery of spiritual education.

A further methodological issue follows from this. *Even if* Carr is correct in his choice of sources and even if they characterise exactly the logic of spirituality within common English usage, that does not *automatically* mean that this logic, emanating from the way in which the term has and may in fact be commonly used, *must therefore* also inform its use within an educational context. To say this would be implicitly to advocate the kind of conceptual universalism which he gave as the grounds for avoiding the search for an educational *definition* of the term 'spiritual'. If the use of the term within an educational context had no resemblance to its ordinary use then that would be very odd, but that does not mean automatically that its logic within the educational context should mirror *in every respect* that which it has in common usage. The view that it should indeed have such a 'mirror' logic itself requires further philosophical or educational justification not provided or alluded to in Carr's account.

In introducing his detailed discussion of the term 'spiritual' Carr suggests that we need to distinguish 'significant' from 'insignificant' features of usage. He criticises John Hull[16] and the NCC document for failing in this respect because of '..an eagerness to accommodate as wide a notion of spirituality as possible'. But, having raised the need to outline a significant sense of the term, he offers only the fact that the two senses of the term which he discerns in Greek and biblical thought are *'separately specifiable'* and that they *'..exhibit interesting and important connections'*. For reasons set out above, I think that he also uses other criteria of 'significance' which are passed over without comment. Later on in this study, I will try to provide a less arbitrary support for the 'significance' of the two senses of the term chosen by Carr.

The two senses of 'spirit', which Carr takes to be significant are first identified as part of Plato's ontology, where they constitute an aspect of his dualistic ontology, and then traced through the thought of Aristotle and linked with the Judeo-Christian tradition. They are also linked etymologically in Greek and Latin with the related ideas of 'breath', 'wind' and 'air'. These ideas which had originally, within the Judeo-Christian tradition, been linked with the presence of life were by New Testament times linked with the notion of that which gives meaning, direction and purpose to human life. Notions associated with what gives life to things in general came to be associated, perhaps directly under the influence of Plato, with the

> ..anthropocentric idea that what drives and gives purpose to human life in particular are precisely motives and intentions- in short, reasons for action which are susceptible of evaluation in normative terms as true or false, right or wrong and so on.. [17]

Carr describes them in the following way:

> The first sense in which we speak of the spirit or the spiritual is that whereby something is referred to in terms of what are taken to be its identifying features or essential characteristics; in this sense the spirit of an entity distinguishes it as, or for, what it is. Thus we may speak of the spirit of the times, of an era, culture, religion or people. The second,..is that in which we speak of a particular quality of motivation- or of the lack of it- in a sense which indicates something more dispositional than identity constitutive, hence, we may speak of a horse possessing spirit or a youth lacking spirit- which..connotes a certain presence or absence of nerve or energy.[18]

Carr is concerned to remove any association between the first of the two uses of the term 'spirit' and the kind of ontological dualism that underpinned Plato's use of the term, as part of his 'tripartite' theory of the person. On the other hand, Carr wants to prevent this non-dualism from collapsing into a crude reductionism that focuses *exclusively* on physical or behavioural phenomena. He believes that Aristotle's understanding of the soul, in teleological terms of function and purpose, as set out in the De Anima, provides a framework for doing just this.

> What Aristotle indicates is the possibility that talk of spirit in either the 'essence' or 'motive' senses does not have to imply awkward philosophical dualism or any of those conceptually embarrassing notions of a ghost in the machine which have notoriously confounded the philosophies of Plato and Descartes.[19]

Having shown that talk of the spiritual does not, even in its 'essence' sense, involve unfortunate ontological implications, he moves on to what he says '..we mainly need to know in the present context..', that is to its epistemological implications for the development of human nature and personality. Carr suggests that there are two important implications of this kind, one relating to each of the two senses of the 'spirit' outlined above.

> Spirit in the first of our senses, as attributed to either a person, a culture or an era, is susceptible of more or less strong evaluation in normative terms- it can be either good or bad, positive or negative, right or wrong.

In order to support this assertion he uses a comparison between the spirit of the North American civil rights movement and the spirit of Nazi Germany. In both cases the use of the word spirit is wholly appropriate despite the fact that while we might approve of the first we regard the second as inherently evil. In the first 'essence' sense the logical relationship between the use of the term spirit and a positive evaluation is purely a matter of contingency. The second of Carr's epistemological implications is that in the 'motivational' sense of the term spirit, this link is a matter of logical necessity. He says,

> ..the possession of spirit in our second motivational sense is a positive quality..even if the ends towards which this kind of spirit may drive people are not always positive ends; ..it is simply better per se to be positively motivated, lively, energetic and resolute rather than depressed downtrodden and listless.[20]

Here it is important to note a significant but implicit acknowledgement in Carr's account of the *authority* of ordinary usage in the determination of the logic of the terms that are central to our discussion. This is indicated by the fact that the above points are tempered by such phrases as *'..we should want to say..'* and *'we are also largely inclined to hold that..'*. For the reasons set out above, the validity of this assumption is not self evident and therefore requires further justification.[21] In addition, his analysis of the logical implications of the motivational sense of the term spirit as used in such phrases as 'she really has spirit' can be questioned. Carr's claim is that the use of the term 'spirit' in this context *necessarily* implies a positive evaluation of the person. But it is only in a very narrow and untypical range of cases that the appellation of 'spiritual' to a person's motivational energy would imply a positive evaluation of the nature of those motives. I would maintain that the question of whether the evaluation is positive or negative would turn rather upon the ends to which such motivational energy were directed. What is meant by describing someone as 'positively motivated' most generally relates inherently to those *ends* rather than to *the fact* that one has energy. Even in the cases which Carr has in mind, the use of this phrase in the sense of 'she is positively motivated' connects with certain views about an ideal form of human living i.e. that it be self directed and active.

One wonders also about the validity of the original distinction once spirit in the 'essence' sense is understood in the Aristotelian, teleological terms for which David Carr states a preference. When *this* move has been made the quality of one's motivation will be an inherent aspect of one's essential nature so that evaluation of that nature will, likewise, be *contingently* related to the *ends* towards which it is directed. Carr appears to recognise this since, in the paragraph that follows he says that the two senses

> ..come together in the root notion of inspiration; to work like a man inspired is generally to be impelled positively towards the pursuit of one's enterprises and projects because one has found higher meaning or significance in them.[22]

While this shows a recognition of the fact that no hard and fast distinction exists between the logic of the 'essence' and 'motivational' senses of spirit, nothing in the analysis so far sanctions the suggestion that the use of the term 'inspiration' makes the user logically bound to a positive evaluation of the enterprises and projects which inspire the person concerned. This is a crucial consideration since Carr proceeds from here as if *that* has been established. However, this can be shown not to be the case. When I use the phrase 'He worked like a man inspired' *of someone else* then it is true that I am committed to the view that whatever the person concerned is inspired by is something which *he* evaluates positively. This 'internalist logic' of the term 'inspired', does line up with Carr's analysis, but this logic is not the only one of importance from the educational point of view. Educationalists are also, and perhaps more, interested in what might be called the 'external' logic. That is, one taking as its perspective the use of the term *by a third party*, but *free of any commitment to the validity of subject's own viewpoint*. It does not follow from Carr's analysis thus far that the user of the term 'inspired' in this context, from a third person perspective, is also necessarily committed to sharing the subject's positive evaluation of their goals and projects. The logical situation here is exactly similar to that which Carr affirms with reference to the 'spirit' of Nazi Germany, earlier on in his discussion. In that case it was said that the relationship between the use of the term 'spirit' and our positive evaluation of the goals and projects is a *contingent* one. What then could be the objection to saying that 'Hitler was inspired to kill Jews' or that 'Hitler was a charismatic person'. While there *is* a necessary connection between our using these terms and *our belief* that *for him* certain things were evaluated positively, that clearly does not commit the user, as a matter of logic, to the view that in fact the goals and projects that inspired Hitler should be evaluated positively. From the external or third party perspective the logical relationship between the use of the language of 'spirit' and a positive evaluation of the subject's goals and projects is one of contingency rather than necessity, as David Carr assumes.

That he does not see matters in this way is demonstrated by the way he spells out the educational implications of his analysis in the next few paragraphs. The tone is set by the following section where he says,

> So inspiration, we might say, has two aspects with discernible educational implications; one concerned with the conception or recognition of higher or perhaps transcendent values which are capable of motivating individuals towards the pursuit of (preferably) positive rather than negative goals; and the other concerned with the formation of dispositions to pursue those goals. [23]

It is important to notice that, firstly, Carr is dealing here with what we have called the external logic of the language of inspiration. This is demonstrated by the use of the phrase 'preferably positive' which suggests a contingent rather than necessary relationship between the elements outlined. Ironically, it might even be said to support the critical point made immediately above *against* Carr's analysis of the language of 'inspiration', since it suggests that, as he says a few lines below,

> ..people are capable of applying themselves optimistically and energetically to enterprises without any clear idea of where they are going.

Secondly, it follows from this that when he talks about the educational implications in terms of a concern for the recognition of 'higher or perhaps transcendent values' he is suggesting that those values which underpin inspiration in educational terms must be 'higher or transcendent' from the third party perspective and this is not justified by the internalist analysis which preceded it.

The logical fault lines noticed earlier widen in the paragraph which follows where Carr moves to the educational implications of the use of the terminology of spirituality. He does not distinguish between the descriptive term 'spirituality' and the process of 'spiritual development', interestingly and quite imperceptibly the faulty analysis which preceded it is given an apparent credibility. It is quite true to say that '*..spiritual development cannot be concerned with the pursuit of any old values or ideals*' since it runs against logic to suggest that someone could be said to be '*developing*' pupils according to a set of values and ideals that the speaker could not themselves evaluate positively. But the fact that Carr can make this statement, correctly, about the process of spiritual development is, in my view, entirely due to the logic of the word '*development*' and has nothing whatever to do with that of the word 'spiritual' itself, as he appears to assume.

In the following section Carr reverts back to a discussion of the educational implications of the word 'spiritual' and, in the section which follows, makes the assumption that this term now carries the full evaluative weight of 'spiritual development'. We are told that while Nazi Germany and Aleister Crowley could be said to have a 'spirit' they could not be said to be 'spiritual', since *we* could not evaluate them positively. Teachers would not want to make either Adolf Hitler or Aleister Crowley their ideal of the spiritually developed person but we are not compelled *because of that* to refrain from saying that these two people were 'spiritual' in some non-evaluative sense. Firstly, the logic of common usage does not sanction it. The word 'spiritual', like the word 'moral' can be used in at least two ways with either an evaluative or a non-evaluative meaning. It is perfectly possible to say of someone *'her moral framework is faulty'*. We are not compelled, by force of logic, to say *of someone* that they are 'not moral' just because they consistently do things which we quite rightly regard as immoral. Perhaps more easily because of its association with 'spirit' and the idea of a constitutive motivational energy, the same analysis can be given of the term 'spiritual'; we might well speak of someone as having a 'faulty spiritual framework' or of being 'inspired by the devil'. If Carr's analysis were correct then such phrases would jar with the spectre of contradiction. He does not seem to recognise these non-evaluative uses and in the case of 'spiritual', he does not see them either as legitimated by common usage or as having any educational use. I have shown that there is no justification, even in common usage, for saying that the word 'spiritual' should always be conceived as a term embodying a positive evaluation.[24]

Given the fact that the non-evaluative use of the term 'spiritual' is not ruled out by the logic of common usage, I think there are other reasons, connected with the political backdrop to this discussion, for wanting to make some educational use of this non-evaluative use of it and I will return to a fuller discussion of these at a later stage. In some contexts it is necessary to use words like 'moral' and 'spiritual' as a terms which identifies some aspect of human life in order that the process of evaluation and development can properly and appropriately be discussed prior to the formulation of policy. In a situation where little doubt exists about the existence of and the nature of those aspects, evaluative terminology would, as it were, speak for itself but in a situation, like that under discussion here, where doubt, uncertainty, controversy surround the evaluations to be made, then the non-evaluative uses have a crucial part to play the construction of a procedural consensus. David Carr rightly wishes to undermine any attempt to use a non-evaluative conception of the spiritual as a basis for some reductionist attempt to suggest that this is all spirituality in an educational setting could or should be. But this is only a danger when the logic of the 'spiritual' is confused with the logic of 'spiritual *development*'. My case for clearly delineating the non-evaluative uses of the word spiritual is that it is an essential precondition for the intrinsically evaluative developmental work to take place since only in exploring the non-evaluative conception will we be in a position to identify, for the purpose of public discussion, the educational 'ground' upon which such development might take place.

One of the preconditions for a successful evaluative use of the term 'spiritual' in an educational context is that there should be agreement amongst members of a particular educational community regarding, firstly, what talk of the spiritual is about and, secondly, about the criteria for its development. While this might well be the case within schools controlled by particular religious communities and perhaps within particular school communities, without such affiliation, it does not seem to me to be wise to start off by assuming that this precondition is fulfilled within say the wider sphere of the educational community of England and Wales. Given that there may be good reasons for assuming that different individuals and groups within the aegis of the nation-wide initiative on spiritual development disagree markedly, it does not seem very wise *to start* a discussion of the area by looking for something *evaluatively laden* solely in the interests of outlining something which is *distinctive*. David Carr however, does not proceed in this way, perhaps because he disagrees with my tentative outline of the national educational context, regarding it as less plural than it might at first appear.[25]

In the following section, in the interests of further conceptual distinctiveness, Carr hones the notion of the spiritual to be even more exclusive and attempts to establish logical links between it and a transcendent perspective, characterised along traditional religious lines. In discussing Marxism and humanism, Carr shows that while, for him, a positive moral evaluation is *necessary* for a set of ideals to be regarded as spiritual, it is not *sufficient*, at least according to the dictates of ordinary usage. His ensuing discussion shows that two further conditions have to be fulfilled. In the first place he tries to establish a necessary logical link between 'spiritual' and 'transcendence'. He says

> ..spiritual values and the dispositions they entail are none the less focused upon those aspects of human experience which look beyond the material and mundane towards what is immutable, eternal, infinite, invisible and immortal....but however morally noble or well meant Marxist or humanist beliefs are....they cannot be regarded as spiritual because-in concentrating exclusively on the things which pass away rather than the word of God which endureth forever- they are not focused on transcendent or spiritual experiences in any relevant sense.[26]

Carr's further discussion of Aleister Crowley suggests that not only do values and dispositions have to be oriented towards a transcendent dimension but they have also to be based upon claims about that dimension which are *true*. This latter claim does seem to confirm that, at this stage in the discussion we must interpret Carr's claims about spirituality as claims about spiritual development. He is not just making a point about the logic of spiritual development but making a claim about the particular developmental *ideals* which we should, in an educational context, build-in to any policy on spiritual development. In doing this he has moved beyond the logic of common usage to what might be described as the *epistemology* of common usage. But, while it is clear that the logic of spiritual development demands that we require a concrete notion of what is true and false, it is not clear *whose epistemology* educationalists ought to be using in this way to determine *which values* and dispositions are spiritual, in Carr's normative sense.

For Carr these questions don't seem to arise, presumably because he feels that at some level *we do*, in the education system, *have* a common epistemology. Consequently, he is so confident about this that he doesn't find it necessary, here at least, to offer any hint of justification for that view. However, the view that there exists, on anything like a national scale, a *common* epistemology, of the kind that this seems to require, is highly questionable.[27] If a more restricted claim is being made for the scope of the epistemological commonality that he presupposes then some indication should be given of its range so that this *empirical* claim can be judged on its merits. In the next chapter we will look at the similar views of another communitarian writer, John Haldane who explicitly makes and attempts to justify such claims on a national scale in cultural and historical terms. For the moment I would just summarise what I take to be the conclusions of my discussion of David Carr's claim that educationalists are required, on philosophical grounds, to work with an evaluative notion of the spiritual which can be shown to be based upon true claims about a transcendental dimension of life, conceived along religious lines. Firstly, there is no *logical* requirement underpinning this claim or, at least, one has not yet been demonstrated. The philosophical argument for such a claim is based, perhaps indirectly, upon empirical claims of a social and cultural nature and, in addition, upon normative arguments which presuppose a particular approach to the *political* philosophy of education.[28] The case against Carr's analysis is just that he has certainly not made out a satisfactory case for the conception of spiritual education that he has outlined.

It is worth stressing here that my argument against Carr does not in any way rest upon the view that moral and spiritual values are not objective. While I have emphasised the importance of what I have called the logic of the internalist perspective, my analysis is not tied to the view that this logic is the *only* logic for spiritual and moral values. My questioning of Carr's alleged assumption that there exists a philosophically significant epistemological commonality within the educational community does not rest on the grounds that moral and spiritual claims are *intrinsically controversial* owing to their subjective nature. This will become very clear as the discussion moves on but for the moment I will say that if such a claim could be made against the arguments put forward here then they would be fatally inconsistent with the overall tenor of the later discussion, underpinned as it is by a strongly objectivist approach to values.

2.3 Ofsted, signals of transcendence and religion

I want now to move on to look at one further philosophical discussion of the nature of spiritual education. This will give us the opportunity in the closing section of this chapter to bring other 'official' views of spiritual education into critical focus and to set the stage for the more positive discussion of the relationship between spirituality, religion and the idea of transcendence, in the chapters that follow.

David Carr is inclined to say that the account of spiritual education outlined in the recent National Curriculum Council discussion document lacks a clear conception of spirituality. He is inclined to think it too accommodating of a very broad range of views to the point where it appears to presuppose that anything value-driven is spiritual. John White, however, says of the outline of inspection criteria for spiritual development contained in various documents published by the Office for Standards in Education (Ofsted)[29] that they embody a very clear and distinctive conception- and one which ironically looks very much like that recommended in the final stages of Carr's discussion. OFSTED's Framework for Inspection has the following definition:

> Spiritual development relates to that aspect of inner life through which pupils acquire insights into their personal experience which are of enduring worth. It is characterised by reflection, the attribution of

> meaning to experience, valuing a non-material dimension to life and intimations of an enduring reality. 'Spiritual' is not synonymous with 'religious'; all areas of the curriculum may contribute to pupils' spiritual development.[30]

It might be thought that any attempt to transfer the word into an educational context, particularly that of state education, would require an excessively stipulative redefinition of the word, effectively depriving it of all real meaning. But the fact that the use of a word by government doesn't line up completely with ordinary usage is not grounds alone for saying that it is inappropriate especially if, as I will argue later, there are other grounds for preferring it to its rivals. There is nothing intrinsically wrong with a stipulative definition as long as it is clear. And although getting clear about what 'spirituality' actually means is no easy task, the same problems face anyone wishing to use rival terms, like 'personal' or 'ethical'.[31]

If one thing is made very clear in all the advice about spiritual development that has been issued by the British government and its agencies it is that, in the context of state education, spiritual development does not mean the same as religious development.[32] There are those, however, who continue to allege that the very use of the word 'spiritual' by government agencies shows that religious development *is* intended.

John White's discussion of the Ofsted document on spiritual development, 'Instead of Ofsted'[33] says that

> There is..a place for what might be called 'the spiritual' in education, but it should be all but uncoupled from religion.

He goes on to give a brief characterisation of his own very secular humanist understanding of what the term might mean. It is perhaps because of its contestable nature that he prefers alternative characterisations. While he certainly recognises that the Ofsted document does decouple spirituality from religion, he is not keen on the use of the overall term 'spiritual development' because he is suspicious of certain things said by Ofsted in their attempt to characterise it.

He finds those aspects of the Ofsted characterisation which encourage 'reflective self-understanding' acceptable but not phrases like *'valuing a non-material dimension to life'* and *'the attribution of meaning to experience'*. The latter, allegedly implies that *'..our lives have a meaning or purpose beyond themselves'* and he claims that this *'..introduces a religious assumption which not all would accept'.* He is unhappy with the former phrase since it might imply the religious thought that *'we are, or have, souls as well as bodies'.* He goes on to comment on the connection between spirituality and 'intimations of an enduring reality' saying that this

> ..might refer, unrevealingly, to a belief that things like trees, rocks, rivers, planets and stars will carry on existing when we are no more, or, more controversially, to a belief in eternity in some religious sense.[34]

He similarly detects the implicit coupling of spirituality and religion in phrases where spiritual development is said to involve leading pupils to *'seek answers to life's great questions'* and of aspects of human nature which may give *'meaning and purpose to human existence'. 'At points like these'*, he says,

> the 'spiritual' seems not to have to do with self-knowledge-which need have no connections with religion, but with questions about why we are here (sic)-which bring us ineluctably back to it.[35]

There *is* something important to be said about the key phrases picked out by John White but for the moment I want to dwell on the fallacy involved in the way he criticises their use in the Ofsted document. He implies that just because a phrase used to characterise the spiritual domain *could* be read in a religious way that this is evidence of an attempt to ensure that children are in fact religiously developed. But it is possible to challenge the idea that the phrases quoted do, in fact, imply an *exclusive* link with religious thinking. Even if such phrases do admit of a religious reading, this is insufficient evidence of an implicit attempt to ensure that educators are being covertly encouraged to develop children towards the acceptance of a religious world view. It might merely be taken as an attempt to ensure that children develop spiritually in the light of *knowledge* of religious responses so that *some* children, who might otherwise be denied the spiritual opportunities offered by religion, might be *enabled* to develop in that way.

In fact, John White recognises that the religious reading is *not* the only reading of these phrases. In most cases he gives us a secular humanist reading before revealing what he regards as the hidden religious agenda behind each one. This, in itself, undermines White's critique since it shows that such phrases *can* be decoupled from any necessary link with religion. Just because a phrase could be given a religious meaning does not, of itself, imply that it *must* be read as such and yet this is the assumption upon which most of White's critique relies. Ironically, it is his own preliminary *secular* readings which show this crucial assumption to be false.

He implies, at one point, a requirement that an educationally suitable definition of spirituality ought to have *no* connection with religion at all. For example it is because self knowledge *'need have no connections with religion'*[36] that *it* is acceptable. In part this desire to impose non-religious criteria of acceptability, is due to the fact that he considers development to be a social matter and that on the issues raised by religion there is no social consensus upon which educators could proceed. This echoes Terry McLaughlin's discussion of the constraints laid upon educators from the liberal democratic perspective. It might be argued that if the state is to be responsible for promoting spiritual development, then it must put forward a set of values which will apply to *all* schools and *all* school pupils, on a nation-wide basis; it should determine both the character *and* direction of spiritual education. If one takes that view of the matter then one must also assume that the Ofsted and NCC documents are to be read, not as broad characterisations of the area of the spiritual but, as *developmental ideals* to be added in full to the educational aims of each school. That this *is* how John White sees these documents is reflected in the fact that he is critical of the fact that many of the phrases are open to a *variety* of readings, inviting confusion as to how 'development' in this context might be interpreted. On this view, any possible reference to religion should be ruled out, in favour of some other, more acceptable and less controversial, developmental ideal based upon national consensus.

If one reads the Ofsted characterisation in this way as both definition *and* developmental ideal, for a national approach, then it also follows that there can be no middle way between a secular[37] and a religious conception of spirituality for that would give national policy makers the impossible task of trying to hold together two contradictory conceptions within a single developmental ideal. John White appears to favour a wholly secular approach to education but it is difficult to see how that would fare any better than a wholly religious approach given his suggestion that the ability of a view of spirituality to command a nationwide consensus is a vital part of any nationally common approach. Arguably, it is *precisely because* of the fact that there is no apparent consensus on issues of substantive value in British society that we require an education system which is not *wholly* committed to *either* secular humanism *or* religion.

I suspect that John White does not appreciate this last point because he is inclined to *assume* that the metaphysical commitments of secular humanism are not controversial and could form the basis of a national consensus view with which the liberal state could operate.[38] Perhaps allied to this is the assumption that liberalism and secular humanism are in some way inseparable. On that basis it might be argued that although there is currently no consensus on this, the assumption that secular humanism is the only legitimate approach to issues of value in the public domain emerges as a *rational precondition* of our particular political system and that a wholly secular approach to educational development is just one implication of that.[39] Firstly, if this is the basis of the argument then it should be stated and justified, especially in the face of the communitarian challenge to liberalism. Many leading liberals have been concerned, in the face of that challenge, to demonstrate that liberalism is not connected with any particular conception of the good.[40] If secular humanism were taken to be an intrinsic part of the liberal democratic perspective then it would have unhappy consequences for those who would want to continue to regard the link between liberalism and *pluralism* as equally important. Quite clearly a pluralist approach would rest upon the assumption that the education system were *neither* wholly secular *nor* wholly religious in its approach to values. A commitment to pluralism is just not *logically* compatible therefore with an educational commitment to secularism of the kind suggested by John White's comments. I suspect that it is precisely because of these considerations that both Ofsted and the NCC produced characterisations of the spiritual which are non-exclusive and 'scattershot' in approach.

2.4 Transcendence, education and the importance of 'spirituality'

One of the reasons for preferring the term spiritual over rival terms is the intimate relationship that exists between 'spirituality' and 'transcendence', where transcendence is associated with aspects of human experience which are related to something other than (located beyond) the realms of the individual, material and of that which is presently experienced. This connection is brought out clearly in both the Ofsted and NCC characterisations of the area of the spiritual, and interestingly, this connection is implicit in several of the key phrases from the Ofsted discussion paper that John White finds particularly problematic. The following phrases from the Ofsted discussion paper and framework for inspection suggest the presence of *'transcendence'*:

> valuing a non-material dimension to life
> intimations of an enduring reality

and the NCC guidance lists the following as 'aspects of spiritual development':

> Experiencing feelings of transcendence
> Search for meaning and purpose

At points in John White's critique it seems as if his objection to these references is the very fact that they contain some notion of transcendence which he associates with religion. It is interesting that both David Carr and John White assume that there is a necessary connection between 'transcendence' and religion.[41] It is also interesting that the secular gloss which John White places initially upon the first two of these phrases itself suggests that 'transcendence' may be open to a secular as well as a religious interpretation. What is clear and crucial to this discussion of the appropriateness of the language of spiritual development is that all parties to the debate appear to recognise that there is a definite and clear connection between *spirituality* and the notion of *transcendence*. *Both* Carr and White believe that this ties the language of spirituality to the language of *religion*. However, I want to challenge this assumption. If we can assert a logical link between a non-evaluative sense of spirituality and a similarly non-evaluative sense of transcendence and, if we can show that 'transcendence' is, or should be, of vital importance to educational practice, then we may have the basis for asserting that spiritual development is also of vital *educational* importance. I will return to the exploration of these issues in chapter five.

For the moment it is worth reiterating the fact that while the phrases pinpointed by John White, in the Ofsted document, seem to be committed to something 'transcending' the mundane and the material, they don't necessarily have to be read as a commitment to a transcendent realm wholly beyond this world, of the kind that underpins traditional religious belief. White's own secular humanist readings clearly demonstrate this much and seem to undermine his own attempt, and that of Carr, to suggest that there is a strongly religious flavour to *any* commitment to a transcendent perspective.

Consider the possible results of a situation in which the school refrained from actively encouraging reflection on the possibility of transcendent aspects of life. This would mean that the school effectively regarded the realm of value itself as something outside its legitimate area of responsibility since many sources of value, religious and otherwise, are *hidden* [42]aspects of human experience, even though their influence is profound. It might be argued that it is important for schools to make a special point of highlighting the hidden and the non-material dimension of life since much of the school curriculum is rightly concerned with giving young people a knowledge and understanding of its material and physical aspects. A spiritual development policy, from this perspective, emphasises the hidden and the non-material, *not* in order to suggest that the material and obvious are unimportant, indeed they may themselves be a legitimate source of spiritual and moral value as John White shows, the aim is rather to counter the possibility of an *unreflective drift* towards the view that material things are the *only* real and important things. This might be considered a very real possibility in our society where such a view is promoted actively by powerful agencies. On something like these grounds the educational importance of developing the transcendent perspective, and therefore the importance of using the language of spirituality within the educational context, might be asserted while *at the same time* resisting some of the educational implications of such an initiative suggested by David Carr.

Earlier on in this chapter I challenged David Carr's strictures against attempting either to produce a particular characterisation or definition of the terms involved for use within the education system or moving away from the strict logic of ordinary English usage in an attempt to develop that usage and its logic via authoritative stipulation for purposes of public policy. In fact, contrary to David Carr's analysis, common English usage does sanction a non-evaluative or descriptive use of the term 'spiritual'. This suggests that an attempt to formulate, either by common consent or stipulation, a characterisation of that type would in fact run *with,* rather than against, the logical tide of common usage. I want now to explore whether such a conception of the spiritual dimension to human experience can be justifiably outlined and whether it might be appropriate or useful within the educational setting.

Before moving on, in the next chapter, to the task of characterising what I will call 'common spirituality', I will spend some time now attempting to say why this pathway should be regarded as a promising one, sketching the broader picture that will put the later detailed work, hopefully, into some, albeit tentative, perspective.

Having thrown doubt on Carr's logical analysis of the term 'spiritual' and particularly his attempt to build an evaluative stance into the logic of even third party uses (that might have direct implications for educational applications of the term), we have undermined a further possible communitarian assumption beyond the boundaries of the present discussion. It might be argued, on the basis of Carr's analysis of the language of spirituality, that it is not possible for educationalists to rely even upon the commensurability of judgements about what spirituality is. This is an epistemological point that would place in considerable doubt the possibility of organising programmes of spiritual development within the state system since there could on this view be no way of characterising the spiritual domain that did not build in some particular evaluative and developmental perspective. In a society like ours where it might be thought a matter of empirical reality that a large number of different and perhaps contradictory spiritual ideals exist then communication about such a programme would be impossible.

Given then that such a perspective is not for linguistic or epistemological reasons ruled out, there might be other positive reasons, hinted at earlier in this chapter, for trying to establish at the outset a purely descriptive and non-evaluative characterisation of the word 'spiritual' and the aspect of human experience to which it refers. We might regard the use of such a concept, able to command a rational consensus on the question of precisely what is meant when we speak of 'spirituality' in an educational context, as perfectly appropriate. In this context we are inevitably committed to the view that the language of spirituality must apply to all, whatever their state of development or their cultural background. If there are children, attending state schools, of whom we could say that they have no spiritual aspect which might be developed, then the language of spirituality obviously has no place in the discourse of state education. This perhaps presents the biggest challenge to the conception of spiritual education put forward by David Carr. Following his analysis, educationalists would be committed to the view that there are many children, even in church schools, to whom the word 'spiritual' just could not be applied since they lack motivation, are morally bereft and have not even a modicum of interest in a transcendent dimension, of a broadly religious type. This position doesn't sit very easily with the support which he expresses for the initiative in the introduction to his paper on spiritual education. If spiritual education is thought to be important or if we are to convince people that it is important, then it must be applicable to all pupils and that will involve the development of terminology which can identify the relevant human capacities that will be the subject of spiritual *development*. It is those aspects of human experience by virtue of which spiritual education becomes a possibility that need to be given rational specification open to all and applicable to all. An evaluative concept of the 'spiritual' is *logically* incapable of doing that since it will embody a particular spiritual *ideal*. To present my argument in Kantian terms, some notion of common spirituality is a condition for the possibility of *any* programme of *spiritual development*.

If we follow the liberal democratic approach to state education, outlined by Terry McLaughlin and implied by John White, we seem to require some discussion of the area of concern that will enable all groups in society to be able to understand and also feel comfortable with the educational initiative based on it. Liberal thinkers who wish to accommodate the promotion of a pluralist society into their thinking about the role of the liberal state are apt to say that it should adopt a neutralist approach to policy. Educationalists of this liberal persuasion will want available the conceptual apparatus by which to demonstrate that a nationally organised programme of spiritual education will not constitute an illegitimate use of state power in order to impose a particular substantive type of spiritual development upon the children of its citizens. From this particular, but influential political perspective, it will be a pre-condition of establishing the legitimacy of any nationally common conception of spiritual education that it can be shown to be based upon notions of human capacity that are not unduly 'tainted' by particular evaluative models of human development. In addition, the arguments outlined above to suggest that the attempt to characterise some conception of common spirituality is a *pre-condition* of any discussion of what spiritual education *itself* might be will, by the same token, appeal to liberal and pluralist thinkers on the grounds that it will also facilitate the most *transparent* discussion of the political legitimacy of each and every scheme of spiritual education that might be proposed. In the face of communitarian critiques of the liberal approach to education and the controversial link between spiritual education and personal formation, bringing with it the possibility of conflicts between the state education system and other important social institutions like the family and the requirements of the democratic process, this need for rational transparency becomes even more important for those both within and outside the liberal fold.

David Carr correctly extols the virtues of having a *distinctive* conception of spiritual education but, in attempting to provide *that,* loses the possibility of building a rational consensus. This is, I think, in large part because he does not allow anything like the kind of non-evaluative conception of spirituality which I will attempt to develop in the next chapter. On the other hand, those educationalists and government advisers who feel that it is essential to establish a rational consensus are apt to proceed in such a way as to undermine the possibility of anything distinctive or adequate from arising, by adopting what Carr has called a 'scatter shot' approach. Terry McLaughlin sees this tension between the demands for rational consensus on the one hand and the need for a distinctive conception on the other and, on that basis, questions whether an initiative of the kind we are considering, connected as it is with substantive personal development, is in fact workable.[43] I believe that the kind of non-evaluative conception of spirituality, which I will attempt to outline in chapter three, is a small, but necessary, part of the conceptual apparatus required to negotiate a way through these logical tensions *without* giving undue consideration to one side and losing sight of the other.

Notes

1 McLaughlin (1996).

2 For the purposes of this discussion this should be understood as a state funded school operating a common conception of education with pupils who represent a range of cultural backgrounds.

3 McLaughlin (1996), p14.

4 They would be required to have the status of what liberal theorists call 'public values'.

5 Ibid., p14.

6 Ibid., p14, cf. P15 and McLaughlin (1994).

7 Elsewhere, in McLaughlin (1995), he offers a detailed discussion of the relationship between the domains of the public and its impact on the non-public domain in the common school. But, while this is sensitive to the subtle ways in which public values may illegitimately intrude upon the non-public domain, his discussion also reflects the fact that the moral rights of parents

with children in common schools appear to be less developed than are those with children in religious schools, where their preferred thick, non-public conceptions of the good are used to determine the personal education of their children.

8 This issue is central to chapters 4, 5 and 7 of this book.

9 For a full account of the communitarian challenge to liberalism, see Mulhall and Swift (1992).

10 Carr, D. (1995).

11 Carr, D. (1995), p97.

12 National Curriculum Council discussion paper (1993)

13 In passing, it is worth taking note of the fact that government representatives have used a third strategy for circumventing the requirements of commonality outlined by McLaughlin. In 1977, the DFE offered policy makers two alternative distinctive characterisations of the spiritual, as follows,

> *1. The spiritual area is concerned with the awareness a person has of those elements in existence and experience which may be defined in terms of inner feelings and beliefs; they affect the way people see themselves and throw light for them on the purpose and meaning of life itself. Often these feelings and beliefs lead people to claim to know God and to glimpse the transcendent; sometimes they represent that striving and longing for perfection which characterises human beings but always they are concerned with matters at the heart and root of existence.*
>
> *2. The spiritual area is concerned with everything in human knowledge or experience that is connected with or derives from a sense of God or of gods. Spiritual is a meaningless adjective for the atheist and of dubious use to the agnostic. Irrespective of personal belief or disbelief, an unaccountable number of people have believed and do believe in the spiritual aspects of human life, and therefore their actions, attitudes and interpretations of events have been influenced accordingly.*

14 Carr, D. (1995), p97.

15 Hegel, G.W.F. (1977).

16 Hull, J. (1993) '..In the body or out of the body?': Spirituality or Materiality. A keynote address to the RIMSCUE conference on Moral and Spiritual Development, held at the University of Plymouth, Rolle College, Exmouth.

17 Carr, D. (1995), p87.

18 Ibid., p86.

19 Ibid., p88.

20 Ibid., p89.

21 Common usage may have a certain *authority* but that doesn't mean that it must necessarily be regarded as *authoritative* in an educational context, as Carr is perhaps expecting the reader to assume.

22 Carr, D. (1995), p89.

23 Ibid., p89.

24 Neither would it appear to be ruled out by the logic of Christian usage. See, for example, Martin Luther's use of the term 'apostate spirituality'.

25 For a classic communitarian attempt to show that British culture has more homogeneity than pluralistsareinclined to assume, see Haldane,J.(1986).

26 Carr, D. (1995) p89-90.

27 On the relevance of such issues to personal education, see Standish, P. (1995).

28 Providing further demonstration of support for McLaughlin's intuition that some reflection upon the political framework being employed ought to be the *starting point* for any discussion of the meaning of spiritual development, within the state funded school.

29 White,J. (1994), p369-377.

30 Ofsted, (1993).

31 White, J. (1990), (1994) and (1995).

32 Even where a distinctively religious definition has been issued, as in the DFE statement of 1977, this has been presented as one alternative understanding of what the terminology might mean in educational terms and not as an exclusive definition (cf. Note 12).

33 White,J. (1994) pp370-377.

34 Ibid., p372.

35 Ibid., p373.

36 Ibid., p373.

37 The term 'secular' is here used as implying an exclusively non-religious approach to public policy. However, I would not wish to imply that the meaning of this term be comprehensively understood in this way. For a fuller, more nuanced discussion of the meaning of the term 'secular' and its application to public policy, see chapter 4 of this study, Haydon, G.(1994) and Mitchell, B.(1980).

38 There is clear evidence for this in White, J. (1995) , especially pp2-3.

39 Such a view of matters is argued in Hirst, P.(1974) and is based upon the view that religious claims are inherently controversial and may only be accommodated into public policy to the extent that they overlap with common values that may be established either through consensus or which are themselves rationally demonstrable.

40 See for example, Rawls, J. (1993), for a discussion of various communitarian challenges to Rawls' earlier anti-perfectionist position see Mulhall, S., and Swift, A. (1992).

41 See, for example, Carr, D.(1995) pp89-90.

[42] In the sense, suggested earlier, that they point beyond a concern with the present, material and individual realms.

[43] McLaughlin, T. (1996).

3 Agency, Experience and Common Spirituality

Summary

This chapter begins with an examination and criticism of John Dewey's attempt, in his book A Common Faith, to outline a concept of 'the religious' that can, in principle, be separated from the beliefs of traditional religion. It is argued that, while it provides a promising basis for the development of a non-evaluative account of spirituality, it is based, as it stands, upon scientism and fails to take account of the historical and traditional dimension of all human experience. In the central sections, several aspects of the accounts of human agency offered by Alastair MacIntyre and Charles Taylor are examined and rejected. It is argued that a conception of narrative unity is not an essential aspect of even the internal logic of human action and that the ability to articulate one's conception of the good is not a condition of agency. Taylor's view that socially constructed frameworks of evaluation are logically inescapable aspects of any attempt by individuals to orient themselves towards the good is examined and shown to be groundless.

In the final section the positive account of common spirituality which emerges from the preceding discussion and which will provide the basis for discussion of the educational issues, is outlined.

3.1 Dewey, religion and religiosity

One attempt to delineate a common and distinctive conception of what spirituality might be understood to be from a liberal democratic perspective is to be found in John Dewey's Terry lectures, published in 1934 and titled *'A Common Faith'*. There Dewey tries to characterise structural elements of traditional religious faith and attempts to distinguish this 'religious' faith from that of religion and suggests that it should be given a 'natural' focus, by linking it with the experimental methods of modern science. He says that traditional religion has the means to 'enchant' the natural world with values and to inspire the arduous pursuit of moral ideals based upon them. But although religion has prompted this commendable and much needed 'ardour', it has been based upon a supernaturalism that is, Dewey alleges, untenable in the modern world. Modern science, on the other hand, has generated the scientific or experimental method which, according to Dewey, is the ideal truth generating methodology. Unfortunately, its use has been accompanied by the marginalisation of values from the natural world which has become 'disenchanted'. This, in turn, has supported a move towards the ethics of subjectivism, relativism and has underpinned a divisive and dangerous individualism. To overcome the shortcomings of these two approaches, Dewey suggests that a truly common faith for the modern world might be developed by merging the *spirit* of traditional religion with the view that locates truth exclusively within the natural world and which adopts the experimental method. This approach which is both truth generating and critical could support the *effective* pursuit of moral value ideals.

Dewey characterises the spirit of traditional religion as the 'religious'. This, he says, '*...signifies a certain attitude and outlook, independent of the supernatural, necessitates no...division between the sacred and profane*'. He is concerned to separate religion from some account of the 'religious' dimension of all human experience and he sets out the contrast in the following way,

> ..a religion..always signifies a special body of beliefs and practices having some kind of institutional organisation, loose or tight. In contrast, the adjective 'religious' denotes nothing in the way of a specifiable entity, either institutional or as a system of beliefs...it does not denote anything that can exist by itself..It denotes attitudes that may be taken toward every object and every proposed end or ideal.[1]

I want to examine Dewey's suggestion that there is a distinctive human capacity, close to that which forms the basic structure of religious forms of life, but which bears only a contingent relationship to those forms and could therefore be instantiated through secular *and* religious frameworks of belief and value. His discussion of the 'religious' appears to provide the raw materials for a more satisfactory and complete account of what I will call 'common spirituality'. However, I have strong reservations about some aspects of Dewey's account, especially his sustained and misguided attempt to discredit traditional forms of religion, on the back of an adherence to a reductive naturalism. This rather negative strand in Dewey's account of religiosity, comes through in the following section where he says,

> It is widely supposed that a person who does not accept any religion is thereby shown to be a non-religious person. Yet it is conceivable that the present depression in religion is closely connected with the fact that religions now prevent ..the religious quality of experience from coming to consciousness and finding the expression that is appropriate to present conditions, intellectual and moral...I believe that many persons are so repelled from what exists as a religion by its intellectual and moral implications, that they are not even aware of attitudes in themselves that if they came to function would be genuinely religious. [2]

However this quotation exemplifies just one aspect of Dewey's account but one which is hostile to religion and suggests that the future value of the religious function rests upon the extent to which it might be from the metaphysical beliefs associated with traditional religion. There is, however, another strand to Dewey's thinking which is concerned to show that traditional religions have, at some level, *also* been animated by the religious attitude. From the educational perspective sketched at the end of the last chapter, it is extremely important that any suitable account of a common spiritual mechanism is both contingently related to traditional religious views, but is also free of any intrinsic hostility to them.

There are two aims of the detailed discussion of Dewey's concept of 'religiosity' that follows. Firstly, I want to establish whether Dewey's account of religiosity is itself free of the kind of secular humanist bias that Dewey's exposition clearly exhibits and therefore whether it is capable of providing the basis of a descriptive account of common spirituality. Secondly, I will attempt to see whether it is based upon a coherent and comprehensive account of human experience.

In outlining his account of the 'religious', Dewey, at several points, uses the terminology of 'spirituality'. And one wonders why, given his obvious hostility to traditional forms of religion and the obvious confusion that results from his extraordinarily counter intuitive use of 'religious', he did not confine himself to the terminology of 'spirituality'. I think there might be two explanations for this. While the terminology of religion has very clear social and institutional connotations, the language of spirituality might have an association with individual experience that might be thought to make it less than helpful from his perspective. In an attempt to contrast his own account of this faculty with the individualistic account offered by William

James,[3] he may well have thought it better to avoid the terminology of spirituality altogether.

In addition, his Terry lectures were perhaps originally aimed at an audience that might have considerable sympathy with traditional religious forms and *this* suggests a polemical purpose in his choice of terminology. He might have considered it better suited to his purpose of emancipating these people from too narrow a use of the term 'religious', offering them a broader, and more acceptable conception of what religion might become. The term 'religious' narrowly defined might be thought a useful polemical device designed to provide a bridge, in Dewey's view, from traditional supernaturalist expressions of institutionalised religion to an acceptable contemporary conception of them avoiding the 'liberal Christian' route, which Dewey condemns for its emphasis on the individual and the subjective aspects of traditional religion. While he did not choose to use the word 'spiritual' in *A Common Faith*, he would probably be prepared to subscribe to the view that, when focused on the religious dimension of each individual human life, the terminology of the 'spiritual' might be substituted for that of the 'religious', without significant loss.

Dewey explicitly says that the religious is a *function*, operating within experience, rather than being a particular *type of experience*. The following quotation illustrates his concern to undermine the widespread assumption that the 'religious' denotes a *common* type of experience. He says that those who hold that

> ..there is a definite kind of experience which is by itself religious, by that very fact make out of it something specific, as a kind of experience that is marked off from experience as aesthetic, scientific, moral, political; from experience as companionship and friendship. But 'religious' as a quality of experience signifies something that may belong to all these experiences. It is the polar opposite of some type of experience that can exist by itself.[4]

To suggest otherwise would, according to Dewey, be to suggest that *'there is but one road'* to the truth[5] and to subscribe to a dualism of the sacred and profane. A religious experience is so not because of its association with a particular object or a particular practice, but because of *'..what it does in and to the processes of living'*. Dewey tells us that a religious experience is one that has the force of bringing about *'..a better, deeper and enduring adjustment in life'*.[6] The 'religious', he says, is much broader than the 'moral' nevertheless it *is* connected with our moral ideals and our desire to achieve them. This is underpinned by a particular theory of motivation which suggests, in line with that of Aristotle, that human actions are motivated significantly by *rational* considerations. These considerations manifest themselves through a series of ends and ideals to which any particular action is directly or indirectly linked.

Traditional religion, according to Dewey, is characterised by a tendency to take the ends inherent in a moral faith and to construct out of them a metaphysics which takes those ends as already existent in a pre-existing supernatural being or as a supernatural dimension of reality. Dewey's argument for this observation is the evidence of psychologists who have documented the human tendency to *'believe is already so'* that which *'we ardently desire to have thus and so'*. *'Desire'*, he says,

> ...has a powerful influence upon intellectual beliefs...When conditions are adverse- it is an easy way out to assume that after all they are already embodied in the ultimate structure of what is, and that appearances to the contrary are merely appearances..weak natures take to reverie as a refuge as strong ones do to fanaticism.[7]

The negative account of traditional religious belief is clear in this quote. Religious people, in holding to its metaphysical beliefs, give in to a weakness of human nature and religions themselves have a natural affinity with fanaticism and, therefore, increase the likelihood of social division.

Dewey's distinction between 'religion' and the 'religious' is not satisfactory, as it stands, for our purposes. His definition of the 'religious' is clearly built upon a negative evaluation of traditional religious views. This is supported by a characterisation of traditional religion which most religious people would not recognise.[8]

Dewey's characterisation of the religious *is*, however, based upon the interesting and defensible view that human action, a crucial element in any account of human experience, has a built-in and integral reference to ideals and goals. Any adequate account of individual human action will *necessarily* make references to aimed for states of affairs that are positively valued by the individual concerned. Two things should be noted about this observation. Firstly, this does not imply an *individualistic* account of human action since the origin of an individual's goals and ideals remains a contingent matter and is therefore commensurate with a whole range of views about the extent to which an individual's goals and ideals are influenced by social factors. Secondly, and referring back to a distinction made with reference to David Carr's account of the logic of the term 'spiritual', it should be noted that the logical necessity built into this account of human action is one which is internalist rather than externalist in character. This means that when we say that all human action is geared, either tacitly or explicitly, knowingly or unknowingly, towards some goal or ideal, that does not mean that *we* are *thereby* committed to those goals and ideas. To say of the junkie that she voluntarily shoots heroin and that, this *logically* entails that she positively values the state of affairs that she would describe as 'getting high', does not *of itself* entail an endorsement of her ideal. This view of human action is therefore promising as an aspect of human experience that might be operated without exclusiveness. The 'internalist'[9] dimension will be an important part of the account of agency to be developed later in this chapter. However, in suggesting that a religious experience is an experience '*..having the force of bringing about a better, deeper and enduring adjustment in life*'[10] and that it is '*whatever introduces genuine perspective is religious*'.[11] Dewey demonstrates that, in his view, these internalist logical considerations operate *externally* (i.e they constrain third party discussion) as well since these remarks imply that a positive evaluation must be built into *any* use of the term 'religious'.[12]

3.2 Beyond Dewey: religiosity and scientism

According to Dewey, the religious attitude is also a *rational* attitude. An exploration of Dewey's account of its rationality exposes two significant and problematic aspects of his account which bring its coherence and adequacy into question.

The rationality of the religious attitude is exhibited in the relationship between the appropriateness of that attitude in relation to a reality, conceived as 'natural', and certain appropriate ends or goals. This means that the rationality of the religious attitude is determined solely by reference to a possible future state of affairs. The future-oriented thrust implicit in Dewey's account of the religious attitude is shown in the contrast that he makes between it and the present or pre-existent thrust of the attitudes that he associates with traditional religion. The problem with the idea of God in traditional religion, he says, is that represents the attempt to locate something from the forward looking realm of ideals in a pre-existing reality. He says these traditional notions of God are due to the conversion of ideal qualities referred to by them '*..into an existent being due to a conflux of tendencies in human nature that converts the object of desire into an antecedent reality*'[13]

Dewey makes it clear that, since reality is an on-going process, the rationality of 'the religious' cannot be based upon some notion of what is pre-existently true. Nature, says Dewey, is in itself a non-rational and a non-moral process; it is human beings alone that bring rationality and value to reality. A religious piety based on naturalism, he says,

> ..is not of necessity either a fatalistic acquiescence in natural happenings or a romantic idealisation of the world. It may rest upon a just sense of nature as the whole of which we are parts, while it also recognises that we are the parts marked by intelligence and purpose.[14]

Dewey recognises that some conception of what is true and therefore appropriately believed is required to counteract the subjectivist and relativist drift of all this. Human beings don't just construct their own rationality and neither are they at liberty as individuals to construct their own values. Nature constrains human creativity in these respects and modern science provides a methodology for generating the appropriate beliefs and that bestows an objective dimension to the Deweyan account of the 'religious'. The appropriateness of any given attitude or action can be rationally assessed by gauging the extent to which it is an appropriate means to the achievement of the ends that are agreed to be valuable in themselves.[15]

As can be seen from this discussion, Dewey *asserts* in his account of the 'religious' that all rationality, value, purpose and intelligence is bestowed upon reality by human beings alone. In his view reality is a constantly changing process, making *absolute* claims to truth inappropriate and the experimental method is the *only* appropriate methodology for generating truths about nature. All this, however, rests upon *metaphysical* claims as absolute and as controversial as any that are embodied in the belief systems of traditional religions.[16] The reason why Dewey fails to see the need to justify his views more fully in *A Common Faith*, may have to do with the cultural climate within which he was operating. The early thirties were a high point for pragmatism and positivism in both the Anglo-Saxon and Continental philosophical worlds. The philosophical fashions dominant when he wrote the book were associated with hostility to the truth claims of traditional religion and with the idea that metaphysical claims could and should be avoided. The self evident technological and medical successes generated by the careful application of the methods of science led many to believe that this method could be applied not only to truths about the physical world but to the world of human affairs as well. In the modern setting where quite different philosophical fashions dominate, Dewey's adherence to the supremacy of the experimental method requires independent justification. In addition, it also threatens the overall coherence of his account of the 'religious attitude'. Dewey lays out the following criteria crucial to the distinction between 'religion' and the 'religious'. Unlike a 'religion' , the 'religious' he says

> ..does not limit access to truth to any church or scheme of things. It does not just say that truth is universal and then add there is but one road to it...[17]

But, as has been shown, modern science and more precisely its 'experimental methodology' *is* regarded by Dewey as the *exclusive* 'road' to truth.[18]

Dewey's claims for universal validity and scope of the experimental method cannot be based upon the kinds of rational principles which he deploys against traditional religion since the experimental method is incapable of adjudicating without circularity about its own status relative to other rival avenues to truth. If this is the case, then the religious attitude shares a common characteristic with the attitude of traditional religion i.e. they *both* rest upon assertions which are neither negotiable nor rationally demonstrable. The *only apparent* difference between the two attitudes is that the 'religious' attitude rests on truths about the universal appropriateness of a certain *methodology* or *truth generating procedure* rather than on truths about the nature of reality, as such. But even this distinction is more apparent than real since the experimental method itself embodies specific truths about the nature of reality that are from its perspective non-negotiable and universally applicable.[19] Dewey's account of the alleged contrast between 'religion' and 'the religious' appears not to take account of the extent to which *any* truth generating methodology is dependent upon a set of non-negotiable presuppositions that are embedded in a tradition and therefore born in the past. Science is but one particular, historically contingent *mode* of human experience. Scientific method does not provide the complete 'view from nowhere' that Dewey's account of religion appears to suppose.[20]

3.3 Beyond Dewey: instrumentalism and tradition

Arising from the future-oriented thrust of Dewey's account of experience is his instrumentalist attempt to overcome the traditional dualism of theory/practice, fact/value, real/ideal by pointing to the primacy of *practice*.

According to Michael Oakeshott any conception of human experience which sees it primarily in practical terms will necessarily be an incomplete account. This is because such a conception would presuppose the existence of two distinct and discrepant worlds; the worlds of 'what is' and of 'to be' or 'not yet'. Such a conception would be based upon an evaluation of the world of 'what is' by reference to the world of 'to be', on the basis that certain needs, desires and interests exist and that these can be achieved in a world of mutable transient fact by the exercise reason and will, in action. Oakeshott conceives of this process differently to Dewey. For Dewey the world of 'to be' is an ideal world, a kind of blue print to be used for the moulding of the real world of nature. Oakeshott regards both worlds as equally real and, as such, to be brought to reconciliation through practical activity.

This difference between their respective assessment of the ontological status of these two dimensions of practice is telling yet it does not alter the effectiveness of the argument used by Oakeshott against the instrumentalist conception of human experience and value. This argument might be paraphrased in the following way: A view of human experience conceived in terms of the transformation of what is into what ought to be will be ultimately incoherent since the achievement of the goals of human action would undermine the separation of the two worlds that are fundamental to the human enterprise on this view. The problem that Oakeshott identifies in the instrumentalist emphasis on practice has been summarised in the following way,

> Practice depends on there being a discrepancy between 'what is' and 'what ought to be'. On the other hand, practice attempts to break down this discrepancy, to resolve it, through action. Thus, what is attempted in practice is the abolition of the condition which makes it possible in the first place. Practice cannot achieve what it aims at without destroying itself.[21]

What this shows us is that any attempt to think about the realm of human experience and human values purely in instrumentalist terms will be ultimately self refuting. And this brings us back to the fact that Dewey's conception of human experience lacks a traditional or historical aspect.

Values are used to guide the actions with which we make our future lives. In turn they reflect the historically given, present character of the persons that we are and the communities of which we are a part. This helps to form who we are and, in moulding the desires, wants and needs that underpin the instrumentalist conception of human action that Dewey uses. In the section that follows I will try to show that attempts to disentangle present experience and our orientation to the future, from the *historical* contingencies reflecting our position as members of particular human communities, would be to that extent untenable. Indeed, to operate in this way would be to fail to recognise an essential component of our humanity. When discussing the nature of personal human experience and any notion of common spirituality that might be based upon it, we must recognise *all* three aspects all three 'temporal dimensions' of past, present and future. Dewey fails in this respect because in his Kantian attempt to purify the realm of value and to associate it exclusively with the exercise of rational will., compells to place too much emphasis on those elements of human experience which relate to the future. I will attempt to demonstrate this, in the next section, by offering an analysis of the logical preconditions of any adequate account of moral agency

3.4 Towards a less partial account of human agency

Action, while being at the centre of any possible account of human experience, is arguably *the* most future oriented of all its aspects. Thus, if a successful account of the logic of human action could demonstrate that traditional elements are logically fundamental to it, it would do so upon Deweyan 'ground'. This is what I will attempt to do in the next section. In passing, I hope also to show that no adequate account of human experience can rest, as Dewey's account of the religious does, upon too strict a distinction between the 'real' and the 'ideal'. In addition, my account will support later discussion designed to show that any adequate account of the moral will presuppose a dimension of *all* human experience best characterised as 'spiritual'.

If we start from the view that human action is the attempt to influence a given situation through intentional behaviour, then all human action will have a rational or cognitive dimension. In some cases, human actions will result from an active process of deciding what is to be done. Other actions are characterised by, for example, an habitual response to a familiar situation. Though the rational dimension of the latter will not necessarily be constituted by a process of active reflection it will arguably *have* to embody cognitive elements. It will have a purpose or telos, linked to a set of ideals or goals valued because they are taken *by the agent* to constitute the good life or some intrinsic element of it. This will involve some conception of the good, together with a notion of what is valuable. Even if the agent is either unable to articulate their conception of the good or if the agent's own view is thought to be mistaken, these will still be the case.[22]

Such an analysis is compatible with teleological moral theories, for example with those of an Aristotelian or utilitarian character. However, it is also compatible with Kantian theories which do not regard the pursuit of the good as a characteristic of moral action. This is because the rational moral will, favoured by Kantian theorists, is *itself*, on this conception, thought to be an embodiment of the *good*. While it rejects the suggestion that the truly moral agent *aims* for the good, the Kantian view is that the rational moral life *is* the good life.[23]

However, further justification is needed to show that *all* actions have some evaluative dimension of the kind that might seem obvious in the case of *moral* actions. This can be provided by consideration, for example, of a man who goes out to reverse the direction of his parked car for no apparent reason. If the piece of behaviour in question is not intentional, then it doesn't constitute an *action* at all and if, on the other hand, it *is* intentional behaviour then it is either done in the *direct* pursuit of something, thought *by the agent* to be good,[24] *or* it is a piece of behaviour which is regarded as something which *itself* good. If this agent, who might be regarded generally as a complete fool, rejects the idea that his car reversal has any point or purpose, thereby denying the observer a link to some evaluative framework, then his eccentricity can still be accommodated. Although it is not aimed at the direct pursuit of some good, it will for him *constitute* an aspect of the good life and, in his case we would conclude that the life of arbitrary and purposeless action *is* the good life, *from his perspective*.

One further point of clarification is necessary before I proceed to build upon these preliminary observations. It might be thought that I am proposing a counter-intuitive view of moral action based upon narrow self interest. If all action, and therefore all *moral* action, is linked necessarily to some good *for the agent* it might be felt that we are lumbered with a very particular and controversial moral theory, that of egoism. At some level, my account might be said to imply an egoist theory of action but certainly not in any strong or controversial way, suggesting that *all* action is necessarily performed on the basis of self-interest and that, consequently, altruism is an impossibility. Several examples spring to mind here to illustrate the need to make a distinction between something's being 'a good *for the agent*' and its being either 'a good to be *enjoyed directly by* the agent' or 'directly *in the interests of* the agent'. The man who, according to legend, formed his body into a human bridge aboard the up-turned cross channel ferry outside Zeebrugge, and thereby enabled perhaps hundreds of others to escape, certainly did not do something which could be described as 'acting in his own interests'. But there is surely nothing counterintuitive, in adding that he must have acted in the way that he did because the escape of those other people did constitute a good *for him*. Consider also the devoted researcher into cancer who does so because she is aiming at a good i.e. producing a cure for cancer. Her actions are aimed at something which, for her, is a good but that doesn't *necessarily* involve our saying that she must be aiming for this good because she expects to enjoy that cure or that she regards the cure as in being in her own interests (though these are *contingent* possibilities).[25]

A second aspect to the cognitive dimension of all human action, in addition to the framework of evaluation set out above, will be some conception of *the situation* that presents itself at any given time. This will have a number of components that take us well beyond the view that the situation is just a set of material *facts* about the world. It will inevitably include, at least, a potentially fallible understanding of ourselves as physical beings and of our world. In the case of moral actions, such facts may be important but largely marginal. They will set limits upon what it is that *might* be done or help to determine, in combination with other factors and to a greater or lesser extent depending upon the context, what ought to be done. In the medical context, for example, natural facts will be largely and uncontroversially determinative whilst in the context of morality they will generally be thought marginal at most and the extent of their influence a matter for debate.

In the moral context, facts about the physical aspects of the situation will, in all likelihood, take the form of a set of *constraints* but they may also suggest *possibilities* that have moral significance. In the area of embryo technology, for example, certain factual discoveries have led to medical techniques which have created possibilities for human agency. Current research into human genetic structure is likely also to present human beings with a range of hitherto unknown possibilities. For the sake of clarity and brevity I will, henceforth, refer to the domain of constraints and possibilities as the domain of *possibility*. The possibilities that present themselves will also include certain facts of a phenomenological kind regarding the agent's understanding of their own life and that of others. It will include *commitments* and these will have to be ordered into a hierarchy and will relate to the evaluative framework that the person holds.[26] In view of this, any attempt to disentangle the realm of facts from the realm of values in any absolute way must be regarded as misguided. The commitments will take the form of an adherence to a particular evaluative framework and they will rest upon factual and interpretative presuppositions while they and, in particular, their interrelationships (for example, their hierarchical order), will become an important factual aspect of any situation that presents itself, to an agent.

Facts about an individual's commitments are a central element in the *self understanding* which in turn constitutes a key aspect of the domain that I have labelled *'the situation'*. They will also necessarily operate as constraints within the sub-domain of possibilities. If we are committed to certain things, perhaps in part to generate important connected possibilities, then some other possibilities will, as a matter of logic, be ruled out while others will just become less likely. If one chooses to enter into a sexual relationship, then, at least for its duration, the possibilities opened up by a life of celibacy are ruled out. Commitments will arise because of the agent's needs, desires and wants. These will be key factors in our decisions to make commitments, as the marriage example self-evidently illustrates. We adhere to certain modes of life because they open up the possibilities that make, or contribute (directly or indirectly) to, the life which we consider to be good.

While individual desires and wants are definitely key elements of any human action, they should not be seen as the starting points for any such analysis. Desires will in turn *reflect* the fact that we are particular kinds of people with a particular physical, social, cultural and individual nature. The wants and desires that a particular agent has at any given time will be affected, in large part, by the society in which they live as well as the facts of their humanity.

The nature of the social dimension just referred to will have been affected by the *history* of the society in which the individual is located. Alistair MacIntyre gives voice to the importance of these constraining and non-individual aspects of human agency, in the following way,

> ..what an agent is able to do or say intelligibly as an actor is deeply affected by the fact that we are never more (and sometimes less) than the co-authors of our own narratives. Only in fantasy do we live what story we please. In life...we are always under certain constraints. We enter upon a stage which we did not design and we find ourselves part of an action that was not of our making. Each of us being a main character in his own drama plays subordinate parts in the dramas of others, and each drama constrains the others.[27]

This rightly emphasises the fact that traditional and social elements within our situation restrict the extent to which we can, so to speak invent ourselves ex nihilo. However, it might be regarded as presenting a somewhat negative picture of the influence of the traditional or historically given aspects of human experience. John Kekes, in addition, makes much of the *opportunities* that are opened up through the effects of our commitments and the constraints that we have noted. Both Kekes and MacIntyre, by drawing attention to the importance and inevitability of these traditional aspects of human agency, highlight the problematic character of Dewey's own future-oriented account. He *is* concerned to locate the individual in a *communal* setting but, for political reasons, connected with his idealised view of the democratic society, he builds into his account the possibility that the community might be freed from the 'burdens' of tradition. In doing this he effectively adopts a non-individualistic version of something which Kekes calls the 'conflict view of moral reflection' and criticises in the following way,

> My opponent's view is that reflection enables us to decide what we really want, as independent, autonomous individuals, and , then to go on to try to extract it from our surroundings..This view is not false or inconsistent, rather it is incomplete and unbalanced..The truth is that our minds and wants are formed by the conventions into which we are born. Conventions are not the traditional gloss upon our wants; wants are given form and articulation by couching them in the moral idioms our tradition provides..We thereby make ourselves into what we have learned to value from our moral tradition.[28]

These comments are applied to those who idealise the situation of *individuals*, regarding them as potentially free from social constraints. But they apply also to those, like Dewey, who idealise the position of communities in the same kind of way, regarding them as potentially freed from traditional truth claims through the exercise of the scientific method. The lesson that such an approach can learn from the philosophical tradition that Kekes and MacIntyre[29] represent is that such a strategy would merely succeed in minimising social diversity by strengthening and extending the influence of a particular kind of tradition, that of science.

3.5 MacIntyre, Taylor and the importance of narrative unity

Moral reflection does not just provide a guide to action, it and the actions which result from it, both reflect our self understanding and contribute to it. The process of moral reflection and moral agency is a process of person construction. Alistair MacIntyre and Charles Taylor link this to the fact that some sense of narrative unity running across the whole of an individual's life is a fundamental aspect of agency.[30] MacIntyre sets this out in the context of a discussion of the existentialist view that actions can be seen in atomic terms and a complete life narrative given only in retrospect, starting from death and looking backwards. Against this he says that it would only be possible for an external observer to make sense of individual actions (i.e. make them intelligible) if, and only if, such actions could be placed within the context of a life narrative, involving some prior reference to the long term *intentions* of the agent. MacIntyre proposes a hierarchy of intelligibility in which those characterisations of an action that invoke longer term intentions of the agent have proportionately *more intelligibility* than those which invoke shorter term intentions. I take him to be saying, in part, that characterisations in terms of *pure bits of behaviour* are insufficient to adequately characterise human *actions*. This is correct and lines up with the view expressed earlier that any theory of human action *must* include a phenomenological dimension invoking the agent's intentions. However, that important point is obscured in MacIntyre's discussion because instead of contrasting *behaviour* and *action* along these lines he contrasts *'intelligible actions'* and *'unintelligible actions'*, proceeding from there to the idea of *degrees* of intelligibility, relating to the temporal scope of the agent's intentions.

MacIntyre uses an account of this *externalist* logic of action to make a case about its *internalist* logic. The argument, however, does not in fact work, *even* for the external perspective, since, on the account of action set out above, and arguably, on the basis of MacIntyre's own account, the idea of an *'unintelligible action'* is *itself* unintelligible. It is a contradiction in terms, since an unintelligible piece of behaviour could not be described as an *action* at all. In addition, the notion that intentions with a longer temporal sweep bestow upon the actions they describe more *intelligibility* requires some further justification that is not provided by MacIntyre's account.

These important assumptions form part of a philosophical strategy designed to classify all those who reject his preferred theory of action as 'behaviourists' who think they can construct an intelligible account of human action on the basis of a description of *behaviour alone*. But clearly it would be possible to accept (as I have done), against the behaviourists, that some phenomenological dimension is a logically necessary *aspect* of any adequate theory of action without accepting the logical priority of action descriptions characterised in terms of *longer term* intentions. One could presumably make the external narrative judgement that a man lived a life characterised by extra marital 'philandering' by reference only to his short term intentions to have a series of extra-marital affairs. Here, we might argue the short term intentions of the agent determined the narrative flavour of his life, despite the fact that the man had no long term intention to live life as a 'philanderer'. But, *even if* this externalist case *did* support the priority of longer term intentions, *that* would not, *automatically*, sanction a parallel set of conclusions (with reference to the internalist perspective) to the effect that *any* account of human agency must attribute *to the agent* some long term narrative perspective. This is the case, however, which MacIntyre intends his preceding discussion to support. He sets out, in the following way, to show that the internalist point appears both to follow from *and support* the externalist case,

> It is now becoming clear that we render the actions of others intelligible in this way because action itself has a basically historical character. It is because we all live out narratives in our lives and because we understand our own narratives in terms of the narratives that we live out that the form of narrative is appropriate for understanding the actions of others. Stories are lived before they are told-except in the case of fiction.[31]

While the significance of a sense of narrative for the internalist logic is largely implicit in MacIntyre's account, it is wholly explicit in a similar account offered by Charles Taylor. Describing the agent's narrative sense of their life as a 'quest' for the good as an *'inescapable structural requirement of human agency'*, he says[32]

> ..because we cannot but orient ourselves to the good, and thus determine our place relative to it and hence determine the direction of our lives in narrative form, as a quest....Because we have to determine our place in relation to the good, therefore we cannot be without an orientation to it, and hence must see our life in story.

Later he acknowledges his debt to MacIntyre's account and endorses the internalist significance of the logical priority of longer term intentions, in the following terms:

> Thus making sense of my present action, when we are not dealing with such trivial questions as where I shall go in the next five minutes but with the issue of my place relative to the good, requires a narrative understanding of my life , a sense of what I have become which can only be given in a story. And as I project my life forward and endorse the existing direction or give it a new one, I project a future story, not just a state of the momentary

> future but a bent for my whole life to come. This sense of my life as having a direction towards what I am not yet is what Alistair MacIntyre captures in his notion...that life is seen as a 'quest'.[33]

Some detailed criticism of this apparently trivial aspect of the MacIntyre-Taylor theory of action is vital to the development of my own and to the validity of the characterisation of common spirituality which I hope will follow directly from it. It is vital, for the reasons set out earlier, that the view of spirituality that I ultimately hope to develop, is wholly non-evaluative. Nothing, therefore, must be allowed into the foundational structure of my account that might be shown to embody certain particular evaluative presuppositions. The views of MacIntyre and Taylor are also influential amongst key thinkers who have contributed to the debate within the philosophy of education regarding spiritual development. I hope to show that the key weaknesses in the MacIntyre-Taylor case are fundamental to the weaknesses of the communitarian position as it is articulated within the philosophy of education. Indeed, it will be remembered that an illicit movement from the externalist logic to an internalist account was the main allegation that I made against David Carr's communitarian approach to spirituality. I hope that another parallel will emerge from my detailed discussion of key passages from Taylor in what follows. Just as David Carr[34] was shown to build a theistic perspective into his account of the logic of spirituality, I believe we can identify an *unwarranted* particularism in the MacIntyre-Taylor account of certain aspects of the logic of human agency.

Looking back at those aspects of the MacIntyre-Taylor account identified above, it might be agreed by many that it is highly *desirable* that a human agent has some sense of the narrative unity of their life. This might be linked to the view that integrity is a virtue and brings a desirable consistency of approach to decision making. We might also agree with the suggestion, made by Taylor in *Sources of the Self*,[35] that someone who failed to have a 'framework' or regarded his frameworks of evaluation as optional and disposable, would be in the grip of some pathological identity crisis. *But*, given that a person in this state is nevertheless regarded as an *agent*, without contradiction, the question of *pathology* is irrelevant to any account of the *logic* of action.[36]

While there might be many good reasons why a person should act consistently and in accordance with a long term point or purpose, there seems to be no *necessary* link between this and the notion of being an agent, as such. One can imagine a person living their life on the basis of momentary whim and being, to a rational observer, wildly inconsistent *and yet* that would not lead us to question that person's status as an *agent*. The central character of Jean-Paul Sartre's existentialist novel 'The Roads to Freedom' springs immediately to mind as a feasible counter-example. In the Zen tradition of Buddhism, the very things which MacIntyre and Taylor suggest are aspects of the *logic* of agency, i.e. long term plans and purposes linked to a strong sense of self identity, are seen as problematic. Certainly, there are questions to be raised about these two examples, but at the very least, further justification is required in order to show that someone adopting this approach to life and acting with only short term point and purpose is, therefore, either not *acting* at all or not articulating their intentions in the most intelligible way. An intelligible account could be given of these actions without begging a reference to some longer term goal, since the 'goals' of existentialist authenticity and Buddhist goal-lessness could be characterised purely by reference to the very shortest of short term intentions, relating to what is conventionally known as the 'present'.[37]

3.6 Taylor on agency, articulation and the inescapability of frameworks

Another aspect of Taylor's account of the internal logic of human agency that makes it particularly problematic is the requirement that all agents must be able to *articulate* their orientation in relation to an evaluative framework. As members of a 'community of interlocutors', all human agents must, necessarily, have a sufficiently well defined sense of their own identity in order to be able to respond to demands for an answer to the question '*who is this speaking?*'.[38] I take this to reflect the rationalistic bias of Taylor's approach, since it appears to embody a particular *ideal* view of human agency rather than its logical structure. It is the kind of condition that might be expected to appertain amongst a group of philosophers on a university campus but not for *all* members of all communities, as his account requires.

There are at least two examples which show that it is incorrect to suggest, as Taylor does, that this is an essential aspect of the *logic* of human agency. Firstly, consider those who, while strongly adhering to a framework of evaluation, would not take themselves to be in a position to give a rationally satisfactory account of their conception of the good. They might, on the basis of faith in a traditional view rather than reason, locate the source of good in some supreme being whose nature is beyond complete rational articulation. They might also see themselves as engaged upon a process of self *discovery* and therefore be unable to play their full part in Taylor's community of interlocutors. The logical upshot of this, for Taylor, is that he is bound to say of such people that they are non-agents. This must also be true, from Taylor's perspective, of anyone who could not, for one reason or another, give an account of the evaluative framework which affected their behaviour, e.g. someone who is severely physically disabled. Given the internalist and phenomenalist nature of the logic of action, this would *have to be* Taylor's view, *even if* an external observer were able to articulate the motivating framework of the person in question. Of course this begs the question of what constitutes 'articulation', but the centrality of the community of interlocutors suggests that anyone would have to be in a position to *communicate* their motivating framework or basic orientation to the satisfaction of some community, in order to *qualify* as an 'agent'.[39]

A few paragraphs back I put the word 'framework' into inverted commas to suggest that its use by Taylor, particularly in the context of discussion of the perspective which he calls 'naturalism',[40] is problematic. Firstly, it demonstrates that the 'evaluative frameworks' that individuals hold or adhere to through their agency are, to a significant and controversial extent, presented as relatively static, *socially* constructed edifices, standing in *authoritative* judgement over the desires, wants and preferences of particular individuals. Taylor rejects the view that frameworks form part of an individually constructed life orientation since on his spatial model of moral action they stand as 'maps' with which individuals judge their moral 'position' relative to the good. *'On this picture'*, he says of the 'naturalist' view, *'frameworks are things we invent, not answers to questions which inescapably pre-exist for us..'*[41]

Secondly, in outlining the 'naturalist' perspective, Taylor identifies it as the view that frameworks are optional and their place in the logic of agency as one of pure contingency rather than of logical necessity. In further characterising the naturalist position he says that it is the view that frameworks are logically unnecessary since agents can and do orient themselves in relation to the good by reference only to their wants, desires and preferences. This reveals, at best, a rather problematic ambiguity at the heart of Taylor's discussion, throwing doubt upon the consistency of his challenge to (what he describes as) 'naturalism' with other aspects of his theoretical progamme. At worst, it masks a deft sleight of argument which enables him to offer an unbalanced account of the relationship between social and individual factors in his account of human agency.

Taylor's position can be stated as follows:

> ...naturalists fail to recognise that those subjective factors that they emphasise (e.g. desires, wants, preferences etc.), in fact presuppose an adherence on the part of the agent to frameworks which are significantly socially constructed and pre-exist both individual agents and any particular moral decision. For individual agents frameworks of strong evaluation are inescapable.

It is by looking to Taylor for answers to the question 'in precisely what way are these frameworks *inescapable*?' that we bring out the ambiguity mentioned in the last paragraph. There are two possible answers to this question. We might say, as Taylor seems to do at points in his text,[42] that frameworks of strong evaluation are pre-supposed when any decision is made or action performed. To suggest then, as the 'naturalists' allegedly do, that an account can be given of desires, wants and preferences, free of *any* reference to their embeddedness in frameworks of value, would to that extent be faulty. On this view it is frameworks, in principle, which are inescapable. On the other hand, it might be suggested that particular pre-existent, socially determined de facto frameworks of value, provide 'answers' to which individual agents within a particular social and cultural setting *inevitably* adhere when they make decisions and act.

The first of these characterisations of the inescapability thesis, is fully in line with the account of human agency that I have, so far, been putting forward. But it is at odds with Taylor's critique of so called 'naturalists' as well as his strong distinction between a 'framework' and an agent's individual 'orientation'. His account of their inadequacies shows clearly that he intends to promote the second stronger inescapablity thesis. It is the possibilities of creative innovation at the level of individual orientation that Taylor finds problematic in the naturalist account, not the view that frameworks as such are unnecessary. In fact his account shows that 'naturalists' *do* assume that all individual choices presuppose frameworks since he is keen to argue that naturalists suppose that agents *invent their own* frameworks, rather than regarding them as 'pre-existent' and socially determined.[43] Taylor's argument with the naturalists is not whether frameworks *as such* are *necessary* but about *who* is responsible for determining which *de facto* framework is embodied in the desires, wants and preferences of particular individuals. The view which he wants to promote and which I think should, at the very least, be subjected to close scrutiny is the stronger inescapability thesis which claims that socially determined de facto frameworks of strong evaluation are *logically prior* to, and not just logically bound up with, the individual and subjective features of human agency (desires, wants, preferences etc.).

That it is the *stronger* inescapability thesis that the reader is being asked to accept, is made clear in his later discussion of the differences between the frameworks found in India and in western societies. It is implied there that all individuals are subject to the same culturally or ethnically determined homogeneous frameworks of strong evaluation. The following quote on the situation of individuals brought up in America demonstrates a clear implicit adherence to the strong thesis,

> It matters that American young people are expected to be independent of their elders, even if this itself is one of the demands of the elders. Because what each young person is working out is an identity which is meant to be his/her own in the special sense that it could be sustained even against parental and social opposition. This identity is worked out in conversations with parents and consociates, but the nature of the conversation is defined by this notion of what an identity is.[44]

Taylor goes on to discuss the radically different definition of identity to be found in India. He says that to suggest that one view of things is better than the other would be 'ethnocentric', suggesting the homogeneity and incommensurability of the frameworks that *in fact* persist in these zones of cultural influence.[45] The latter is an empirical claim but the reference to ethnocentricity denotes an adherence to the view that no culturally neutral account of individual identity can be given, thus confirming that social factors are logically prior since the very notion of what constitutes the individual will be socially determined.

There are three strands in Taylor's account of human agency that might be taken as supporting argument for the strong thesis. There is firstly an attempt to show that, for any given individual, the de facto framework they acquire will be strongly influenced by, and embedded in, the framework which is exhibited by those who, in the broadest sense, educate them. Individuals will inevitably start out by imbibing a framework over which they exercise no control as individuals. This relatively uncontroversial thesis clearly grounds the discussion of the way in which the American young person will be inducted into a culture of individual independence outlined above. But it is important to note that it is possible to accept, in full, the empirical thesis that the frameworks of others will be accepted by individuals *before* anything like an individual orientation emerges (this might be called the *pre-existence thesis*) without accepting the strong inescapability thesis which states that those frameworks are *logically prior* to anything which the individual produces for herself.

That the genetic thesis might be thought to imply the stronger logical one rests upon the second element of Taylor's supporting discussion mentioned above. Taylor makes much of the analogy between the evaluative framework in relation to individual moral orientation and that between a language and its use for the purposes of individual articulation and expression. The use of the linguistic analogy for discussion of moral behaviour is an extremely useful one, first introduced by Michael Oakeshott and recently used to effect by John Kekes. However, it will not support the strong inescapability thesis, in the way that Taylor intends. It is in the context of language, rather than in a discussion of moral frameworks as such that Taylor explicitly sells the reader the strong inescapability thesis, which is then taken by analogy and implicitly to apply to frameworks of *moral* evaluation. A key point of crossover emerges later where the discussion moves to the way in which the *learning* of 'languages of moral and spiritual discernment' depends upon social relations while the ability to *communicate* and to be *innovative* in one's self understanding depends upon the fact that certain judgements are shared. On this Taylor says,

> I can only learn what anger, love, anxiety, the aspiration to wholeness etc. are through my and others' experience of these being objects for us, in some common space.[46]

The historical dependence of self understanding and innovation upon the acceptance of a shared set of judgements regarding what certain words and phrases should *mean* is uncontroversial in the context of a discussion about the logical preconditions of my being able to *articulate* and *communicate* my self understanding. However, this is used, without any further supporting argument, to underpin a logical point about the *nature* of the self; this is determined by its position within what Taylor calls *'webs of interlocution'*.

Notice that this is, in the first place, a move from the *genetic* presuppositions of self-understanding and innovation, directly to the *logical* preconditions of all action which, without independent support, is fallacious.[47] Secondly, there is a move from the logical preconditions of my *articulation* and *communication* of my self understanding to the *nature* of *that* self-understanding. While it is certainly true that both of these aspects of my acquiring a self-understanding (as a child) and communicating it, require some agreement between the individual and some wider community neither offers support for the thesis of strong inescapability.[48] In other words, we can accept all that Taylor says regarding the learning and communication of our individual moral and spiritual discernment without, at the same time, accepting his view that this logically presupposes that all agents must *agree* to the framework of strong evaluation that is held widely in the society to which they belong.

This analysis, influential among communitarian writers, follows a popular, but in my view misguided reading of Wittgenstein's later philosophy.[49] This takes it for granted that any agreement about the *meaning* of language, presupposes agreements of a substantial kind on the *judgements* which that language is used to make. In the case of a moral language it can be argued, as Taylor does, that effective communication of my innermost self understanding presupposes public agreement about what is to constitute, for example 'anger' or 'sadness'. This does not however mean that I have to agree with the judgements of my society about what constitutes the good life nor does it presuppose that it is impossible for the public understanding of those notions to be altered directly by a particular individual. And it is these things which the strong inescapablity thesis rules out since on that view the logical priority *must* run from the social to the individual. The form of the Wittgensteinian[50] argument that is used by Taylor here and which is to be found in much communitarian writing runs something like this:

1. Language is an inherently social phenomenon.
2. The nature of reality can only be articulated and communicated, logically, using some particular language or another.
3. Communication can only take place between members who share a language and sharing a language requires agreement about what terms mean.
4. Articulation of judgements about the nature of reality requires substantial agreement about those judgements. Therefore the nature of reality is socially determined.

While the first three aspects of this argument seem to me to be uncontroversial, the last embodies an illegitimate leap. The only thing which members of a language community have to agree about in order to communicate their self understandings are the *meanings* of the words that are used and the criteria used for purposes of identification. Beyond that there is plenty of scope for radical disagreement about *particular judgements*. Wittgenstein may well be correct in saying that we can never invent or create our own set of meanings as it were privately, even for a language used to refer to intimate aspects of our personal experience. This does lead us to deny that the relationship between words and the things to which they refer is a purely contingent one; it is one of logical necessity and socially, rather than privately, determined. However this does not imply, and should be clearly distinguished from, the stronger thesis that consequently any of the significant judgements that a language is used to make are *themselves* socially determined or have to be agreed to in order for communication to take place.[51]

Also important for the distinction which Taylor draws between framework and orientation is the spatial analogy, on the basis of which frameworks are regarded as *maps* by means of which individuals orient themselves in *moral* space. The use of this analogy is further confirmation of Taylor's adherence to what I have described as the strong inescapability thesis. An examination of its implications will show the extent to which Taylor's account of human agency is biased towards social factors and significantly at odds with a picture of the individual required by pluralism. As such it is an aspect of his account from which I wish to disassociate my own.

The assumption which lies behind the use of the spatial analogy is that an individual's relationship to the socially given evaluative framework is similar to that which exists between, say, a Londoner and their street map of London. And this analogy *appears* plausible partly because of the arguments based upon the relationship between language and reality discussed above. In order to *communicate* their self understanding all individual agents must *agree* to use a *single* framework of meaning which is socially determined. The most interesting and controversial aspect of this analogy is that it *assumes* that there will be just *one* framework of evaluation for a particular language using community. We saw above that the general linguistic arguments intended to sustain this assumption are not in fact equipped to do so.

The spatial analogy which likens an evaluative framework to a socially constructed map cannot be justified from these linguistic arguments. This is because, as has been shown, the assumptions upon which it rests are false. It is counter-intuitive to suggest that an agent cannot have a moral or spiritual orientation or self understanding unless they can articulate or communicate it. And, the view that sharing a common language requires a person to share significant judgements is unsustainable.

However, the above discussion refers to discourse which is primarily *descriptive*. It might be argued that even if the weaker Wittgensteinian thesis is applied to the language of strong evaluation, then it still offers striking support for the notion that a *single* moral framework is authoritative for the members of a given community, and that would offer some support for the limited application of the spatial analogy in the moral domain. Since the language of evaluation has a central concept, that of the 'good' and some agreement on the meaning of this term is a fundamental logical presupposition for all evaluative statements, it might be argued that individual actions and decisions, while they might be very different, will have to be logically underpinned by some *agreed* conception of it. While he doesn't argue for this point, it is clearly presupposed in Taylor's use of the map analogy. This view gains plausibility by running a number of things too closely together and it is worth just re-iterating the correct elements contained within it. Firstly, for reasons set out above, it *is* correct to say that all action logically presupposes or embodies *some* specific view of the good. Secondly, any articulation or communication of an agent's self understanding will rely on some shared notion of how evaluative language is to be used and this will include agreement about the socially determined meaning of the grammar of the word 'good', as well as a range of other evaluative terms. However, the monistic strand in the argument cannot accommodate a recognition of the open-ended and essentially contested nature which the concept of 'good' has in certain societies. The meaning of 'good' is such that those who use it regard it as fundamentally open in that it is not specifiable, in advance on the basis of widespread agreement, precisely what the criteria are that will satisfy its *correct* use. While the notion of good does embody some element of agreement, its grammar is such that it may *correctly* be used *in a wide range of perhaps contradictory ways*. It is this which undermines the monism which is built into Taylor's view that the socially determined framework provides 'answers' to the questions that are thrown up by our need to orient ourselves in moral space.

Taylor's view may well be true of those who adhere to traditions existing *within* otherwise open and plural societies but the logical necessity which he posits, *follows from,* rather than underpins, an individual's *contingent* adherence to any such tradition. It may also apply to those who have been, or are being, brought up in closed traditional communities, but then the necessity which he posits once again clearly rests upon the *contingent* fact that these societies are the way they are. Certainly, the picture of a global, closed traditional society binding individuals within a web of common evaluation is not thought by cultural analysts to characterise the state of a western society like that of Britain. Although Taylor's implicit adherence to the strong inescapability claim in his discussion of the American tradition of the independent individual might be thought to suggest that he *does* view even the common archetype of 'openness' as evidence of its being, in some sense, a closed traditional society.[52]

Consideration even of individuals brought up within closed traditional communities (e.g. American Amish people) still fails to support Taylor's inescapability thesis. The logical necessity which he posits for the relationship between the orientation of such people and a particular, traditional and socially determined notion of the good, will at all times rest upon the *contingent* fact that they *remain* part of such a closed community. The *possibility remains* that such people may, through personal decision or through force of circumstance, come to act on the basis of a radically different notion of what constitutes the good, from the one they hold at present.[53]

3.7 Kekes, weak inescapability and pluralism

While any agent necessarily acts on the basis of some particular notion of the good, irrespective of whether they are capable of articulating it, the relationship between the framework or tradition within which that particular conception of the good is embodied, and the individual who acts upon it, is one that is purely contingent. It is, therefore, possible, in my view, for individuals to radically change the frameworks which are, as a matter of necessity, embodied in their actions.

It is something like this view of things which underpins the pluralism of John Kekes. If we conceive of our society as one where a whole plethora of incompatible and incommensurable traditional conceptions of the good co-exist, then Kekes argues, we can acknowledge *both* the thoroughgoing influence of social factors, tradition and personal history on the nature of our current wants, desires etc. *and* that one of the valuable aspects of a plural society is the opportunities that it provides for individuals to move between traditional frameworks of the good, developing new and uniquely personal frameworks. This suggests a path between the voluntarism of the choosing, unencumbered self of non-cognitivist moral philosophy and the social monism of extreme communitarian thinking. Following Kekes along this path will enable us to develop a conception of human agency which moves beyond the future-oriented, individual and social aspects of human agency, discussed earlier, to recognise the fundamental importance of an historical dimension.

For Kekes there are three distinct elements which impinge upon the moral situation which confronts the agent. These are tradition, character and social morality; all three constitute a backward looking aspect or dimension to the understanding of any moral action. They might be regarded, though Kekes doesn't use this terminology, as important *sources* of present experience. The third of these elements, social morality, alludes explicitly also to the social dimension that might be visualised as an outwards or sideways looking aspect to the understanding of moral action. But all three of the elements just mentioned embody both an historical and a social backdrop to human agency.

But Kekes' communitarian arguments, against voluntarism,[54] avoid the social monism that the writings of MacIntyre and Taylor seem to support. This is because he says that tradition is both a source of individuality and the framework which enables individual expression. He does not regard the voluntaristic view as false or incoherent, as MacIntyre alleges, it is merely *incomplete* since it works with a view of human agency that has no source or genealogy since it lacks the historical dimension, mentioned earlier. Agency, on the voluntaristic view, is consequently a liberation from the *limiting* constraint of tradition. The mistake of the extreme communitarian, on the other hand, is to see traditional and social elements as co-extensive with the entire domain of human *possibility*. The relationship between the individual and their moral tradition is not characterised by the conflict model which in fact underpins *both* the voluntarist *and* extreme communitarian views. An agent's relation to a moral tradition is similar to that between a speaker and their language; it is one that is best characterised in terms both of *possibility and limitation*.

Just as an individual may choose to communicate through a number of different languages, provided that they are multi-lingual, so might an individual, living in a society with a plurality of co-existing moral traditions, use a number of them in order to interpret moral situations and through them construct a good life. Just as an individual might move during the course of their lifetime from the language of their birth to communicate exclusively in an entirely different language, through a process of learning and practice, so might an individual exchange one moral tradition for another by a similar process. Thus, if the analogy between language and moral tradition, first developed by Michael Oakeshott[55] and developed by Kekes, can be sustained, then it both undermines the conflict view of the relationship between the individual and tradition *and* supports the view that this relationship is one of contingency rather than logical necessity, as some communitarians suggest.

3.8 Agency, experience and a common conception of spirituality

At the heart of the picture of human agency set out above is the notion of a framework of ideals, beliefs and values, affecting an agent's relations with others, her self understanding and her understanding of the reality of which she is an indwelling part. Intrinsic to this framework, and rooted in a conception of what is real and ultimately significant, is some conception of human well being or 'the good'. I want to suggest, in what follows, that this framework should be regarded as a *spiritual* framework and as the cognitive dimension of an aspect of human experience that is most appropriately denoted as 'spirituality'. I believe that the frameworks that underpin all human agency cannot be adequately characterised by any other terminology since they significantly incorporate but also transcend the domains of the 'personal', the 'moral' and 'the ethical'.

The domain of human experience which I wish to identify in what follows can be linked to human agency. However, it would be wrong to think that the domain that I am identifying, for educational discussion, is merely the domain of *action*. It rather identifies both the sources and the overall direction of human action and therefore has personal, social and temporal aspects that are largely hidden from view when any action is described. The domain in question has both epistemological and ontological aspects which are an implicit in any action but which are by no means co-extensive with the domain of action since they are also present, in the same hidden manner, when a person is passive, for example, when reflecting or just 'doing nothing'.

Neither do I think that the domain identified by the frameworks suggested above could be adequately characterised as 'moral'. The relationship between what I wish to call the spiritual and the moral domains is not simple or straightforward. Since the moral traditions with which an individual is associated inevitably have some formative effect upon the character of their spirituality and the latter will, in turn, affect the way in which one conceives one's obligations to others as well as one's behaviour towards them, the moral domain is clearly both an *influential* as well as a *resultant* aspect of the spiritual. However, the domain outlined above is much more extensive than that denoted by the term 'moral' and could not, therefore, be adequately denoted by this term.

The framework and domain identified above seems to combine the personal domain with that of the moral. And it may be that some combination of these two terms would be adequate to identify the area with which we are concerned. John Kekes seems to operate in just this way disavowing all comprehensive terminology while speaking of the moral and personal aspects of our pursuit of the good life. Bernard Williams has recommended that moral philosophers should give up talk of the 'moral' in favour of talk of the 'ethical',[56] in recognition of the fact that holistic personal and social factors have an important interactive effect upon our moral obligations and our relations with others. Some might suppose, following Williams, that talk of 'the ethical' will adequately cover the domain that might otherwise be denoted as 'the spiritual'. There are a range of reasons why I think this would be a mistake, some of which cannot be articulated adequately at this stage of our investigation and I will return to those later on. At this point I would merely observe that the activity of ethics is one of *rational* reflection upon the kind of cognitive framework which undoubtedly underpins all answers to the Socratic question: *'How should I live?'*. The ethical domain points to, and is influential upon, that of the personal and moral but it is one that is essentially about *rational reflection upon* the cognitive aspects of these domains, rather than being something which can be *identified* with them. Thus, to identify the area with which we are concerned as 'the ethical' would, firstly, narrow the focus onto the *cognitive* frameworks which map out that domain and, secondly, build in a judgement about the correct *development* of that domain within an educational context. It would imply that the 'engine' of personal development should be the *rational* examination of the cognitive aspects of human experience. This would be to build in the respectable, but not uncontroversial, Socratic dictum that '..the unexamined life is not worth living'. Perhaps a policy of spiritual development *should* involve ethical reflection, but, even if this were so, it is something which should not be added at this stage, where the intention is to be significantly impartial and *descriptive*, avoiding all evaluative presuppositions. Since this is something which *is* inextricably linked to the terminology of the 'ethical' it should therefore be rejected as unsuitable as a descriptor of the domain identified above.

A terminology is required for this domain which is able to incorporate the domains of the moral, personal and ethical but which is not limited by all or any of them. Charles Taylor recognises this need for a terminology which both impinges upon the realms of the personal and the moral but which is significantly capable of pointing beyond them. This leads him to refer to the frameworks of strong evaluation as 'spiritual'. He says that his concern is with a domain which stretches beyond that of the 'moral' and forms something like a 'background picture'. This 'dimension of our moral consciousness and beliefs' has been ignored, he says, by much contemporary philosophy. In line with what I said above about a personal dimension, he goes on to suggest that this dimension raises questions not just about justice and our relations with others (the concern of the moral) but also with

> ..our sense of what underlies our own dignity, or questions about what makes our lives meaningful or fulfilling...these are too concerned with the self-regarding,..too much a matter of our ideals to be classed as moral issues..they concern, rather, what makes life worth living.[57]

In the following paragraph Taylor goes on to identify exactly what it is that makes these concerns *'spiritual'*. His explanation suggests that they are spiritual because they point beyond the personal and moral domains, to a set of standards which are independent of them. This involves, he says,

> 'strong evaluation', that is, they involve discriminations of right and wrong, better or worse, higher or lower, which are not rendered valid by our own desires, inclinations, or choices, but rather stand independent of these and offer standards by which they can be judged. So while it may not not be judged a moral lapse that I am living a life that is not really worthwhile or fulfilling, to describe me in these terms is nevertheless to condemn me in the name of a standard, independent of my own tastes and desires, which I ought to acknowledge.[58]

I have already criticised Taylor's account of the nature of the independence between the personal domain and what I take to be the social nature of these inescapable frameworks of strong evaluation. Where Taylor uses the notion of 'independence' as the key characteristic of the 'spiritual', I would wish to introduce that of 'transcendence'. This suggests both the *importance* of the frameworks which Taylor identifies *and* the fact that they *both participate in and stretch beyond* the realms of the personal and moral. And, this pointing beyond is the key to the nature of a *spiritual* framework and a key feature of the dimension of the spiritual; there is a link, in my view, between the spiritual and the significantly *hidden*.[59]

Our individual experience can therefore be thought of as constructed around a spiritual framework, which transcends any given experience, is non-material and contains elements that are hidden in a range of ways. The spiritual dimension might be regarded as a hidden, non-material source of *inspiration*. As David Carr has pointed out, the etymology of the word 'spirit' is suggestive; it is derived from the Greek word for 'breath', that is, that which is both the *source* of life and *constitutive* of it. Spirituality has a motivational aspect that can be linked to the notions of inspiration and aspiration. The foregoing discussion suggests the following characterisation of common spirituality,

> Spirituality is that quality of being, holistically conceived, made up of insight, beliefs, values, attitudes/emotions and behavioural dispositions, which both informs and may be informed by lived experience. The cognitive aspects of our common spirituality can be described, at any particular time, as being a 'framework' of ideals, beliefs and values about oneself, ones relations with others and reality/the 'world'. Logically intrinsic to this framework, and rooted in a notion of what is real and ultimately significant, is some conception of the good life (possibly, but not necessarily, related to a supreme will and agency), which informs (implicitly, via a network of unexamined assumptions/ prejudices or explicitly, via rational justification), but may not determine, all action.

This definition is non-exclusive, it successfully characterises an essential aspect of human life that schools are inevitably concerned with (whether they admit it or not) and it does so in such a way that no one could allege that any particular developmental ideal were being built into it.

While this is not the only, or the best, possible characterisation of spirituality that might be used by educational theorists, it does provide a more adequate basis for the discussion of spiritual development than we have at present.[60] It will enable policy makers to articulate its importance and to inspire the confidence (or at least to allay the suspicions of) both secular humanists, and of those from a traditional religious background.

It is clear from the characterisation outlined above that it embodies a view of the spiritual mechanism which is, in principle, open to being 'fuelled' by a transcendent and enduring reality beyond this world, in some supernatural sense, as required by certain religious views. This is the view of what transcendent means which suggests itself immediately to most readers and beyond showing that my characterisation does not *exclude* it. Some, however, might find it difficult to see how any other form of transcendence could emerge from the development of this spiritual mechanism. John White rightly points out that the mental apparatus that we bring to our present experiences is itself non-material, even when the object of the experience is material. But the way in which even our most mundane experience of material objects transcends the realm of the material is arguably much more extensive than this picture suggests.

The character and meaning which a physical object has for any given individual will itself reflect a framework of belief, understanding and evaluation which in some very real sense *transcends* both the object and the individual who perceives it. The question of what we see the object *as*, perhaps the most mundane question of all, will itself, according to the most persuasive and popularly held theory of perception[61] be answered, in part, at a level which is logically prior to the perceptual situation itself. Both the experience of any individual, as well as the language in which ideas are expressed, contain elements which are irreducibly social and traditional. And this is as true of the radical critic as it is of the most temperamentally conservative person.

Having now outlined an educationally suitable characterisation of the *meaning* of the 'spiritual' and having justified the metaphysics of human experience upon which it is based, I will move on in the following chapters to consider the issues that appertain to its *development* in schools, especially those controlled by the state.

Notes

1 Dewey, J. (1934), pp9-10.
2 Ibid., p9.
3 James, W. (1985).
4 Dewey, J. (1934) pp14-15.
5 Ibid., p26.
6 Ibid., p15.
7 Ibid., p22.
8 Moreover, this characterisation is unsupported by anything other than references to the alleged weakness and fanaticism of religious believers, together with unsubstantiated psychologism. And such criticisms of Dewey's distinction, while significant from our presently uncommitted perspective, should be regarded as fatal by those committed to that of liberal democracy. This is because, on their view, state policy makers are faced with a clear choice, either to use a characterisation of religion which is acceptable to adherent citizens or one that is defensible on purely rational or procedural grounds: it is clear in my view that Dewey has done neither. For further evidence of an in-built hostility to certain kinds of religious belief, that is those that challenge a naturalist metaphysics based on scientific method, cf. op cit, p28.
9 This could also be described as a 'phenomenological dimension' and the logical considerations arising from it the 'phenomenologic'.
10 Dewey, J. (1934), p15.
11 Ibid., p25.
12 Ibid., p27.
13 Ibid.,p43, cf., p23-4.
14 Ibid.,p25, cf. Dewey,J.(1958), p113 and Tiles, J.F.(1988), ch7 and p213ff.

[15] Ibid., p26-7, for a full exposition of Dewey's advocacy of faith in scientific method as the best and only procedure for generating appropriate metaphysical beliefs.

[16] The definitive statement of Dewey's metaphysics of experience is to be found in Dewey (1958).

[17] Dewey,J.(1934), p26.

[18] Ibid., p26-7, passim.

[19] For support of this view, see Banner, M. (1990), Newton-Smith, W.H. (1981) and Polanyi, M. (1958).

[20] Dewey's account of human experience is defective partly because it embodies a dualistic perspective inherited from the Kantian modernist tradition. In Dewey's theory of experience this Kantian perspective manifests itself, firstly, in a radical separation of the realms of 'nature' and 'culture', and secondly, in a distinctively forward looking (future directed/ futuristic) conception of human culture, linked to a theory of human action itself disproportionately characterised in terms of the exercise of will and reason. These aspects of Dewey's Kantianism come together in the essential contrast between the logically distinct realms of the 'real' and the 'ideal'. This contrast is inextricably bound together with Dewey's elevation of the scientific method (both underpinning and following from it), as final rational arbiter of what can fall into the category of the 'real', and with his devaluation of tradition in general and of religious tradition, in particular.

It is interesting that while Dewey follows a Kantian modernist path in these respects, he follows an Hegelian modernist path in suggesting that all human experience has a social dimension, an emphasis on practice being the tool used to overcome the dualisms that had haunted pre-enlightenment modernist accounts of human experience.

As such, Dewey represents the philosophical tradition which underpins much educational thinking in modern Britain. This *may* reflect the fact that Dewey has had a huge influence on the philosophy of education, but that is of little importance here. My main contention is that as far as Dewey does stand as a representative of the predominant philosophical presuppositions that underpin any discussion of spiritual education in modern Britain (and here I am making a vulnerable empirical judgement about the educational culture), then, *to that extent* a critique pinpointing the shortcomings of his account of human experience will be of more than merely historical interest. It is to this task that I will now turn as an essential step in the exposition of my suggested account of common spirituality. Accepting that Dewey's account of human experience does recognise transcendent elements that go beyond the merely present, particular and individual, it will be my contention that his account lacks an historical and traditional dimension. Stated in this way my view of what is inadequate about Dewey's modernism is precisely the critique that Hegel made of Kant's classic statement of enlightenment modernism.(cf. McDowell (1994), p109-126, Houlgate (1991), p5-40 and, especially, Pippin (1989), passim.).

[21] Franco, P.(1990), p63. See also Oakeshott (1933), p247-321.

[22] cf. Kekes, P.(1989) p135.

[23] Kant, I. (1785) trans. Paton, H.J. (1953) and Nell (O'Neill), O., (1975)

[24] This could be, in turn, *either* completely misguided *or* linked to the agent's commitment to some obscure aspect of the highway code, momentarily forgotten when the car was originally parked earlier in the day.

[25] When the distinction offered earlier between the external and internal logic is kept in mind then it will also be clear that my account does not involve an endorsement in absolute terms of the internal evaluative framework of any given agent; I am not advocating a subjectivist approach to values.

[26] Kekes defines commitments as allegiances to the conventions which guide the realisation of some selected possibilities. When these commitments cohere and form a hierarchy, we have what he calls a 'moral perspective'. While it is possible for someone to have only conditional commitments, Kekes takes the view that it is better for a person to have some unconditional commitments. Unconditional commitments are necessary in order for individuals to develop a strong sense of self (see, for example, Kekes (1989) p169). This point is somewhat at a tangent to our current concerns with human agency but it does support the argument that an educational commitment to autonomy may *presuppose* rather than undermine an education for commitment.(See also the argument presented in chapters four and five).

[27] MacIntyre (1981), p213.

[28] Kekes (1989), p151.

[29] A philosophical tradition that includes such thinkers as Aristotle, Hegel, Polanyi, Oakeshott and Berlin. The fears about the social consequences of the kind of approach advocated by Dewey were perhaps given their most powerful literary expression in Aldous Huxley's Brave New World.

[30] Just here it is worthwhile emphasising the difference between the accounts of human agency given by these two thinkers and that offered by John Kekes who, while emphasising the fact that moral reflection and moral agency is, in fact, a process of person construction, contributing to the narrative that might be offered of any particular life, does not suggest that a sense of narrative unity is a fundamental pre-requisite of the agent's moral perspective or self understanding. See, for example, Kekes (1995), p124-5.

[31] MacIntyre (1981), p212.

[32] Taylor (1989), p51-52.

[33] Ibid., p48, and cf. Ibid., p47, 50-51.

[34] cf., chapter two for detailed discussion of Carr (1995).

[35] Taylor, Op cit., p31.

[36] Ibid., p27.

[37] John Kekes develops a similar view to the effect that while a person must have self-knowledge of some sort in order to act, that self-knowledge does not have

necessarily to be coherent or rational in the way that the MacIntyre-Taylor thesis under discussion seems to presuppose. See Kekes (1995), ch7.

38 Taylor, Op cit., p38.

39 Consider the position of a space explorer who can articulate himself only in earthly languages. While in space, the earth is destroyed, along with all his extra-terrestrial companions. Thus, he is deprived of his own community of interlocutors and he is unable to articulate himself to a group of aliens who confront him on the martian wastes. He reaches for his weapon and fires at the aliens. As a direct consequence of the thesis just outlined, Taylor would be forced to make the absurd and counter-intutive judgement that this man did not 'act'. The interesting fallacy being committed by MacIntyre and Taylor in the passages under discussion is one by which the reader is being illegitimately asked to accept a *logical* point on the basis of some *commonly held notion* of what is *desirable.* This might be labelled the 'communitarian fallacy' the tendency to ascribe the status of logical necessity to that which is merely commonly agreed. It could be seen at work in the writing of Haldane (1986) and Carr (1995).

40 Taylor (1989), p30-32.

41 Ibid., p30.

42 See, for example, ibid., p35-36.

43 As was demonstrated in the quote just given, see note 40.

44 Taylor, Op cit., p40.

45 Perhaps also throwing doubt about the *depth* of his commitment to moral objectivity. From this vantage point it looks as if it might be, at best, rather parochial and rooted in something like social consensus.

46 Taylor, Op cit., p35.

47 It is an example of the so-called genetic fallacy.

48 That is, the view that any expression of an individual's moral or spiritual orientation through action (self understanding) will logically pre-suppose an agreement with the social group, to which they happen to belong, about the framework of strong evaluation with which that person maps the direction of their life.

49 See, for example, the remarks collected together in Wittgenstein, (1969). For arguments to show that the meaning of words must be socially rather than individually bestowed, see Wittgenstein (1953) sections 202, 256-281 and 290.

50 I am not suggesting here that this is a view which Wittgenstein actually held. For the suggestion that Wittgenstein held only a very weak version of this view in relation to scientific discourse and did not appear to regard it as applicable, in the way that Wittgensteinian ethicists often suggest, to moral discourse, see Cavell (1979).

51 Cf. Mulhall's discussion (in Horton and Mendus (eds), (1994), p210-220) of MacIntyre. MacIntyre may hold a similar view to Taylor as regards the inescapability of tradition, on the grounds that, unless substantive judgements are shared, it is

impossible for an action to be 'rational'. It appears to be a characteristic of communitarian thinking to see moral disagreement as a threat to the objectivity and rationality of the moral enterprise itself. Mulhall, following Cavell, says that this is based upon a false model of rationality which is underpinned by an overly scientistic approach. All that is in fact required, according to Cavell, even within the realm of science, are agreed canons of appropriateness and relevance (Cavell, (1979), p261-2.)

52 Taylor, Op cit., p40.

53 Taylor takes up the question of just how strongly inescapable his socially determined frameworks are in chapter IX of his later book, The Ethics of Authenticity. The particular chapter in that book which deals with this question is called 'An Iron Cage?' and suggests that indeed *he* regards the strong inescapability thesis as contrary to the notion of personal autonomy which is a necessary aspect of the ethics of authenticity that he wishes to advocate. However, this, in itself, does not show that my interpretation of his position in Sources of the Self is incorrect, since it may be that he has not realised the extent to which these two aspects of his project are incompatible.

54 Kekes is keen to confront the advocates of groundless individual choice that were also prime targets for MacIntyre and Taylor. These views, which he labels 'voluntarism', rest upon a conflict view of the relationship between the individual and their moral tradition,

'..my opponents' view is that reflection enables us to decide what we really want, as independent, autonomous individuals and, then to go on to try to extract it from our surroundings. '(Kekes, 1989, p.151)

55 Oakeshott (1962).

56 Williams (1985).

57 Taylor, Op cit., p4.

58 Ibid., p4.

59 The educational importance of a weakly conceived notion of transcendence is discussed further and linked with realism at the end of chapter six.

60 In Britain at least, where government backed initiatives in the area spiritual and moral development have been discussed for some time.

61 See, for example, Mulhall (1990) and McDowell (1994).

4 Culture, Politics and Education

Summary

This chapter is something of an overture to all that follows since all the issues that are explored at length later on are, at least, raised here. I begin with an attempt to summarise the state of the argument so far and I end with a look forward to the content of the following chapters.

Each of the writers featured here, John Haldane, Mike Newby, John White and Stephen Macedo, make recommendations for educational policy that rely significantly upon claims about national or political culture. In exploring their use of cultural references, I will identify some structural similarities in their approach to education that appear to unite 'liberal' and 'communitarian' writers and which, arguably, dominate educational theorising in general. I link these similarities to a political perspective which is characterised in detail and dubbed 'social democratic liberalism'.

All three writers have significant things to say about religion and in discussing their views I identify two versions of 'secularism', one based upon a commitment to impartiality and another which is hostile to some forms of religion when used uncritically to formulate educational policy.

4.1 Introduction

In the second chapter I argued for the importance of establishing a notion of common spirituality that might enable a more fruitful discussion of what the development of spirituality within the state education system might involve. In addition, I resisted the assumption found explicitly in communitarian writings and implicitly in the writings of others that somehow this might prove either a logical or practical impossibility. In the third chapter I set out an appropriate and workable characterisation of what I have called 'common spirituality' that will be used to underpin the discussion of spiritual *development* and its organisation that be undertaken later on. I believe this account of common spirituality, while it may not be impartial in any absolute terms, does not include any significant cultural or traditional bias that might make it unacceptable to some groups. This makes it a valuable resource for the discussion of spiritual development within the state education system and significantly improves the prospects for the exploration that I am about to pursue in the pages that follow since it will allow me to maximise the transparency of that discussion and enable me to illuminate the exact nature of the developmental assumptions being made at each stage.

Readers who are disatisfied with the arguments offered so far and who therefore feel unable to join wholeheartedly in the explorations that follow will, I believe, do so for one of three reasons. Some may object to my account on the grounds that *no* characterisation of spirituality can be given that does not logically depend upon or necessarily entail some particular conception of spiritual *development*. In response I have tried to suggest that a moderate and defensible communitarianism would not support the kind of bold universalist proposal that this kind of objection to my account would constitute.[1]

Others might object to the characterisation given here on the grounds that it is wrong or in some important way inadequate. A third objection might be that my characterisation claims to be impartial but that this is not in fact the case. The first thing to note about these two kinds of objection is that to the extent that they recognise both the conceptual possibility and value of separating the question of *meaning* from that of *development*, they do not prevent the reader from following the path that I will lay down in the pages that follow. And, in as far as the third objection rests on the assumption that significant impartiality is at least possible then it offers some support for the overall strategy even in objecting to some of its particulars. The characterisation as it stands may have significant imperfectections but I think that it is about the best, significantly impartial characterisation of spirituality that can be set out to facilitate further discussion. If others have better accounts that live up to the criteria set up at the beginning of the last chapter then I will happily defer to them. If the previous arguments form the starting point for a debate that eventually leads to a more useful characterisation moulded by other hands, then this aspect of my study will have been successful in at least one of its aims.

In offering a broad characterisation of spirituality in such broad terms I hope that I have forced a recognition of the fact that *any* educational programme will embody implicitly, if not explicitly, certain developmental effects that impact upon the domain of the spiritual. Schools have always and will always be agencies of spirituality, affecting the spiritual life of those who pass through them. Philosophers of education have long been aware that this kind of analysis can be applied to the school in terms of its effects upon the personal, social, moral and civic development of the child; they have been and remain more reluctant to acknowledge the educational validity of a concern for the spiritual domain. I believe there are two main reasons for this reluctance. Firstly, the lack of a clear notion of what that domain is and what its development might involve. Secondly, the link in the common imagination between spirituality and religion. I hope now to have removed *both* of these barriers to the acknowledgement that talk of spiritual development has a place in all education institutions, even those run by the state. In addition, I have tried to show that, rightly understood, spiritual development certainly overlaps with and arguably incorporates those aspects of personal development outlined above. My own view is that one cannot offer *purely rational* justification for a preference for the language of the spiritual over that of the personal or ethical. My reasons for preferring the former are as follows. Firstly, it would appear that as a matter of legal and educational tradition those responsible for framing educational laws and setting up a state funded education system in Britain, at least, preferred to couch things in these terms. Secondly, many liberal educational thinkers tend to assume some association between a liberal approach to education and the kinds of secularism that are hostile either to religion per se [2] or to particular types of religion. In this chapter I intend to show how this association between liberalism and secularism is exemplified in recent papers by Macedo and Newby. And to facilitate more effective discussion of this, I will make a distinction between two types of secularism (1 and 2) which I will show to be essential in pinpointing liberal equivocation in the use of the term. In view of this the fact that the language of spirituality does have the ability to incorporate the religious while not being identified with it is useful since it reminds those liberal educational thinkers who are inclined to assume otherwise that, in the words of Amy Gutmann, *'a liberal state cannot rightly mandate an exclusively secular education for children'*.[3]

In addition, towards the end of chapter three, I set out arguments designed to show that the language of spirituality describes an important domain of human experience which incorporates the language of the 'personal', 'ethical' and 'moral'.[4]

All those mentioned so far who have written specifically about spiritual development within the state education system, rightly, make explicit reference to its cultural and/or political context. David Carr and John White both make quite clear *empirical* claims regarding the nature of the *culture* which exists in Britain.[5] In addition, John White and Terry McLaughlin make claims about the nature of the political parameters within which any educational initiative is expected to operate. The latter puts forward a balanced account of the two main alternatives, as he sees them, and is content to spell out the kinds of constraints that each might impose upon the education of the whole person as the necessary groundwork for any future account of spiritual development.

Further discussion of these cultural and political aspects of the matter is of vital importance and, in my view, needs to be given a more closely argued and nuanced treatment than it has received thus far, at least to my knowledge. This is because, as McLaughlin makes clear, any discussion of spiritual development will inevitably have a determinative effect upon the *personal formation* of young people. As such the principles, whether explicit or implicit, which govern its implementation and character will require clear justification that must involve considerations of a political and cultural nature.

Though the political questions might be regarded as essentially ideological, empirical claims about the nature of British society will have some bearing on them, since education is, in part, a preparation for life within a particular cultural community. The *political* culture will be an important aspect of this and will, for example, define the extent to which the state might be justified in exerting a determinative influence on the formation of future citizens through its ability to control the education system. This will add a cultural and empirical dimension to the political discussion of the nature and extent of state control over education, the relationship between the rights and duties of the state and the relationship between these and the rights of other important parties like, for example, parents and local communities.

In this chapter I want to deal with the cultural and political issues that must be considered before any positive account of spiritual development can be developed. These issues have critical bearing upon the very possibility of producing a *common* conception of spiritual development for use in state schools. And the results of this discussion will form important criteria which will be used in the chapters which follow to judge a sample of suggested common spiritual development packages. But, as exemplified by Terry McLaughlin's cautious approach, it is of vital importance that the cultural and political constraints are identified and laid out *first* so that the various candidates for spiritual development can be evaluated, as it were, objectively with reference to educational criteria. When discussing these political aspects of the debate, I will follow the lead of Carr, Haldane and McLaughlin[6] and attempt to set out a range of alternative conceptions of the political-cultural context within which the education system exists. But I intend to offer a significantly broader range of alternatives than has been identified, I believe, by any of these writers, all of whom work within a rather rigid 'liberal or communitarian' framework.

4.2 Haldane, Christian communitarianism and state education

I begin, however, by examining claims made by John Haldane, in a recent discussion of the role of religious education and church schools in the context of modern Britain. Haldane's paper[7] was prompted by attacks upon the place of religious education in the state school curriculum and the existence of church schools by advocates of multicultural education.[8] Haldane sets out to defend the current arrangements for the provision of religious education in British state schools against reformist calls for it to be removed from the statutory curriculum in the face of the increased secularisation and pluralisation of British society. His defence of religious education is multi layered and relies in part on a particular cultural analysis.

In parts six and seven of the paper Haldane says that British culture,

> ..remains broadly Christian; not, of course, in the sense that the majority are members of Christian churches but in the deeper sense that our institutions and values can only be rendered intelligible by reference to the creative and sustaining influence of this religion...the principles of our social life by which all are bound are those derived from the Christian religion.[9]

In making this claim Haldane is not trying to deny the fact that Britain is in some senses a pluralist society since it *'..contains people of different ethnic groups and of different social, political and religious loyalties'*.

Haldane's argument to show that those groups and individuals that would not regard themselves as Christians should nonetheless be legitimately subjected to institutional arrangements which do embody an allegiance to Christian values seems to embody three types of argument.

The first argument offered by Haldane to support this is that the social and political principles that underpin that culture are *historically dependent* upon it. Haldane says that

> The notions of freedom, moral equality and social responsibility which feed into law and government through concepts of Justice and Democracy, themselves derive both meaning and justification from Christian doctrines.

Having stated this thesis in fairly strong terms, Haldane then sets about the task of giving it more concrete illustration, but in doing so significantly tones down the strength of the claim. In the next section he says,

> In claiming that all men are created free children of a loving God, Christianity gives content and support to the idea that each person is a moral agent and thereby the bearer of responsibilities and entitlements...Likewise, the thought that...there is some respect in which all are equal..flows naturally from

> Christian teaching. Again the notion of democracy is fed from two sources deep within this religious tradition: first, the dignity of man, as possessor of freedom and reason: and second, his propensity for evil as inheritor of original sin..[10]

This 'historical dependency argument' is bound together with others. Most particularly and obviously, it derives its force from the thesis that without some reference to Christianity British culture and its social institutions would be *unintelligible*. The reference to the 'intelligibility' of British institutions and values, seems to suggest that we could make no sense of the concept of 'British' culture without reference to Christian values. Without reference to these values it would be impossible to speak of 'British' culture at all since they bestow some conceptual unity upon what would otherwise be unintelligible. It should be noted that this 'intelligibility argument', as it is presented by Haldane, amounts to no more than an assertion and one that presupposes exactly that which a pluralist or liberal interpretation might wish to challenge.

However, I think that the view that British culture could not be comprehensively understood without *some* reference to its historical dependence upon the Christian tradition and that *this* has clear implications for educational practice is largely uncontroversial. But while this claim may be well founded, the educational implications of it are more limited, in my view, than Haldane appears to assume. Such considerations may well sanction some requirement that children of whatever ethnic or religious group be given lessons in religious education in order that they have *knowledge and understanding of* the Christian tradition and Christian values, as part of a broader commitment to ensuring that they have such an understanding of British culture and its values. However, that *in itself*, will not be enough to sanction an educational commitment to the *promotion* of Christian values. Yet *this* is precisely what Haldane takes his cultural arguments to support, as the following quote shows,

> The conclusion of the present argument therefore, is that religion should be taught in state schools since it is the duty of government to provide education the aims of which derive from the common values of the society.[11]

While this might be open to more than one interpretation, the most obvious is that since the common values of our society are Christian values, it is the duty of government to provide an education *the aims of which* also derive from Christianity. He explicitly denies that his arguments are intended to advocate 'religious formation' within the state education system, but it is clear that this is inconsistent with his communitarian approach to the educational process which calls for *'partiality in favour of certain agreed social virtues'* and is necessarily *'partisan'*.[12] This may not amount to religious formation, but it does, at the very least, mean that Christian values should have some significant impact upon the *personal formation* of *all* children in British state schools.

The bolder educational claims embedded in this quotation may well be thought to follow from the third kind of argument which Haldane deploys in his attempt to assert the cultural importance of Christian values. He says that these form the social principles 'by which all are bound'. This embodies the view, which he attributes to communitarian thinking, but which undoubtedly underpins much liberal educational thinking as well, that,

> ..society is only able to function because..diverse groups of which a pluralist society is made up,..are worked together into a unity.[13]

Any society requires for its effective functioning a set principles of social life to which and by which all are bound together. For British society, according to Haldane, those principles are derived from the Christian religion. It is clear, however, that this falls very far short of what will be required to convince anyone wishing to affirm the pluralist nature of society. Many advocates of pluralism would agree wholeheartedly with Haldane's view that a society requires *some* principles of social life by which all are bound. Presumably the constitutional and legal arrangements that currently exist and which have de facto jurisdiction over all those who are a part of British society do, in fact, constitute just such a set of principles. But the question remains as to whether the principles which hold British society together do, in fact, derive from Christianity.

The claim that there is some causal link between the notions of democracy and justice as such and the Christian tradition is obviously false. These notions were being discussed by classical philosophers well before the Christian tradition emerged and were, in all probability, conceived independently of the Jewish tradition. The suggestion that there is a causal connection between the way in which these classical notions are understood in Britain and Christian ideas, is perhaps more defensible or at least less easy to disprove. The argument here is only worth having if it is being claimed that there is not just a causal link but that without a *continued commitment* to a Christian view of things, i.e. the kinds of doctrinal commitments suggested by Haldane, our particular understanding of these classical notions would collapse *along with those institutions themselves*. And here the language which Haldane uses to make his case suggests that he is less than confident about the plausibility of the kind of claim which is needed.

For we can agree that Christianity gives *'content and support'*, that the idea of equality of treatment *'flows naturally from Christian teaching'* without making any commitment to the view that either of these ideas derive from, or are in any significant way logically dependent upon, an allied *commitment to* Christian teaching. Even Haldane's claim, further down the page, that the notion of democracy is 'fed from two sources deep within' Christianity falls short of making the kind of claim to *logical* dependency (albeit unsupported by substantive argument) that his broader educational argument requires and which some of his statements suggest. Though the language used to set out the detailed case is open to and perhaps inclines towards a weaker claim, Haldane is aware that the stronger case must be made. It is not just that 'they continue to derive sustenance' from the Christian tradition,

> ..it remains the case that the values presupposed in social life have their source in this religious tradition and this is not simply a fact about its historical origins.[14]

Indeed, further on, he claims that the church 'created' certain important institutions and it *continues* to be the '..main source of reflection upon the meaning of public virtue'.

The foregoing discussion shows that the educational implications that Haldane wishes to derive from his particular cultural analysis, in fact, require further independent support. His educational arguments in fact rest upon a *political* claim that is, in principle, independent of the particular cultural analysis that he gives and which is compatible, as we shall see, with a range of rival cultural claims. Haldane sets out the political principle on which his educational case rests in the following way,

> Since government is charged with providing education it must determine and implement public policy. As in other areas this is in part a matter of legislation including the imposition of statutory duties on local authorities and also of providing guidelines. Of course, the determination of public policy is a complex affair but earlier argument shows that in general this must be a matter of looking to the nature of the culture and to its traditional value.[15]

I will eventually critically examine the validity of this politico-educational principle. But, clearly, this does not *follow from* a particular cultural analysis but rather is used by Haldane to give the particular, and perhaps quite correct, cultural analysis that he offers, educational credibility.

4.3 Newby, White and secular approaches to education

In adopting this approach Haldane is not alone. In a recent discussion of spiritual development for the maintained school entitled 'Towards a Secular Concept of Spiritual Maturity'.[16] Mike Newby sets out an analysis of our common culture which is quite contrary to that of Haldane. Its explicit starting point is a conviction that *'our common culture is not religious'*.[17] In Newby's view the aims of spiritual education must be redefined with reference to the nature of our culture and these will influence educational policy makers who have,

> ..long realised that education cannot be values free. To write policy documents is not only to commend certain values, it is to explicate that culture into which the school should initiate pupils.

He sets out to offer an account of spiritual maturity that might inform school policy makers by referring, firstly, to a cultural and political perspective. It is, he says, *'..an explication of the values perspective of our common secular culture as liberal democrats'*. It demands a recognition of the fact that

> ..spirituality has become, thanks to the pluralism and post-traditionality of late-modernity, focused upon the preservation of individual, national and international identity rather than religious development.[18]

The political-educational principle at work here is similar to that used by Haldane even though they hold quite different views about the character of the national culture. For both Haldane and Newby, despite the differences between them, educational policy should be influenced by, perhaps even determined by, some *empirical* analysis of the nature of national society and culture.

The same kinds of political-educational assumptions are to be found in John White's discussion of the OFSTED discussion paper.[19] As we saw earlier, he is critical of its *alleged* conflation of spiritual development with 'religious development' on the grounds that *no national consensus could be established on that basis* to support the nationwide implementation of spiritual development. His response is to suggest that a secular approach might command such a consensus, presumably because the values of secularism could not be denied by any rational person.[20] I argued elsewhere that this embodied an unnecessary hostility to religious views that would be unacceptable within the British system of education or any system that considered itself committed to liberalism or pluralism.

This illustrates the way in which the debate about spiritual development, and therefore personal development as well, is almost always bound up with certain assumptions of a cultural and political nature. They are to be found in both liberal and communitarian writers and are found explicitly, as I have shown, in the discussions of Haldane and Newby. I will call these assumptions 'social democratic liberal' and I will approach a discussion of their implications for the organisation and nature of a programme of spiritual development by way of further discussion of the claim of both Mike Newby and John White that any analysis of our culture leads to the conclusion that it is 'secular'.[21] For these writers the fact that our culture can in some significant way be truly denoted as 'secular' has important implications for the values to be promoted or nurtured by the state through its influence on the education system.

An examination of Newby's recommendations for a secular approach to spiritual development demonstrates that considerable care is required in the use of this quite difficult term. We can, I think, determine two distinct uses of the term 'secular', when describing the values inherent in a public institution like a state school. Obviously, the very notion of 'secular' implies some distance from religious values. But this distance might take one of at least two forms. I shall call Secularism 1, in this context, the view that *public institutions should operate as if religious views or some particular religious viewpoint is either false or, in some way, problematic. From this perspective, it would be justified for representatives of the state to act as if a particular religious view were untrue and to operate in a way that discouraged children from coming to hold it.*

As should be clear this kind of view has its origin in a particular and hostile view about religion and its truth claims. Secularism 2, on the other hand, is the more moderate view that *the state cannot act as if religious truth claims are true on the grounds that it would be inappropriate for the state to act as if any comprehensive view of the good is true.*

The grounding for this kind of secularism is not a particular negative attitude to religion, as such, but in a particular and characteristically *liberal view of the nature and scope of state action*. In summary it is the view that the state can rationally justify its interventions, particularly in the context of a plurality of sincerely held values, *if it acts impartially* with respect to any particular conception of the good. Alongside this commitment to the impartiality of the liberal state, it is recognised firstly that it is in the interests of all that the state acts but that it is constrained to act only on the basis of a set of procedural values that all rational citizens should support.

In line with Secularism 2, Mike Newby welcomes the openness shown in recent government pronouncements to the 'secular possibilities' for spiritual development. This demonstrates an implicit recognition of the fact that it would be wrong, from the liberal perspective, for a government to exhibit some partiality towards *religious* development, as such.[22] The following quote starts off in the same way but soon begins to exhibit the kind of negativity towards religious perspectives that is a characteristic of secularism 1.

> One central feature of the liberal society is its commitment to openness of enquiry. Integral to this is the valuing of critical and imaginative thought which is not restricted by refusal to question accepted authorities. That this rules out certain religious and ideological attitudes should be clear at the outset..It is important, however, if we are to develop an integrative system of values, that we give up pretending to show respect for authorities that inhibit change by repressing unrestrained enquiry. This requires no supporting argument unless we remain convinced that the only spiritual hope lies in a revival of tightly defined tradition...[23]

The ambiguity between the two notions of secularism is brought out in the following quote which I think could just about be given an interpretation compatible with secularism 2.

> If we feel so convinced that our common culture is not religious, and that the development of children into maturity cannot be religious in any realistic sense of the word...[24]

This *could* be read as: Given that the set of agreed common values that it might be legitimate for the secular liberal state to act upon, could not include those of religion, then it cannot require a school to operate with a notion of spiritual maturity derived from a religion. The same could be said of the following, *'Indeed, spiritual maturity cannot be religious, if religion is understood in the traditional realistic sense'*.[25]

It very soon becomes clear, however, that Newby regards traditional, realist interpretations of religion as fundamentally unsustainable in the modern age of 'critical thought'. On page 97 he says that *'..today the supernaturalist dogmatic has to be transcended if one is to go on caring in a climate where beliefs evaporate like dew in the critical sunshine'* and Sigmund Freud is cited as an authority for the view that religious beliefs are mere *'comforters and motivators'*.

Thus Newby takes himself to have established, in the case of what he calls 'traditional realist' interpretations, a logical connection between a version of secularism 1, which should perhaps henceforth be known as 'Non-realist'[26] Secularism 1, and Secularism 2. In taking up this position, Newby doubtless takes comfort and inspiration from the fact that some Christian theologians also believe that the only rational approach to religion, appropriate to our modern age, is one that is non-realist and 'expressivist' in its use of God-talk.[27]

Newby makes the move from non-realist secularism 1 to secularism 2 in the following way:

> The religious life, as traditionally conceived, is a life for which the celestial view is pivotal. the believer's life derives meaning and direction from a theological perspective determining language, thought and values. Once we remove this framework and begin to entertain the notion that God's will is valid only in so far as it can be identified on grounds independent of scripture and tradition (Hirst,1974) we sense that the age of religious realism is ending...[28]

That the nature of the secularism 1, embodied here, involves a thoroughgoing commitment to theological non-realism is confirmed by the fact that elsewhere Newby advocates that the secular state should encourage what he calls a '..debate about religious meanings' but under an *'expressivist umbrella'*.

But while the proponent of secularism 2 may wholeheartedly support the view that the state cannot legitimately adopt the realist theological framework (contra the Christian communitarian thinking of Haldane) and operate 'on grounds independent of scripture and tradition', she may wonder why the state should have *any* interest in either, firstly, the empirical fact (and let's assume, *for the sake of argument*, that in cultural terms it is true) that the 'age of religious realism is ending' or, secondly, in siding up *with a particular strand of theological thinking* and against theological realism. For while such a state might not be licensed to act as if certain controversial religious views were true, it does not follow automatically from this that the state is licensed to act to undermine such views through the state education system.

A secular state committed to impartiality would *only* be licensed to take up such a particularist theological perspective, *if* one or more of the following conditions were fulfilled:-

1. It could be shown to be *an inevitable and unavoidable* consequence of its acting impartially in the domain of education.
2. It could be shown that those types of religious belief excluded by it were harmful.[29]

Newby clearly fails to offer any adequate argument to show that either of these two important conditions are in fact fulfilled with regard to theological realism. In part this is due to the fact that he regards some reference to culture as sufficient.[30] It appears, in addition, that he regards the *rationality* of certain forms of religious belief to be in doubt and he may therefore regard this as sufficient to satisfy either or both of the conditions set out above. This stance is of great interest since 'theological realism' would be the most accurate description of the theological perspective of a *significant minority* of British citizens, from a wide range of religious traditions, with children of school age and, arguably, the majority of religious leaders and thinkers. It is a view which contradicts any moderate secularism since it recommends that the state use its offices to *promote* a particular conception of the good designed not just to reflect but to also to ensure, for no apparently legitimate political reason, that the 'age of religious realism' does in fact end. And, when we consider the context of Newby's comments, as the basis for proposals about the nationally organised conception of spiritual maturity to be used within the state school system, then there can be no doubt that his proposed programme would have profound effects upon the personal development of children from religious backgrounds educated within the state system.

Secularism 1, rooted in a negative attitude towards religion, can only be shown to be compatible with secularism 2, rooted in the values of liberalism, if it can be shown that religion in general or some particular type of religious adherence is irrational or harmful. Those wishing therefore to say that secularism 1 is an integral aspect of secularism 2, must *at the very least* construct some argument to show that religious belief is irrational. And reference to the attitudes of people within the British population, a decline in theistic belief, church going etc. will not be sufficient. Political and educational theorists who wish to assume a logical connection between these two kinds of secularism, on the grounds that the state is justified in excluding or undermining forms of religious belief that can be demonstrated to be irrational or harmful must, firstly, justify *that* controversial view[31] *and then* construct arguments to that effect, based upon or similar to those of philosophers like Ayer and Flew.[32] The burden of proof in this respect does not lie with the religious believer but with those who would attempt to exclude religious views from the public arena through the linkage of the two forms of secularism outlined here. Anyone familiar with the recent history of discussion in the philosophy of education will know that arguments designed to question the very rationality of religious belief will be very difficult to sustain and will have to meet the rigorous rational defences of religious belief constructed recently by Basil Mitchell, Stephen Banner and others.[33] I have no intention here of rehearsing any of these arguments, but merely wish to point out that the kind of logical connection that some working in the philosophy of education wish to establish between the two kinds of secularism, or between secularism 1 and liberalism, will require some reference to this on-going debate within the philosophy of religion.

Without the kind of argument required to show that the two kinds of secularism are logically linked, the two views must, in fact, be regarded as logically incompatible, since adherence to secularism 1 would then constitute an unjustified partiality against religion and in favour of humanism.[34]

The tendency of Newby and others to underestimate the need for further justification of the link between the two kinds of secularism that he deploys may be connected to the fact that he also supports the educational-political principle that was identified in the earlier discussion of Haldane. We saw there a tendency to place a very high value on the relevance of empirical cultural judgements when attempting to justify particular approaches to educational policy, accompanied by a distinct lack of justificatory argument. But independent argument *is* required to show that any value that is integral to the general or political culture of a particular society should *also* become one of the common values to be promoted or nurtured by government policy. It is perhaps easy to see why communitarians are sympathetic to this conservative position, it is not at all clear why liberals should support it, especially in the context of pluralism, where a range of often contradictory value systems co-exist within the same polity.

4.4 Macedo, civic education and the culture of liberal democracy

However, some liberals will be sympathetic to an allied principle, one which states that *certain* cultural ideals should be embodied legitimately into government strategy. They will also argue that a common conception of education is required as an essential aspect of state education. These liberals will see that a common conception of education should embody certain important values, not because they embody the common culture of a particular society, but because they are essential to a particular liberal view of the *political* culture. These values will be those which underpin the kind of impartial approach to policy that formed the roots of secularism 2. The classic modern statement of this 'anti-perfectionist'[35] liberal view is to be found in the political liberalism of John Rawls. Rawls says that liberalism must start from a recognition of the facts of pluralism and operate impartially *only* on the basis of values derived from the *overlapping consensus* of all groups within the society that live up to the requirements of what he calls *public reason*.[36] This kind of liberalism will be committed to a common conception of education quite specifically because it will be important, from that political perspective, that citizens are educated to play a full and active part in the life of a polity described as liberal and democratic (i.e. a political culture which is constituted by the collective decisions of free and equal citizens, from a variety of values backgrounds). Anti-perfectionist liberals will wish the state to have no interest in promoting a particular comprehensive conception of the good. They will, however, be prepared to sanction the promotion of certain *procedural* values as part of a common conception of *citizenship* education. *This* will inevitably have consequences for the personal formation of pupils in state schools. While this common conception of spiritual development will not be actively hostile to religious viewpoints, and will line up with the principles of secularism 2, outlined above, it *will* operate in a hostile way towards comprehensive conceptions of the good life which are deemed to be either intolerant or which otherwise prevent future citizens from taking up their place as free and equal citizens of the liberal democracy.

Stephen Macedo has written two papers recently which have attempted to outline and defend the values derived from this kind of liberalism as they will operate within a common conception of education to transform future citizens along lines laid down by the constitutional (i.e. political) requirements of a liberal democracy. The commitment to the development of tolerance and freedom embodied necessarily in a satisfactory civic education will have consequences for the education of children from certain religious groups within society.

> Successful liberal constitutional institutions must do more than help order the freedom of individuals prefabricated for life in a liberal political order: it must shape the way that people use their freedom, and shape people to help insure that freedom is what they want.[37]

This means, according to Macedo, that liberals will seek actively to promote certain values that conflict with the wishes of certain otherwise law abiding citizens. He recognises that an anti-perfectionist liberal programme, fully committed to the principle of impartiality, will nonetheless sanction a certain approach to education built upon a particular characterisation of the good society. This will be legitimate if *that* action is only limited to the promotion of a certain desirable *political* culture and the transformative changes that occur will be merely a necessary 'double effect' of the requirements of political impartiality. Macedo acknowledges the communitarian critique of the *neutralist* liberal approach to education and sees that the public institution of a common conception of education will have a direct effect upon the constitution of individuals. Education is perhaps one of the few areas of policy where the dividing line between the public and the private domains is straddled. It therefore presents a particular challenge to those wishing to follow Rawls' political liberalism. He says,

> If a constitutional regime is to succeed and thrive, it must constitute the private realm in its image, and it must form citizens willing to observe its limits and able to pursue its aspirations.[38]

Macedo believes that an adherence to a particular political culture will have direct educational implications. He is also uncharacteristically candid in stating that liberalism's commitment to pluralism is necessarily limited, individual and communal diversity being promoted only within the parameters laid down by certain liberal and democratic values.[39]

This is well illustrated in Macedo's discussion of the Mozert case in a recent paper. Here Macedo supports the view that it was correct to overrule the desire of a group of religious parents who objected to a multiculturalist reading scheme, offered by their state funded school. The principles which he lays down in the course of this discussion focus on the problematic nature of *any* attempt to work the commitment to impartiality, that is at the heart of Rawlsian anti-perfectionist liberalism, together with a commitment to a programme of *common* civic education based upon the common values agreed for the *public* sphere. While anti-perfectionist liberalism thrives upon a distinction between the public, non-public and private spheres, a certain form of liberalism[40] is tied to the view that the provision of education is primarily an aspect of the *public* sphere.

This problem is presented clearly by Macedo and is resolved in characteristic social democratic fashion by an assertion of the overriding importance of *public* values within a common conception of education. Unfortunately, Macedo fails to see that this resolution of the problem is in conflict with the very principles which appear to make political liberalism a truly liberal and pluralistic approach to public policy. Those basic principles are spelled out in Macedo's characterisation of political liberalism which he says,

> ..is not..based on a single account of the whole truth of the human condition. It holds that all reasonable people will agree on certain fundamental principles of justice, which justify democratic political procedures and a range of basic freedoms, but it does not assert the truth of one account of the meaning of life as a whole. It insists at the very base, indeed, that there are *many* reasonable answers to the deepest questions of meaning and value, religious and philosophical views of mankind's highest ends.[41]

This is, I think, an excellent statement of the Rawlsian anti-perfectionist position. It is the version of liberalism which has, in my view, the best chance of accommodating cultural and individual diversity and therefore is that version of liberalism that best embodies a commitment to pluralism and is closest to the classic liberal position. It lines up with the perspective that I described above as secularism 2 and it does demand an allegiance from those holding religious views, even those of a fundamentalist or totalistic kind. This is because this kind of liberalism strictly aims to *confine* the imposition of common values to the political domain thereby disavowing any attempt to impose those values in the *non-public* or *private* domains. It should be noted here that its ability to command the allegiance of those with strongly held views, at odds with those upheld in the public domain, *depends* in turn upon its ability to make the distinction between the 'public' and 'private' spheres, in a way that is *acceptable to all*. I think that this distinction would just have to be made to the satisfaction of public reason in order for full allegiance to be demanded. However, I think it is arguable that if we wish to see the political order as a fully rational order, something to which Rawlsians aspire, then *the distinction itself* would have to be shown to be part of a de facto overlapping consensus since it is obviously more fundamental in the Rawlsian scheme of things than any exclusivist conception of 'public reason', which would seem logically to require rather than support it: it is not possible to conceive of 'public reason' without some *prior* reference to a conception of the 'public' domain.

In view of this I think Macedo is quite right to say that

> Political liberalism furnishes grounds for not supporting those who insist on the whole truth of their particular cultural or religious belief system at the expense of a system of mutually respectful liberal multiculturalism..[42]

Under this conception of things a person who objects to abortion, may be required to show an allegiance to a democratic process of public policy construction that eventually not only permits abortion but, as in the case of Britain, uses tax payers' money to *fund* abortions. Here, as in the case of pacifist objections to the funding of nuclear weaponry, the liberal 'toughmindedness' that Macedo claims to be necessary in the case of the Mozert families *can* I think be be justified. The argument to support this might run as follows: While private policy on these matters may take a number of rationally justifiable forms, public policy *has* to follow a particular line. We have a method of resolving this, the democratic process, to which all have full, free and equal access. Unfortunately, given the facts of pluralism it will inevitably reach conclusions to which *some* loyal citizens will have sincere objections. There are good reasons why it would be impractical and expensive to have a system in which conscientious objections of this kind might be allowed to impact upon the payment of personal taxation, appropriately and effectively. And on questions of public decency, it would not be correct to cut the fit of public policy to suit the sensitivities of a minority, and so on.

Note that this justification of liberal toughmindedness *applies only* where the overlap with the private is *strictly limited*. It also *only applies* where *diversity of public provision* is just not an option. The British legal system and National Health Service must either permit and fund abortions, or not. In the same way a country must choose between holding nuclear weaponry or not. The democratic process is a way of resolving these important and intensely controversial issues into a *single* policy stance. The anti-abortionist and pacifist may object most strongly to being part of a society where a democratic decision has been made to support something which, *from their private perspective*, are morally wicked policies. However, the liberal will be compelled to say that this is 'tough'. She will insist that such objections must, in Macedo's words, be *'put aside'* since

> ..political power is.. thought of as a trust held in common (held by us all in our capacity as fellow citizens), which may not be disposed of for our private purposes.[43]

We are then required, in such cases, by this liberalism to separate our private and public selves in rationally justifiable ways.

The question that arises immediately is whether *education policy* falls into the category of *public* policy in the same way. This is a question that Macedo fails even to recognise and he assumes, wrongly in my view, that the provision of education shares the key characteristics outlined in the last paragraph and that it is self-evidently and primarily an issue within the public domain. He argues that common civic education is necessary because the state has the right to promote the *'political supremacy of liberal and democratic values'* and to ensure that children are educated towards *'..the virtues needed by liberal citizens'*. He spells out what form that common civic education should take in the following way,

> ..we must remember that children cannot be good citizens of a diverse liberal polity unless they are taught that critical thinking and public argument-reason giving and reason demanding in public- are the appropriate means of political justification.[44]

Notice that this is a normative claim, depending on the view that the polity in question is correctly characterised as 'liberal democratic'. This is a particular claim which cannot in my view be made about any particular political culture without further justification. Macedo's comments are made in respect of the USA but it would be wrong to think that this characterisation were automatically true also of Britain, despite the fact that aspects of the British constitutional system have inspired liberal democratic systems around the world. The second thing to notice about this statement, is that it presumes the educational-political principle that was identified earlier in relation both to Haldane and Newby. It is the view that empirical truths about the nature of a culture- in this case the *political* culture- should automatically, and without further argument, be used to determine the values to be nurtured within the educational system associated with that culture.

Certainly, it might be desirable for to be given and understanding of the culture in which they are likely to pursue their lives. However, I don't see that a liberalism of the kind outlined above should wish to ensure that children are educated to have the virtues which the advocates or servants of that particular political system deem to be 'appropriate'. This would seem to presuppose the flawed view that a *good citizen* could not, as part of their comprehensive system of values, entertain a complete loathing for the democratic system and a loathing for the views of their fellow citizens. Neither can I see that this stance is implied, or justified, by Macedo's own characterisation of the anti-perfectionist liberal position. It is not clear to me why the state, *especially one based on liberal and democratic values*, should have any interest whatsoever in *private attitudes* to liberal democracy as a system.[45] Surely, only if such attitudes were to lead someone *to interfere with that system* would the state have *any* grounds for constraining a citizen in this way. In the absence of this kind of justification it might be argued that any move by the state to alter the beliefs and attitudes of its child-citizens through a compulsory education system *would itself be undemocratic*, since it would be an attempt to constrain freedom of thought, by constraining it within a rationalistic conception of 'the requirements of the current system'.

Macedo suggests that another essential characteristic of a liberal democratic education is an exposure to a programme of multicultural education. The 'political' justification for this is that

> ...children must..be exposed to the religious diversity that constitutes our polity for the sake of learning to respect as fellow citizens those who differ with them in matters of religion. The crucial thing is that their civic education should be guided by civic imperatives: the question of religious truth should simply be left aside. Children must be taught that all religions are equal in the eyes of the state.[46]

This is the principle which Macedo draws upon to justify liberal toughmindedness in the face of objections from fundamentalist parents claiming that such a programme conflicts with their religious views about the personal development of their children. In this case, says Macedo, it is the common public values which must override those of the parents. Appeal is made here to a principle which *appears* to line up with secularism 2[47] *but*, in the context of *common* civic education, it in fact amounts to a version of secularism 1 and therefore runs against the principles of impartiality which are central even to Macedo's own account of political liberalism.[48]

Given that the Mozert parents have reasonable grounds for arguing that a programme of civic education which exposes their children to a range of views at odds with their religious tradition and given a commitment only to secularism 2, as exhibited in the statement that '*..religious truth should simply be left aside*', it is difficult to see what grounds there could be for arguing that children must be inculcated with the religious belief that '*all religions are equal in the eyes of the state*'.

Several points should be noted here. Firstly, this comment embodies the view, pointed out above, that citizens of the political liberal state are not only to comply with and support the procedures of public reason and decision making but also *privately to agree* with them. I don't see why we should expect a good citizen to do any more than the former, purely on the basis of anti-perfectionist liberalism.

Secondly, there is a question of overall consistency here. If the state should leave questions of religious truth aside, as he suggests, then it should not, by the same token, take up the view that 'all religions are equal' and make belief in it part of a programme of civic education. In my view this would be extremely hard to justify in any case but most *especially* when it additionally, as in the Mozert case, runs against the expressed wishes of parents.[49]

Thirdly, and linked to the first point, this comment embodies a commitment to a version of secularism 1 since it says that logically allied to the adherence to the view that all religions are equal is a concomitant hostility to religious and other ideological traditions which are either intolerant of other rival beliefs or who refuse to recognise in their *private* lives, as well as their public conduct, the division between the public and the private self which is central to the political culture of political liberalism. This is parallel to the version of Newby's apparent, but implicit, hostility to traditional *realist* interpretations of religion. In justification of this adoption by the state of what might be dubbed '*tolerance promoting secularism 1*', as one of the key values underpinning its common conception of civic education, is that this disposition to tolerate the views of others *is essential for the smooth running of a democratic system*. Its justification might be alleged to be *purely* procedural.

This disposition towards tolerance, found more often, according to Macedo, in traditional protestant Christianity than in traditional 'undemocratic' Roman Catholicism, must be one of the key procedural values of a liberal democratic state. In addition, Macedo argues that because John Locke, the founding father of modern liberalism, took the view that the promotion of tolerant forms of Christianity supported the liberal system, then the same view can be said to be an intrinsic part of classical liberalism. This of course is an inverted form of the ad hominem fallacy. Just because a great philosopher says that two things are connected and because we wish to adopt one of them *it does not follow*, on those grounds alone, that we have also to accept the other as well.

Macedo argues that tolerance is an essential aspect of a democratic pluralist state. As a statement of fact this seems uncontroversial, especially when it is almost certainly true that some loyal citizens who recognise the authority of the liberal state will loathe some of its policy decisions, as we have demonstrated with reference to pacifists and anti-abortionists earlier on. But when we look closely at what is meant by 'tolerance' and what the 'tolerance requirement' consists of, in this context, it is difficult to agree that its promotion by the liberal state has the kind of educational implications *for the personal formation of children* that Macedo alleges. This is made particularly clear if we adopt the kind of definition of 'toleration', put forward recently by John Horton,[50] which states that *'toleration is a deliberate choice not to interfere with conduct of which one disapproves'*. On this account toleration is connected with *actual behaviour* or at most with a temperamental disposition not to interfere and it is clearly a necessary condition of one's being tolerant that a person cannot (logically) be tolerant of behaviour of which they personally approve.

This has the following destructive implications for Macedo's educational programme. Firstly, Macedo must show why this desirable state of affairs requires any inculcation of particular virtues. If the liberal democratic state requires tolerant behaviour, it might be argued that a disposition towards this could effectively be encouraged through the rule of law and a deterrent system of punishment. This could be sufficient to ensure that democratically sanctioned policies can be put into place without unnecessary interference from those who disapprove. On that basis further justification must be found to show that there are *any* educational implications *beyond* the inculcation of respect for the rule of law. Secondly, Macedo's programme of civic education involves a programme of multicultural education premised on the notion that 'all religions are equal'. This will be designed to ensure that children from families who hold a strong belief in the unique truth of a particular tradition are encouraged 'to put that on one side'. Note here that just because a person holds strong beliefs about the wrongness of other people's rival beliefs does not necessarily lead them to be *intolerant* of others i.e. to interfere with behaviour that is disapproved of, and yet

Macedo's case seems to rest upon a conflation of these two through deft use of the term 'fundamentalist'.

The behaviour based definition of intolerance offered by Horton would appear to undermine the very *possibility* of someone or a religious group being described as 'intolerant' *merely* on the basis of their beliefs and practices. Given that this is true, it is difficult to see how an active programme of education designed to promote *a very particular theological viewpoint* with radical effects upon the personal formation of particular groups of children can be justified in social or political terms.[51] Thirdly, if the programme of tolerance inculcation via multiculturalism succeeds then it will serve the needs of liberal society not by producing people with a disposition to tolerance but whose disapproval of certain rival traditions and forms of behaviour has been removed through the agency of the state. This is because the effects of the kind of multiculturalist programme that Macedo wishes to put in place will be to promote, on his own view, certain forms of religious belief and to undermine others and that *will not so much promote tolerance as remove the need for it* by undermining those belief systems which sincerely disapprove of others. By encouraging all children to approve of rival belief systems a programme of multicultural education will *logically* remove the possibility of those children adopting a tolerant attitude by, *ironically,* using state power to restrict de facto multicultural diversity.[52]

4.5 Social democratic liberalism, cultural interventionism and education

I want now to draw this chapter on the relationship between cultural or political claims and particular nationally common conceptions of personal education to a close by trying to say why Macedo is led to undermine the political liberalism to which he is at some level committed. Firstly, I will try to characterise that set of assumptions political, educational and cultural that I want to denote as **'social democratic liberalism'**.[53] I will do this by highlighting certain features of the three educational thinkers that have been discussed in this chapter. This will demonstrate that I have not just invented this alleged and influential perspective despite the fact that it hasn't been identified before to my knowledge within the field of education. This, I believe, is because the assumptions that I shall identify are widely assumed to be beyond rational question by those currently responsible for determining the main currents of thinking in the field of educational theory.

Following that I will use it to construct, in the next chapter, a general argument, born of my reflections on Macedo's recent work, to the effect that:

1. The educational programme of Social Democratic Liberalism (SDL) is logically incompatible with the most attractive and the most viable version of John Rawls' political liberalism, which,

2. Must, logically be compatible with real pluralism or 'thick multiculturalism' (Tamir) or collapse into comprehensive or perfectionist liberalism and thereby lose its stated basis of justification.

3. Social democratic liberalism, if it can be described properly as 'liberalism' at all rather than a species of socialism/ collectivism is compatible only with comprehensive (Rawls) or perfectionist (Raz) versions of liberalism that embody a particular view of the good life via the conception of what is the good or ideal society. This last aspect of SDL will bring it into considerable tension with other perfectionist forms of liberalism based on the promotion of autonomy.

4. Both SDL and Comprehensive liberalism can logically have only a limited commitment to real pluralism and therefore subscribe only to a 'thin multiculturalism'.[54]

We noted that all four of the writers mentioned in this chapter made certain statements about the nature of the culture, outlined in national terms.[55] In all cases this was done without adequate justification and without discussion of the wisdom of making any claim of the kind. Nor was it done with any recognition of the question of whether such claims could possibly be rationally justified, empirically or normatively.

It is a defining characteristic of social democratic liberalism to start with some such rationalistically conceived characterisation of *our* culture or society and to see that as embodying positive values or cultural ideals that must be nurtured in future citizens through a common system of state funded education. This requires the active promotion of 'positive' cultural change in order that the social ideal be embodied more effectively and it also involves the task of identifying negative cultural features that need to be undermined so that the ideal can be realised more fully. In this latter process the personal formation of a certain type of individual, the ideal citizen, will be crucial to the SDL project.

For social democratic liberals the key to this cultural ideal, and the determinant of future open ended cultural growth, is the democratic process. Commitment to this process embodies a commitment to the desirability and possibility of establishing a consensus about the best course of action where differences of opinion currently exist. Agreement based on rational discussion is regarded as an ideal that can and should be achieved for peaceful co-existence.

Cultural elements which reduce the chances of *all* playing an *equal* part in these processes are to be eliminated through reformist measures enacted by the democratically elected state, according to its ideals. Crucial to the political ideology of social democracy, then, is the view that the democratically elected government should have as one of its significant aims the determination and development of national culture.

The two key features of progressive cultural change, from this perspective, will be *democracy* and *rationality*. This will emerge as a commitment to extending the scope of rational and democratic change. These two factors will be seen to have unlimited scope in the vision of the ideal society upon which the social democratic approach to political-educational policy is based. This will lead to a wish to restrict or limit those cultural influences which are regarded as irrational, authoritarian and are likely to include those based on a respect for tradition. The de facto social structures thrown up by the contingencies of history (e.g. the constitutional arrangements of a country like Britain, the family and religion, are all likely to be regarded, by social democratic liberals, as things to be tolerated and reformed. Where possible the influence of such institutions will be restricted.

The SDL ideology will be opposed by those who feel that these things are important aspects of the good society and that the democratisation, rationalisation, consensus and the interventionist state have a rather more limited value in that quest. In political terms, this is a brief characterisation of the conservative or libertarian liberal traditions. Perhaps *the* most important cultural bulwarks against the influence of the social democratic ideology will be religion in its traditional, realist and 'fundamentalist' forms.

Central to social democratic liberalism's programme of cultural development is the commitment to a common conception of personal education, democratically sanctioned and nationally determined. The classic statement of the aims and ideals of a common programme of education based on this political perspective is to be found in the educational writings of John Dewey.[56] Allied to this is, obviously, a commitment to the state education system and the ideal of common schooling. The so called common or comprehensive school, with a non-selective intake, is seen as a significant microcosm of the wider national society and a 'public' institution for the propagation of positive cultural change towards ideals of agreement, rationality, equality and freedom[57]. Particularly threatening to the SDL conception of the ideal democratic society will be groups and individuals who don't recognise the need for the kind of personal and ideological *uniformity* that is idealised by the SDL. Since such groups will hold the belief that certain publicly common values and democratically constituted decisions are just wrong, their attitudes will be branded as socially harmful by SDLs and one of the aims of a common conception of education will be to prevent such attitudes and beliefs from being passed on through a diverse and unregulated education system to the next generation. The notion of human well being that will be used to determine the interests of the child will be based upon values determined democratically or rationally which will be taken to be overriding where there is a conflict between parents and the common conception of education.[58]

The following extract from the concluding section of one of the two papers mentioned earlier should leave the reader in no doubt about Macedo's commitment to the entire political-educational vision set out above.

> Liberal constitutionalism is not only about rights and freedom, after all, it is also about sustaining political and social structures that work to educate individuals and shape communities in ways that are congruent with liberalism. This is not only legitimate but essential political work, which will nevertheless have very unequal consequences for different religious communities.[59]

The fact that the educational writing of John Haldane, a sophisticated and politically astute Christian communitarian writer, also embodies several of the important structural elements that also characterise this perspective is both surprising and telling. He holds that some rationalistically conceived notion of common cultural values has important implications for the kind of educational values that should be propagated across the nation via a common conception of education, though he is obviously less committed to the importance of the common school as such. He is clear that where parental inclination comes into conflict with the state, this should be supported, but *only* in the case of religious families by a system of state funded schools, run according to alternative *religious* conceptions of education. The structural similarity between communitarianism and social democratic liberalism is that of a cultural monism. It states that there is one, single, appropriate or rationalistically justifiable, conception of our national culture, which should be given national educational scope. This is interesting because it shows that the division of political perspectives into those which are 'communitarian' and 'liberal' is often, at least in educational terms, less than helpful. It tends to place the critical focus on differences which are often more apparent than real.[60] Unfortunately it also reduces the chances of drawing the attention of educationalists to the more important divisions that exist between social democratic liberalism and conservative communitarianism, on one side, and the political traditions of libertarian conservatism and pluralism, on the other.[61]

4.6 A look forward

In this chapter I have attempted to raise a whole range of issues around the development of spirituality within state schools. I hope to have highlighted the important impact of cultural and political considerations upon these developmental issues, and to have given them some brief discussion. On the political front, I have identified three broad approaches: communitarianism, social democratic liberalism and anti-perfectionist liberalism. In addition, I have indicated the existence of further political perspectives that raise interesting questions for those which currently dominate educational writing in the field of personal and spiritual development.

Allied to these political issues are those relating to national culture and the idea of secularity. In rejecting, at least for the purposes of this study, John Haldane's views about the relationship between Christianity and British culture, I have accepted that viewed nationally, the state education system in Britain should be regarded as 'secular'. But, at the same time, in discussion of Macedo's and Newby's educational recommendations, I have highlighted the extent to which this word may be translated into a hostility to religion, in general, or to quite particular forms of legitimate religious belief and practice. And this echoed earlier discussion of the views of Dewey and White. By delineating two differing versions secularism, I hope to have produced a conceptual tool that might be deployed within the liberal framework to distinguish between hostile and benign uses of the term and to pin down the kind of liberal equivocation that was identified in Newby's writing.

All this has been by way of an overture to the remainder of this study, where several of the issues and themes touched upon here will be brought into sharper focus. In the next three chapters I intend to confine my enquiries to the broad framework of liberalism. I want to expose some of the logical tensions that emerge when it is used to underpin educational policy. In chapter five I will explore the extent to which Rawls' anti-perfectionist liberalism is capable of legitimately sustaining the kinds of programmes of civic education that many liberal educationalists, like Macedo and Rawls himself, *think it requires*. I will offer a general argument, based on a fairly detailed examination of Rawls' programme, to the effect that common civic education programmes, that impact upon the personal development of children, effectively violate the constraints upon state action required by political or anti-perfectionist liberalism.

Following this exploration of anti-perfectionist liberalism, I will move to a discussion of the perfectionist liberalism of Joseph Raz, which candidly embodies a positive commitment to the development of autonomy. It is based upon a socially open ended conception of human well being that might help to justify the use of empirical cultural claims to underpin programmes of personal development. But I will attempt to show that his arguments open up rather than settle important issues about the nature and scope of the *relevant* cultural domain. Communitarians and social democratic liberals are inclined to focus at a global or national level when deciding which are the developmentally relevant cultural phenomena but Raz's communitarian liberal view of human well-being may not be able to sustain this in the way that many educationalists are inclined to assume.

I will end this section of the study, as it were from within the liberal framework, by examining the prospects for any attempt to produce common conceptions of spiritual development, including those based upon the kind of non-realist approach identified in our discussion here of Newby's paper. I will argue that any such attempt would be a violation of liberal requirements and that liberalism appears, rather, to be logically tied to the metaphysical doctrine of critical realism.

In the final section of the study I will move out beyond the liberal-communitarian framework and attempt to construct an approach to spiritual development that might be described as thoroughly pluralist.

Notes

---

1 The 'communitarian' style of theorising and philosophising is based upon the view that rationality is inextricably tied to local and contingent factors. Any claims that are made on the basis of the practical reasoning style consistent with communitarianism should therefore resist rationalistic universal judgements. The claim that 'no characterisation can be given' embodies just such a universalism and is therefore at odds with communitarian thinking. For arguments to show that none of the arguments offered by David Carr support the claims made in this paragraph, see chapter 2, section 2 of this study.

2 See, for example, White,J.(1995).

3 Gutmann (1980), p352.

4 See also, Taylor (1989), p4.

5 See also, Newby (1996), passim.

6 Carr (1993), Haldane (1986), McLaughlin (1996).

7 Haldane (1986).

8 The Swann report (1985) and NUT, Discussion Paper (1984).

9 Haldane, Op cit., p194-5.

10 Ibid., p193.

11 Ibid., p193.

12 Ibid., pp196, 194 ,191.

13 Ibid., p195.

14 Ibid., p193.

15 Ibid., p192.

16 Newby (1996).

17 Ibid., p96.

18 Ibid., p94-95.

19 White (1994) and cf., Ofsted (1994).

20 White, J. (1995).

21 cf., Hirst (1974).

22 Newby, Op cit., p94.

23 Ibid., p95.

24 Ibid., p96.

25 Ibid., p97.

26 It is worth making it clear at this point that non-realism of this kind, making reference to theological or moral claims, is compatible with, and often accompanied by, a rather hard nosed realism regarding the truths of science.

27 Spong (1994), Cupitt (1980), (1991) and Phillips (1976).

28 Newby, Op cit., p97.

29 These might be called 'Secularism 2's conditions of legitimate partiality' (S2CLP).

30 This may, in part, be due to the fact that his writing is also built upon the assumption that I outlined earlier in relation to the communitarianism of John Haldane i.e. the view that empirical judgements about the nature of the culture of a society should have a direct effect upon the political culture of that society. Independent argument is required to show that any value that can be shown to be an integral part of a society's culture should also become one of the common values that should be promoted or nurtured by government policy. It is perhaps easy to see why communitarians will be sympathetic to this political assumption. It is not at all clear why liberals should accept it. It looks particularly difficult to sustain in the context of pluralism, where contradictory value systems co-exist within the same cultural milieu.

31 A view which will be discussed at length further on with reference to the work of Rawls and Macedo.

32 Ayer (1932) and Flew (1971).

33 Mitchell (1980); Banner (1990). See also Alston (1991); Plantinga (1993) and the discussion of the views of J.H.Newman in Dunne (1993). Perhaps the most accessible discussion of these matters is to be found in Newbigin (1995).

34 It will eventually become clear that I take there to be no link between liberalism, as such, and the exclusion of viewpoints that can be demonstrated to be irrational. This approach can only be associated with a very particular, but highly influential brand of liberalism, that I will call social democratic liberalism.

35 This appellation is rarely, if ever, used by those American political philosophers, whose views are categorised with it, in England. Anti-perfectionist liberals themselves (e.g. Dworkin, Rawls and Nozick) are, rather, inclined to talk about a commitment to the *neutrality* of the state, the priority of basic rights and the exclusion of *any* substantive conception of the good. For a fuller characterisation of this technical term and its appropriateness with respect to John Rawls, see Mulhall and Swift (1992) , p25ff and see also Raz (1986), pp110-162.

36 Rawls (1993).

37 Macedo (1996), p7.

38 Ibid., p7.

39 For another candid account of the limited nature of the liberal commitment to pluralism, see Raz (1986), p369-395.

40 This is the form of liberalism which I will characterise fully towards the end of this chapter and will be named 'social democratic liberalism'.

41 Macedo (1995), p228-9.

42 Ibid., p229.

43 Ibid., p226.

44 Ibid., p226.

45 Except where it could be shown that this is an unfortunate but unavoidable double effect of its otherwise acting impartially in the educational domain or where the beliefs and attitudes concerned could be linked to sufficiently harmful behaviour or personal harm (see also p 86 and note 29, on what I called 'Secularism 2's conditions of legitimate partiality').

46 Ibid., p226.

47 Especially when considered alongside Macedo's distinction between religious equality from 'the perspective of the state' and from 'the perspective of God'. However, this abstract distinction cannot hold when consideration is given to the educational consequences of the state's perspective. What appears legitimate in the abstract becomes illegitimate when applied in this particular public sphere. This is because of the impact which the state's view will have upon the personal (non-public) domain of attitude and belief, having direct or indirect effect upon the metaphysical perspective of child-citizens.

48 What I offer here is just a sketch to demonstrate the educational impact of some interpretations of the Rawlsian programme. In the next chapter I will offer a detailed examination of the tensions that exist between the justificatory aspects of Rawls' political liberalism and the approach to civic education, exemplified here by Macedo, which it is commonly thought to require.

49 It might be thought that the reference to equality implies no metaphysical implications or particular theological truth claim. However, it does embody a religious stance stance since, according to Macedo's view, a commitment to the equality of all religions is the same as saying that, for public purposes, they will all be regarded as *equally true*. This is not consistent with an attempt to leave the question of truth 'aside', since it embodies a substantive theological/ metaphysical, and highly *controversial*, claim. The view that all religions are equally true is a religious claim since it is a claim about religious truth even if it is not one made, in this context, by those who hold a religious belief. In the same way the claims of atheism could be classified as religious claims since they are claims *about* the religious belief in God.

50 Horton (1993), p3.

51 The parallel and more detailed criticisms made of Newby earlier are obviously also applicable here.

52 In so doing the liberal state in his vision would contravene his own view that the state must think of all religions as equal.

[53] Sometimes referred to hereafter as 'SDL' for brevity. For a critical characterisation of this prevalent political tendency, see Gray (1996).

[54] The distinction between 'thick' and 'thin' multiculturalism can be found in Tamir (1996).

[55] Macedo explicitly refers to the USA and addresses his remarks to that context.

[56] Dewey (1915), ch1 and Dewey (1916).

[57] Conceived as positive freedom or autonomy, reflecting social ideals about the maximally empowered person.

[58] This is not to suggest that rival political perspectives will include no conception of the best interests of the child. Libertarian and conservative approaches, however, will be disposed to articulate the state's view of this in negative terms making reference to a conception of harm or abuse which might legitimate an intervention in extreme cases. The prime facie disposition of these political perspectives will be to identify others better placed to determine the best interests of a particular child, e.g. the parents. For a classic statement of the SDL position see White,P (1994) and for criticisms of this from the libertarian-conservative perspectives see Almond, (1994) and Crittenden (1988). See also chapter 7 of this study.

[59] Macedo, Op cit., p236. Note that Newby's work also clearly embodies many of the political, cultural and educational assumptions of this SDL vision.

[60] Something which is brought out strongly in Mulhall and Swift, (1992).

[61] SDL assumptions, apparently held uncritically, are I believe apparent in most hostile discussions of recent Conservative government education policy in Britain. (A classic example of this is W.Carr (1996) and also the TES review of that book by Fred Inglis (March 1996.) These asumptions also underpin Ruth Jonathan's monograph, *Illusory Freedoms* (1997).

5 Varieties of Liberalism, Public Values and Education

Summary

After exposing, through a series of detailed arguments, the tensions that appear to exist between the justificatory apparatus of Rawls' political liberalism and the types of civic education that are alleged, by Rawls and others, to follow from it, I move on to examine the educational implications of a perfectionist liberalism, built around a commitment to the value of autonomy. In the final sections I attempt to outline some of the paradoxical educational implications of a commitment to the development of complex autonomy and its links with the concepts of transcendence and spirituality.

5.1 Three cultural justifications for liberal civic education

In the last chapter I suggested that while Macedo's particular conception of civic education would be unacceptable to loyal citizens holding illiberal and undemocratic viewpoints, the particular general liberal principles that he proposed, and which were derived from John Rawls' political liberalism, ought not to be problematic. This suggests that it may be possible to construct at least two conceptions of political liberalism, having quite different implications for educational practice. The following discussion is designed to show, firstly, that political liberalism of a broadly Rawlsian type is logically distinct from the kind of social democratic educational programme which Macedo and Rawls tie it to. Secondly, I think it is possible to show that if anti-perfectionist liberalism is used to underpin an educational programme based on Social democratic liberal assumptions, then it necessarily embodies a particular comprehensive conception of the good, ceases to be anti-perfectionist and therefore loses the only feature which recommends it to those interested in nurturing a fully, pluralist or multi-cultural society; and perhaps the only basis upon which liberalism might be regarded as the appropriate political underpinning for policies on personal development in the context of British state education.

It is possible to make three types of cultural justification for the view that the political values that should underpin any policy on personal development in British state schools are those of liberal democracy. These are outlined below.

Perfectionism

Underpinning this kind of justification is the claim that our culture is liberal and democratic and that this is significant for both private and public life. Therefore, in order to live a good life in this context it is necessary to be educated to be a certain type of person.[1] It embodies a particular comprehensive ideal of the good life that must be based on a normative or empirical claim about the nature of our national culture. The cultural claim upon which any such account depends will be open to rational empirical challenge. The approach is parallel in form to the communitarian approach of John Haldane, discussed earlier, though it embodies a different claim about the nature of British culture. This approach will be examined at the end of this chapter.

Liberal constitutionalism

This embodies the view that Liberal Democracy is the constitutional basis of our society and particularly its political culture. This is the kind of justification of civic education used by Macedo and he makes it clear that his comments may be exclusive to the context of the USA.[2] But while educational philosophers working in some countries, especially those with a written constitution like the USA, could use such a justification successfully, it is not at all self evident that this would be acceptable within the British context, as I suggested earlier. Despite the fact that many people working in the field of education undoubtedly *assume*[3] that this *is* an appropriate description of our political culture this can be disputed as our political system has no written constitution out of which an educational allegiance to liberal democratic theory as such could be developed.[4] Most political theorists would, I think, agree that in some way or other this combination of terms could be correctly applied to *some aspects* of our political system. However, the attempt to suggest either that it is the most appropriate comprehensive description or that the particular account of the nature of anti-perfectionist liberalism, used by social democratic liberals, has any relationship to that of British liberal democracy requires further justification. And any such attempt would be strongly and rationally opposed by constitutional conservatives,[5] Oakeshottian conservatives,[6] libertarian liberals,[7] as well as pluralists.[8] This suggests that in order to legitimise the application of Rawls' political liberalism to a broad range of societies, and to avoid strong objections to its application to the British political and educational culture, we need to look beyond the kind of constitutional justification offered, and relied upon, by Macedo.

The inevitability of pluralism

The basic justification offered by Rawls for his political liberalism is that it is the only political conception that is viable, given the fact that it is not possible to establish, on a rational basis, that one particular comprehensive conception of the good should be regarded as correct for all the citizens within a society characterised by social diversity. He argues that it is just an undisputed fact that *'..diversity of reasonable religious, philosophical, and moral doctrines..is a permanent feature of the public culture and not a mere historical condition soon to pass away'.*[9] Thus the justification that Rawls actually uses to ground his political liberalism relies upon the fact that it offers a conception of the legitimation of policy that is maximally compatible with 'pluralism' or what Tamir has labelled 'thick multiculturalism'. [10]

5.2 Rawls, impartial liberalism and the extent of civic education

Rawls offers a cultural and rational explanation for what he calls the liberal principle of legitimacy and it is this which *underpins*, and therefore cannot be justified *from*, particular constitutional arrangements. And the liberal principle of legitimacy is grounded in a particular cultural claim which differs markedly from the two others that have been examined so far. It is the claim that

> Under the political and social conditions secured by the basic rights and liberties of free institutions, a diversity of conflicting and irreconcilable- and what's more, reasonable-comprehensive doctrines will come about and persist if such diversity does not already obtain...These are the doctrines that reasonable citizens affirm and that political liberalism must address.[11]

This cultural claim has two important aspects which set it apart from those examined in the last chapter. Firstly, it states that we live in a society where *as a matter of fact* reasonable people hold very different comprehensive views about what constititutes the good life. Secondly, given that a society guarantees certain freedoms, especially freedom of thought, this situation will *inevitably* continue. Rawls claims that reasonable disagreement will always exist because of what he calls 'the burdens of judgement'.[12] Under this heading Rawls offers a series of facts about how rational people might come to disagree. They constitute a disavowal of the enlightenment ideal of pure rationality detached from contingent factors.[13] The burdens of judgement include the fact that the evidence bearing on a case is often conflicting and complex, that rational people may disagree about the weight to be given to different considerations otherwise agreed to be 'relevant' and that all our concepts are 'vague' and 'subject to hard cases'. This *'indeterminacy means that we must rely on judgements within some range where reasonable persons.. may differ'*. Rawls says that the

> ..way we assess evidence and weigh moral and political values is shaped by our total experience, our whole course of life up to now; and our total experiences must always differ.

It follows from this that, especially in a modern society, it is possible for our judgements to diverge radically. On some occasions an individual will have to give up one of their cherished values since it comes into conflict with another and it is impossible to say which value should be passed over, as it were, from some rationally privileged vantage point. Alluding to the work of Thomas Nagel,[14] Rawls refers to the fact that certain judgements may reflect the fact that there may be rival and equally powerful reasons on both sides of a particular moral issue. This will militate against any attempt to reach an overall and impartial judgement.[15]

Given this background of legitimate rational disagreement and the need for political decisions to be made, which may involve *'the exercise of coercive political power'*, state intervention may only be legitimated by way of a *political* conception of liberalism. This conception disavows any 'comprehensive' conception of the good for individuals, as such, that might *'extend beyond the political and include non-political values and virtues'*.[16] It is designed to demonstrate, to the satisfaction of a diverse range of citizens, the rationality of subscribing to a just democratic political culture that operates with a set of overriding procedural values that embody the interests of all as free and equal and which has jurisdiction *only* in the public domain.

Rawls says that the education of children is to be regarded as lying within the domain of the 'public' and that this extends to their personal education, as well as to their intellectual understanding.[17] He admits that the public requirements of a civic education may, therefore, come into conflict with the wishes of parents and he says that the public values must be regarded as overriding in such cases. There are three things to notice here. Firstly, there is a clear but unstated assumption that the state has a legitimate interest in the personal education of all children. This represents a commitment to at least some very thin common conception of personal education. But from this

Rawlsian perspective the state can claim no legitimate interest in the *whole* child but just the child *qua citizen*. Secondly, Rawls says that where these derived public values come into conflict with those of parents it is the public values which must take priority. This is because at some very basic primordial level, represented by what Rawls calls 'the original position', those parents who disagree with them ought *rationally* to agree to their priority in the public domain. Rawls concedes that civic personal education may have significant effects upon the non-public development of individual citizens and may amount to the promotion of a partially comprehensive conception of the good. This can be legitimated under political liberalism since it is *unavoidable* and is loosely articulated (not part of a 'rather precisely articulated scheme of thought') and affects only some (but not all) non-political values.

Thirdly, since the Rawlsian programme does not say that the state should attempt to control *all* aspects of the development of the whole person but *only* their development as a citizen, it is not incompatible with a situation where publicly funded schools provide a programme of personal education based upon a *particular* set of non-public values, *in addition to* a civic education. This might appear to be quite an oblique point, but it is nevertheless important because it might be thought, by those who subscribe to the social democratic conception of liberalism, that the state conceived in such terms could *only* legitimately concern itself with the personal education of individuals as citizens. On this view teachers in state funded schools should remain silent or impartial on the non-public values that might be of great importance for the development of their pupils. It would follow from this that teachers should not intentionally promote any non-public values, deriving from a comprehensive conception of the good, since they are representatives of an anti-perfectionist liberal state. But this is not sanctioned *even* by reference to Rawls' own social democratic conception of state education. The British state's current partial funding of religious schools does not conflict with the anti-perfectionist view of state education. It would come into conflict *only if* the programme of civic education required by Rawls were either not being put in place in such schools or if the implementation of the programme were compromised because the public values were not being given priority in cases of conflict with the comprehensive conception of the good otherwise being promoted by the school. By the same token, and in line with the same constraints, it would be consistent with the anti-perfectionist liberal view for the state to urge all schools to develop their own values policies based upon comprehensive conceptions of the good. There is therefore no *logical* link between anti-perfectionist liberalism and the liberal 'silence' identified and criticised by Kenneth Strike.[18]

Arguably the only basis upon which the state could restrain the promotion of particular non-public values (for example, particular moral stances on issues like abortion and homosexuality) or promote public values that undermined those otherwise preferred by the school community, would be by reference to one of the two conditions of legitimate partiality (S2CLPs), outlined with reference to secularism 2 in the last chapter.[19] The view that state funded schools should either seek to undermine certain non-public views or remain silent or scrupulously impartial on all matters appertaining to the non-public domain is not required even by anti-perfectionist liberalism which makes much of the impartiality of the state.

It is only when this liberalism is combined with social democratic assumptions about education that such conclusions appear inevitable. Since the commonality of personal education should be confined, within the anti-perfectionist liberal perspective, to the personal education of the child as citizen, there is scope even under this political umbrella for extending the 'state funded constrained perfectionism', presently enjoyed *only* by religious schools, to *all* state schools. This provides a Rawlsian challenge to the widespread assumption amongst liberal educationalists that *all* personal development must be *confined* to the promotion of a set of *common* values and that state schools should disavow the promotion of comprehensive conceptions of the good in favour of a common conception of spiritual development compatible with a national or cultural consensus. The pressure for such a common conception only comes about if anti-perfectionist liberalism is supposed to imply a system of *common schooling*[20] in addition to a common conception of civic education. The question of the logical link between these two things will be dependent upon the ability of social democratic liberals to provide a substantive argument to the effect that common civic education *can only* be delivered adequately within common state schools, within a particular type of admissions policy. Such an argument would satisfy Rawlsian criteria since it would suggest that the 'unavoidability' condition (S2CLP1) had been satisfied. Such arguments would involve, in the British context, arguments to the effect that *all* children should be educated in such schools. And, any argument of that kind would have to contain supplementary arguments against privately funded and denominational schools, since as a matter of logic children in those schools could not, on the grounds set out above, be receiving an adequate civic education of the kind required.

5.3 Rawls' political liberalism and the attempt to justify the 'regrettable' effects of the SDL approach to civic education

As I suggested earlier, Rawls is inclined to concede that there is a 'partially comprehensive' conception of the good built into the procedural values that are required for the just government of a democratic society. It is very interesting that where Rawls tries to justify this claim, he is inclined to rely upon a *cultural* justification which emphasises, not the pluralism that is so prominent at the beginning of his account of political liberalism, but the fact that it operates in accordance with the 'basic structure of a constitutional democratic regime', is 'reasonable' and that it is consistent with 'certain fundamental ideas viewed as latent in the public political culture of a democratic society'.[21] In attempting to legitimise the common values that will be given overriding priority in the field of education, it is telling that Rawls makes no reference to the way in which its hostility to certain forms of life might be justified to the representatives of a richly plural society in what he calls the 'original position'. He relies instead upon a constitutional 'justification' that merely *asserts* as an empirical cultural fact precisely what he is attempting to justify as a normative political doctrine; that is, that we live or ought to regard ourselves as living in a democratic society, with certain latent fundamental ideas.

The concept of the original position has the role of demonstrating that the procedures and restraints imposed upon citizens by Rawls' political liberalism are legitimate. It embodies a certain notion of justice and equality, since all the representatives who make legitimate the procedures that Rawls thinks real life citizens ought to accept, have to operate in a situation of pure rationality independent of any particular comprehensive conception of the good and without any notion of what position they might hold in the actual society over which the results of their deliberations will have effect. This is designed to impose on the imaginary representatives certain constraints which might be said to embody certain moral and political ideals. They will not make decisions designed to favour any particular group or individual in society nor will they make decisions that favour particular comprehensive notions of the good. Ironically they will do this because, as actors in the original position, not knowing which actual position in society they will occupy, they will be moved by the exercise of rational self interest to ensure that the widest possible range of real interests are accommodated. Rawls is not bound to the view that such a situation ever really existed, nor does it constitute an ideal end of his political programme. It is offered as a means of justifying certain procedures from the perspective of no one in particular, giving due and therefore maximum consideration to everyone on an equal basis. As such the procedure of placing the representatives behind a 'veil of ignorance' might be criticised. People clearly do not make real day to day decisions in this way. The procedure starts with some unjustified assumptions about justice and Kantian assumptions about the role of reason in the legitimisation of moral and political decisions. But, as I have indicated, the procedure does not recommend itself to real life citizens just on the basis of detached rationality alone but also appeals to self interest. Given the brute fact that we live in a society where political decisions are to be made and given the fact that it is, at the very least, unlikely that the one comprehensive conception of the good that any individual actually holds will ever come to dominate, then it is, according to Rawls, in our interest to submit to a *decision making process* that favours no particular conception or interest group.

For the present, I am not particularly worried about establishing Rawls' own view on this issue. I think Rawls would say that his original position procedure recommends itself to real citizens on a purely rational basis and disavows any reference to self interest, at all. This could be criticised by those inclined to adopt a less Kantian approach but my own criticism will accept, for the sake of argument, the entire original position procedure as unproblematic. I will then attempt to show that some aspects of Rawls' political procedures will be unacceptable from the perspective of those who have subjected themselves to the jurisdiction of the original position, on *either* the 'interest' or 'pure rationality' view of its legitimising 'force'. For the purposes of this argument, I will accept Rawls', perhaps controversial, claim about the original position and assume with him that,

> ..there seems no better way to elaborate a political conception of justice for the basic structure from the fundamental idea of society as an ongoing and fair system of co-operation between citizens regarded as free and equal.'[22]

If we think of education as part of the public domain, as Rawls and other social democratic liberals are inclined to do, then I think we can draw out the nature of the particular partially comprehensive claim about the good to which citizens are being invited to subscribe and which will constrain the personal (and therefore spiritual) education of children in state schools. Effectively it is a personal commitment to the anti-perfectionist claim that:

1. Any conception of the private good or comprehensive good, including your own, will be considered good only if it complies with the partially comprehensive conception of the good advocated by the anti-perfectionist state.

The nature of the perfectionism that is incorporated here is the demand that the citizens of the anti-perfectionist state must incorporate the values of anti-perfectionism into their own comprehensive and rational conception of the good. For example, this may mean that an otherwise loyal religious fundamentalist who recognises the value of a division between the public and the non-public, must personally subscribe, for example, to the burdens of judgement even though they are in conflict with her own comprehensive religious doctrines. This involves no direct partiality towards a particular conception of the good life for individuals but, rather, a partiality towards a very particular view about what constitutes the good *political society* underpinning those values. It is *that* partiality which is used indirectly to legitimate hostility towards certain forms of life. The perfectionist bias of this conception of the work of the anti-perfectionist state can be drawn out in the following claims each of which would have to be promoted actively:

2. The one, true good for all citizens is that they live in a liberal democratic society, where they are maximally free, equal and personally constituted by 'democratic virtues' which dispose them to

a) accept this belief as true,

b) be willing to adjust any personal, traditional, cultural or religious comprehensive conception accordingly and in particular to give up any political dimension of such conceptions, if they conflict with the conception of the anti-perfectionist state.

Note that 2(b) will not just involve a demand that someone should not act to interfere with the implementation of decisions and policies made according to this conception but involves the claim that,

c) One should accommodate this into one's own personal belief system and be willing for one's children to be educated according to the common values of the anti-perfectionist state through a common conception of civic education in such a way that they too will accept the truth and priority over the non-public considerations of 1 and 2(a), (b) and (c). This means that parents should be prepared to accept that the common values of the anti-perfectionist state should determine the child's development qua citizen. Any 'unavoidable consequences' of this common programme of personal civic development that might hinder a parent in their attempt to develop their child according to a comprehensive personal, traditional, cultural or religious conception of the good is a matter of regret but must be justified as a 'reasonable requirement'.[23]

Several questions arise from this analysis. Firstly, one wonders why this aspect of Rawls' programme with its encroachment into the non-public of a particular comprehensive conception of the good relating to the notion of the good *society*, might recommend itself to the representatives of a rich pluralism, in the original position. Secondly, it is not at all clear why the representatives of citizens in the original position should accept, or come to acknowledge as reasonable, the necessity for regarding the beliefs and personal characteristics of loyal citizens and their children as falling within the *public* domain. Thirdly, the notion that *the state* should be able to determine the personal development according to *its* favoured conception of the good society is, to say the least, controversial and some would argue that such a view is inconsistent with the basic tenets of liberal democracy, as classically conceived or commonly understood in Britain. I will deal with each of these thoughts in turn and my argument in the next section will be aimed at showing that it is possible to accept Rawls' anti-perfectionist notion of just political procedures, legitimised in the idealised setting of the original position, *without, at the same time*, accepting the social democratic liberal claim that a good citizen must *believe in an anti-perfectionist conception of the good society* (as set out in claims 1,2(a), (b) and (c) above) with its implications for a common conception of civic education, including its 'regrettable' effects on the non-public domain.

Central to Rawls' attempt to suggest that coercive political power might be used in order to ensure that all citizens are inculcated with the virtues of democratic citizenship, via a programme of civic education, are two sets of concepts that themselves require some justification. These are the dual concepts of 'reasonable' and 'unreasonable' comprehensive doctrines, on the one hand, and the 'public' and the 'non-public', on the other.[24] These two sets of concepts play a very important part in underpinning Rawls' educational claims but he makes undefended assumptions about where exactly the line between the two poles is to be drawn in each case. According to his account this does not appear to require any legitimising reference to the adjudicating forum of the original position. Instead, as I will show below, he assumes that his own elaboration of the distinction would be acceptable. This is problematic, particularly with reference to the distinction between a 'reasonable' and 'unreasonable' doctrine since the justification which he offers *assumes* the notion of reasonableness that he is trying to justify as most appropriate to the public domain. It therefore effectively excludes the kinds of doctrines which he takes to be 'unreasonable' not just from the domain of public reason in which political decision making is to take place, but he also assumes that they can have no voice in the important task of deciding what doctrines are to be taken as 'unreasonable'.[25]

It is 'reasonable', Rawls says, to accept any one of a number of comprehensive conceptions of the good, and that those holding other doctrines are also 'reasonable'. But a person may also be termed 'reasonable' even if they don't endorse any particular doctrine. *'Beyond this'*, he says *'reasonable persons will think it unreasonable to use political power, should they possess it , to repress comprehensive views that are not unreasonable'.*[26] Rawls does make explicit reference to the original position in justification of two additional claims that are relevant to this. Firstly, he says that 'reasonable persons see that the burdens of judgement set limits on what can be reasonably justified to others' and secondly, that '..it is unreasonable for us to use political power, should we possess, or share it with others, to repress comprehensive views that are not unreasonable'. The second of these two claims sanctions the use of coercive state power, perhaps with regret, to 'repress comprehensive views which are, in public terms, unreasonable'.

Rawls outlines further up the page what is going to count as an 'unreasonable' comprehensive view and he couches his explanation implicitly in the language of the original position. But he does not do this *explicitly*, as he does for the two claims which use the distinction, outlined above. Rawls sets out his notion of what it is for a doctrine to be 'unreasonable' in the following way,

> Of course, those who do insist on their beliefs also insist that their beliefs alone are true: they impose their beliefs because, they say, their beliefs are true and not because they are their beliefs. But this is a claim that all equally could make; it is also a claim that cannot be made good by anyone to citizens generally. So, when we make such claims others, who are themselves reasonable, must count us unreasonable.[27]

It is this definition which underpins the second claim outlined above and, eventually, the view that certain democratic virtues may be promoted by the state at the expense of certain comprehensive doctrines. It *is* true to say that, as members of a democratic society, we would think it 'unreasonable' for a particular group *having achieved political power* to use that power to *'impose'* their own comprehensive conception of the good upon the rest of society. This definition of unreasonableness might well be accepted *even* by those who, if *they* had such power *would* exercise it in that way.[28] But that limited and uncontroversial definition will not do the kind of work that Rawls requires of it since it assumes an imaginary context in which the condition of democratic decision making had been overtaken by political events as, for example, in the case of a military coup or the election of a repressive regime. The sense of 'unreasonable' in that case would link logically to the *use* of coercive state power *by those with the means to deploy it.* The question is, however, whether or not that sense of unreasonableness can be attached without further justification to those *within* a democratic regime, and without even the remotest possibility of finding themselves in a position where they could wield such power, but who 'insist that their beliefs alone are true'. Is it fair that those who do not subscribe to the democratic and liberal values of Rawls' anti perfectionist state, by continuing to believe the *political implications* of their comprehensive conception of the good should have their voice excluded from the democratic decision making process and their views repressed and undermined by a programme of common civic education?

It might be asked why representatives in the original position should accept this. Being behind the veil of ignorance, they would not know whether their own rational and sincerely held views might incorporate illiberal and undemocratic political implications but would know that such views would be subjected to 'regrettable' treatment by the state. They would therefore conclude that it would *only* be 'unreasonable' to use *whatever power one had at one's disposal*, personal or political in order *to impose* one's own view on other citizens or to discriminate against them. Representatives in the original position would, I think, regard it as 'unreasonable' for coercive state power to be used to undermine any sincerely held view, of an otherwise law abiding citizen, *even if* it were at odds with the common values of society. Thus the original position methodology actually discredits an important aspect of the social democratic liberalism that Rawls himself supports. [29]

These remarks deal with the first of the concerns raised earlier about the overall coherence of Rawls' social democratic programme with the basic tenets embodied in his anti-perfectionist liberal position. I want now to consider the second concern raised there by returning to Rawls' use of the distinction between the 'public' and the 'non-public' domains. He asserts clearly that education should be regarded as part of the 'public' domain and attempts to say why society should have an interest in the education of children, implying that this will have implications for their personal development.[30] It follows from this view that where public values enter the domain of education they should be given priority over other values derived from the non-public domain in the development of the person. But Rawls does not offer *any* further justification for the fact that the education of children should fall into the area of the 'public'. Nor does his characterisation of the various non-public domains, include perhaps the most important source of non-public values, certainly in the lives of children, the family. Interestingly, his exemplification of non-public *'associations'* does feature another educational institution, the university. He is keen, given communitarian critiques of his earlier work, to emphasise that the non-public is not equal to the domain of the private. And, in addition, he emphasises the fact that it is a series of domains of rational association.

> First of all there are many non-public reasons and but one public reason. Among the non-public reasons are those of associations of all kinds: churches and universities, scientific societies and professional groups. As we have said , to act reasonably and responsibly, corporate bodies, as well as individuals, need a way of reasoning about what is to be done. This way of reasoning is public with respect to their members, but non-public with respect to political society and to citizens generally. Non-public reasons comprise the many reasons of civil society and belong to what I have called the 'background culture', in contrast with the public political culture. These reasons are social, and certainly not private.[31]

Given that many intermediate associations of a voluntary or rational kind are offered as examples of the non-public domain, it is puzzling firstly that the family is not mentioned as a source of 'non-public reasons' and more importantly why some educational establishments are seen as part of the non-public while 'the question of children's education' is to be answered '*..entirely within the political conception.*'[32] Rawls' distinction between the 'public' and the 'non-public' may itself be unworkable, but I will not concern myself with that. I am going to assume that it works and attempt to ask whether Rawls' assumption that the education system should be seen as significantly part of the public rather than the non-public domain can be supported, *independently* of his mere assertion of it, from within the framework of his political liberalism. At first glance the prospects for this look bleak since the whole edifice of political liberalism can only be set out and accepted on the basis not just of some acceptance of the distinction between the two domains, but also some precise indication as to where the line between the two domains is to be drawn. The drawing of this line especially on the question of education will be extremely difficult and controversial. It is therefore interesting that a thinker of Rawls' stature has not attempted to offer some *internal* justification for it. It seems quite consistent with Rawls' overall programme to say that the line between the public and the non-public should be drawn by representatives in the ideal sphere of the original position.

In my discussion of Macedo's tough-minded liberal approach to the Mozert case, I suggested that minority groups might be willing to accept the priority of common public values in the public domain. This would mean, for example, an ardent anti-abortionist, accepting the fact that it would be illegitimate for political power to be used to uphold her favoured view, agreeing to the kinds of procedural values that might put in place a legal framework tolerant of abortion, as viewed from her personal moral perspective. Public decisions impinge upon the non-public background culture of a society, and that might be of concern to someone with strongly held views, but this might not, of itself, affect their loyalty to the democratic state. However, I suggested, that this acceptance would be dependent upon the *inevitability* of any non-public 'double effect'. Loyal dissenting citizens might accept that, as Macedo says, '*..political power is a trust held in common..which may not be disposed of for our private purposes*',[33] but they will require that the issue in question falls, *inevitably*, within the domain of *public* decision making. In the case of whether or not abortion is to be permitted, whether or not Britain should possess nuclear weapons, how much tax is paid, this inevitability-condition *is* arguably fulfilled. These issues are *clearly* 'public', despite the fact that they have varying degrees of non public 'double effect', because the law, spending and charge involved in each must be of a single and inevitable kind. This may not seem clear in the third case but where a decision is required, as with a law or a policy on nuclear weapons *a diversity of approach is just* ruled out. In such cases a monovalent policy outcome is inevitable and therefore priority has logically to be given to one set of values. Britain cannot *logically* have nuclear weapons and not have them. Likewise a society either permits abortion or rules it out.[34]

If sense can be made of this attempt to offer a purely rational distinction between the public and the non-public, on behalf of political liberalism, then it might inform judgements made in the original position and not require justification *from* that perspective. However, I don't think that the character of a child's education would come into the domain of the public, as defined in this way. The state education system might be thought to mirror some elements of the obviously public issues mentioned above. It resembles the nuclear weapons example in that the decision as to how much might be spent to fund the system must be a public one. But the relevant resemblance ends just there *unless* we continue to conceive of the character of that system along social democratic lines by making two crucial assumptions. *Only if* we suppose that *all* state schools *must* be *common* schools with a common conception of education can the resemblance between the provision of education and the obviously public examples cited above be maintained. In those examples diversity of provision was *just not a possibility* so difficult choices had to be made, based on common values and public reason. But in the field of state education *diversity* of provision clearly is *a possibility*. However, most people who think about education, especially in Britain, tend to *assume* that some common system is inevitable. It is *this assumption*, a fundamental tenet of social democratic liberalism, which apparently moves the provision of state school values into the public domain. Once this assumption is challenged then the possibility of a system of state schooling which is not common schooling is opened up. It follows that liberals must offer *independent* reasons to show that state education must have the organisational structure favoured by the social democratic conception *before* state education can be assumed to reside fully in the public domain. To do so, without further argument, in the current context would involve circularity since we are exploring the validity of using the liberal framework to *underpin* the common conception of civic education that social democratic liberals think desirable.[35]

Social Democratic Liberals, like Macedo and Rawls, who wish to demonstrate, rather than merely assert or assume, that education should be conceived as part of the public or political domain from the perspective of political liberalism, will have to show that this is an essential procedural requirement of a just liberal democratic order, from behind the veil of ignorance in the original position. Representatives in the original position must leave behind all knowledge of their own social position and their personal conception of the good but, in order to judge correctly, they must be allowed some knowledge of the *outcomes* of the various options before them. In this case, they will have to know what the decision to place the education of their children in the public or political domain will involve. In particular they should be told of the worst case scenarios that were discussed above and which tough-minded liberals regard as both possible and 'regrettable'. I think that two versions of the social democratic liberal programme could be formulated and placed before the adjudicating forum of representatives in the original position in an attempt to capture a stronger and a weaker 'regrettable' worst case scenario (RWCS). They are as follows:-

RWCS 1: *Children will be required to enter schools where they will be educated according to public values as part of a compulsory programme of civic education that will significantly affect their personal development and will positively undermine the comprehensive conception of the good held by their parents, if that conception is deemed, from the public perspective, to be 'unreasonable'.*

RWCS 2: *Children will be required to enter common schools where they will be educated according to public values as part of a compulsory programme of civic education that will significantly affect their personal development and will positively undermine the comprehensive conception of the good held by their parents, if that conception is deemed from the public perspective to be 'unreasonable'. However, the common values underpinning the programme of civic education will be 'thin'. Therefore, even where this programme will not undermine the values of the home, the programme of personal education offered by the school will not foster the* *positive conception of the good held by the parents of any particular child, either. This is because any programme of personal development must reflect common values as well.*

It is clear that RWCS2 is much stronger than RWCS1 since it, not only, reflects the social democratic liberal commitment to a programme of common civic education, but also builds in further social democratic assumptions regarding the scope or relative authority of public and non-public values. RWCS1, on the other hand, while committed to the basic idea of a common programme of civic education does not restrict the extent to which publicly constrained state schools might reflect and support the values of parents whose views are otherwise deemed 'reasonable'. It is worth noting that *even* where the requirement for a common conception of civic education is accepted, it is possible to separate *that* from a range of further requirements[36] which might be assumed in fact to be inseparable and therefore otherwise *inevitable* aspects of it.[37]

However, I think that *even* the weaker version of the worst case scenario (RWCS1) would lead rational representatives in the original position to decide that decisions about the *character of the personal development* offered in schools ought to remain outside the public or political domain.[38] Not knowing, from behind the veil of ignorance, what in fact their own cherished values would be, but knowing that unless these were to meet certain criteria of reasonableness, laid down by others, they would be undermined in the personal education of their own children, they would *certainly* reject the view that education should be seen as 'exclusively' part of the public domain and also, arguably, the minimal conception[39] as well. This may not be sufficient argument to put the case which I am trying to establish, i.e. that Rawls' political programme *cannot* support the educational agenda of social democratic liberalism which he and others favour, beyond rational doubt. However, it does despite its partial reliance upon an appeal to intuition show, firstly, that a counter case running against Rawls' own assumptions is at least arguable on the basis of his own political programme and, secondly, that the onus is on social democratic liberals to provide their own arguments, accommodating and challenging the case made out here. If they cannot provide such arguments then their programme of toughminded civic education, even when minimally conceived, will fail to satisfy the conditions laid down in the last chapter which might otherwise legitimise its hostility to certain forms of life under the ambit of secularism 2.[40]

I have shown that we can speak correctly of two versions of political liberalism. The first, a truly anti-perfectionist version, is incompatible with a social democratic liberal commitment to common schools,[41] and even to a

Rawlsian programme of civic education. It would be compatible with a diversity of schools whose programmes of personal development would be regarded as non-public and strongly led by the wishes of parents. The second form of political liberalism is covertly perfectionist and the perfectionism that it embodies is characterised by the social democratic liberal assumptions that I outlined earlier and elaborated in the course of the foregoing discussion.

5.4 Perfectionist liberal approaches to personal education

While Rawls and other 'neutralist' liberals might find all this rather irksome, many liberal theorists find the conclusion rather congenial and unsurprising. They take the view that liberal toughmindedness should focus not upon propagating anti-perfectionism as public dogma but upon justifying the particular *kind* of perfectionism that all liberalism, in their view, *inevitably* embodies. William Galston, for example,[42] gives three reasons why the neutrality thesis is misguided. Among these he cites the absence of the kind of

> *consensus concerning the substance and importance of key secular goods such as the minimization of violent conflict'* and the fact that each of the proponents of neutrality *'..tacitly relies on a more than formal and more than instrumental conception of the good to move his argument forward.*

We have seen that Rawls and other anti-perfectionist liberals are inclined precisely to assume that a consensus of the required kind either does exist or could exist if everyone adopted their very particular ideals of 'reasonableness' and 'democracy'. Having done that they are inclined tacitly to rely upon the latter in order to move their argument onwards in the name of 'Liberalism'. Galston outlines his more explicitly perfectionist account of liberalism in the following way:

> I shall argue..that liberalism does in fact rest on a distinctive conception of the human good. This conception differs from the 'perfectionism' of classical antiquity. It does not, for example, culminate in a depiction of the summum bonum or of the best way of life for all human beings...It demarcates a capacious but nonetheless determinate sphere of public possibilities'. The problem with the neutralist anti-perfectionist programme is that it pre-supposes a 'two-value model' to the effect that 'either a society is neutral or it must be restrictively partisan even covertly perfectionist.[43]

In a formulation of his own brand of *perfectionist* liberalism, which allowing for a wide though not unconstrained pluralism among a range of conceptions of the good life, Galston demonstrates that *it* would not support the kind of common civic education programme advocated by Rawls and Macedo. He says that, according to the liberal perspective,[44]

> ...the proposition that 'A knows that X is good for B' does not by itself warrant the conclusion that 'A is justified in coercing B to do B or to be X'. Coercion for public purposes, like raising tax to fund a public health programme, is distinguishable from coercion directed at individual ways of life.[45]

One important aspect of the perfectionist liberal view of the human good is the value of human freedom seen as choice, *'unencumbered by claims of need, desert or other duties'*[46] It is this commitment to freedom or autonomy which Joseph Raz sees as *the* key aspect of liberalism. Indeed, he, with some justification, sees the Rawlsian programme while disavowing a perfectionist commitment to the autonomous way of life, as resting covertly on the intuitive idea that

> ..advocates not neutral political concern as a principle of restraint but neutrality between those conceptions of the good which greatly value an autonomous development of one's life in accordance with one's rational nature'.[47]

There is some support for this view in Rawl's own discussion of what he calls 'the political conception of the person' which appears to rest upon a tacit endorsement of the autonomous way of life, but couched in different terms.[48]

For many educational thinkers working within a liberal framework it is a commitment to *autonomy* that constitutes the key value to be legitimately promoted as part of a common conception of personal education. While Rawlsian commitment to a certain kind of civic education would have significant double effects upon personal or spiritual development, it would not warrant explicitly, at least, a commitment to the development of autonomy as a primary aim of a common conception of personal or spiritual education in the state school. A very interesting debate has taken place in recent years among those liberals who take 'democracy' as their starting point. All see *some* form of civic education aimed at the perpetuation of the democratic society as an essential aspect of the common educational programme. However, differences have appeared about the extent to which such an education should bring the non-public values within the scope of critical discussion within the common school.[49] This debate is largely about the extent to which the state should require schools to take responsibility for the development of *autonomy* in young people. William Galston believes that a programme of civic education should require schools to take responsibility for inculcating certain personal characteristics. He expresses this as follows,

> ...the liberal state has a right to teach all children respect for the law...Similarly, the liberal state has a right to inculcate the expectation that all normal children will become adults capable of caring for themselves and their families.[50]

Where *this* requirement comes into conflict with the values or expressed wishes of parents the state, in his view, may legitimately override them. This is required by the liberal purpose of ensuring the *conditions* of a democratic society in which free and equal citizens can make the lives which they see fit. This image of what might be called a 'capacious liberalism', where the state guarantees the conditions of autonomous action, must however stop short of any perfectionist commitment to the *development* of young people *who are themselves committed* to the liberal value of autonomy. Other theorists of civic education believe that a liberal state cannot commit itself to the protection of the conditions of a free society without making a positive commitment to the development of autonomy in young people and that this commitment might lead the state to override, legitimately, the wishes and values of parents in this respect. Amy Gutmann is the leading exponent of this view, though a tacit adherence to something like it underpins Macedo's 'tough-minded' response to the Mozert case.[51] Amy Gutmann spells out the position in the following way :

> The same principle that requires a state to grant adults personal and political freedom also commits it to assuring children an education that makes those freedoms both possible and meaningful in the future. A state makes choice possible by teaching its future citizens respect for opposing points of view and ways of life. It makes choice meaningful by equipping children with the intellectual skills necessary to evaluate ways of life different from that of their parents.[52]

As a consequence, the liberal state is rightly committed to raising children who have been given the ability to exercise that choice and it is made clear that this requirement of our *'valuation of liberal freedom to pursue differing conceptions of the good'* will *'justify limitations on parents rights'*.[53] Gutmann's view is endorsed by Meira Levinson who has argued that schools should be conceived as 'autonomy driven communities',

> ...detached from the inevitably partial values, beliefs, and commitments of children's families and home communities [making available] an essential space in which children are enabled to start defining themselves on their own terms, encouraged- as well as repeatedly challenged- by an educational community structured by the norms of autonomy alone.[54]

5.5 Raz, human well-being and the educational importance of autonomy

Educationalists who give a central role to the development of autonomy in any conception of education and believe that this might be justified on rational grounds, might derive support from the political philosophy of Joseph Raz. who constructs a perfectionist liberalism, built upon a picture of human well-being that is committed to the centrality of the exercise of choice. And this means that the perfectionist liberal state must commit itself to the development of rational self determination or autonomy amongst its citizens. It is this fundamental commitment, according to Raz, which leads liberals to favour and nurture certain autonomy supporting political institutions. It is that commitment and the conception of personal well-being that underpins it that would, I think, lead him to support the view that a common conception of education should be *autonomy-driven*.[55]

It is interesting to note that Raz supports his advocacy of the value of personal autonomy through a rational account which includes *some* reference to its cultural predominance. His attempt to incorporate some reference to a de facto cultural setting into an otherwise universalist account of personal well being, might rekindle the hope, examined in chapter three, that it might be possible to read off certain aims of personal education from an empirical cultural analysis of modern Britain. In fact Raz's account of personal well-being can be seen as an attempt to unify the liberal taste for the construction of universal principles, with the particularism associated with its communitarian critics. He offers an account of personal well-being which is summarised through four conditions.[56] These four conditions establish the foundations of the activities of the perfectionist liberal state, envisaged by Raz, and obviously provide liberal educationalists with an important starting point for the personal development of all pupils. The question of whether such a basis is 'thick' enough to provide a comprehensive account remains to be seen. But, at the very least, those responsible for personal and spiritual education of pupils within the state system should take account of the requirements and constraints which this account might impose upon their task.

Raz says that it is a condition of any one's personal well being that they should be able and willing to pursue self-determined goals, *'whose value is believed to be at least in part independent of the fact that they were chosen and are pursued'*[57] This, in itself, is sufficient to confirm that Raz believes himself to have found a rational and culturally independent justification for the promotion of the ideal of the autonomy characterised as 'uncoerced, rational self-determination'. But he sets out a fourth condition which attempts to disassociate his view from asocial individualism by affirming the universal importance of community membership and cultural embeddedness for the ideal of personal well-being.

This fourth condition of personal well-being states that

> A person's well-being depends to a large extent on success in socially defined and determined pursuits and activities.

Raz uses a cultural reference to make explicit his support for the link between personal autonomy and personal well-being. He says that the ideal of autonomy has 'acquired considerable popularity' in 'western industrial societies'. This particular cultural ideal, according to Raz, goes beyond the limited autonomy of his first three conditions of well-being and *'holds the free choice of goals and relations as an essential ingredient of individual well-being'.*[58] The ideal is

> ...suited to the conditions of the industrial age and its aftermath with their fast changing technologies and free movement of labour..its suitability for our conditions and the deep roots it has by now acquired in our culture contribute to a powerful case for this ideal.[59]

Raz rejects the view that the autonomous life is itself just one of the many options that exist within our society,[60] a view which might be thought to follow as part of an adherence to the importance of autonomy itself. He argues that this would underestimate the fact that the exercise of choice is central to the very character of our society and that this will, in line with the fourth condition of human well-being, have a marked effect upon the well-being of individuals. Individuals who do not themselves value autonomy will find it difficult 'to prosper'.[61] Raz is inclined to extend the classical liberal conception of harm[62] so that liberal governments are required to guarantee the conditions required for the exercise of autonomy in an attempt to prevent individuals from being harmed by the deprivation of *opportunity* that might arise from a failure to see the fundamental value of the autonomous life.[63] A liberal government on this view, and given the social conditions which actually exist in western industrial societies, would be *required* to support the individual capacities as well as the institutional infrastructure required for the autonomous lifestyle to thrive. And Raz is clear that this remains the case even if it means that the government's action would undermine forms of life currently in existence and based on a non-autonomous conception of the good, causing them eventually to be eliminated.[64]

Raz does not discuss the educational implications of his political programme so it is difficult to see whether or not he would share the view of many educationalists that the government's promotion of the conditions of autonomy should be extended to the development of autonomy as an aim of a common conception of personal or spiritual education. Clearly this would raise a host of questions that he does not directly consider. I would just note that even if arguments are provided to show that a liberal government has a duty to intervene to guarantee the conditions that support the autonomous life, those same arguments would have to be supplemented by others in order to support the active advocacy of the development of the capacity for autonomy through a system of common schooling. In particular, given his view that the cultural embeddedness of individual choice is essential to personal well-being, questions arise about the effects of interventionist educational strategies to promote the capacity for autonomy on the cultural fabric via its indirect consequences for families and communities. Raz derives his justification of the value of this capacity from a national or large scale cultural analysis of 'western industrial societies', but in an educational context the use of such an analysis is questionable. Firstly, it appears to translate an empirical analysis into a normative one in a way that would appear to align government intervention with a strategy of cultural conservation.[65]

Secondly, it appears to suggest that *the* culture of a given individual is necessarily best determined at the *national* level. This is to beg a question of vital importance to the whole process used, at least by Raz himself, to show the importance of autonomy. In the educational context of personal development it must be shown that *national* cultural considerations, which are arguably of overriding importance to the way in which *governments* should view the question of personal well-being, are *also* of overriding importance for *individuals* served by schools. This last point raises the question of *who is best placed* to *decide* the answer to the questions about the cultural framework within which any particular child ought to be nurtured. This, in turn, raises questions about the extent to which the state might legitimately override the wishes of the parents in situations of conflict. Social democratic liberals, wishing to take advantage of Raz's overall perfectionist liberalism in order to support a programme of autonomy driven personal education, will need to offer supplementary arguments on these issues and I will examine some of these in the last part of this study.[66]

5.6 The development of autonomy and pluralism

For the moment I want to forget these crucial questions and to ask what it might mean to develop a common conception of personal or spiritual education committed to the value of developing autonomy. This is to envisage, for the sake of argument, that a nationally common programme of personal development, along the lines assumed by social democratic liberals, is desirable. In the last part of this chapter I would like to examine what the implementation of such a developmental ideal would mean for state schools.

Raz does not think it a problem that the state should act to maintain the conditions which support autonomy even if at the same time it prevents the continuance of certain non-autonomous forms of life. While his commitment to this form of perfectionism must sit in tension with his commitment to pluralism itself but it is both compatible with and, indeed depends upon, a commitment to the maintenance of a limited pluralism. This is because a limited pluralism is a necessary condition for the exercise of the capacity for autonomy. It provides individuals with a range of values and lifestyle options some of which will be incompatible. However, given the fact that the plurality of lifestyle options available can in fact be limited while the conditions for autonomy are satisfied, the exact minimum extent of the required range of values is open to question. This is of vital importance when it is combined with the fact that cultural embeddness is crucial for personal well-being and that attempting to expose individuals to a wide range of different values and lifestyle options might undermine the possibility of an individual successfully developing into a *particular* cultural tradition. If the perfectionist liberal state were committed to the perpetuation of a limited pluralism, then this aim might be undermined where too high a value were placed upon the presentation of a plurality of value systems within the context of a common conception of education. The reason for this flows from consideration of the fact that the successful *development* of individuals into *any* particular value system, apart perhaps, from that of pluralism itself,[67] will require some restriction in the range of lifestyle options and value systems to which they can be exposed. This suggests, paradoxically, that the commitment to autonomy should not be stressed to the point where it might undermine the adequate development of individuals into the small cultural traditions reflecting their home life. And this consideration is especially pertinent since these cultural traditions, embedded in family life, actually help to constitute the limited pluralism that Raz sees as an essential aspect of the culture of autonomy.

In discussing the value of autonomy within a liberal framework, Macedo identifies the two poles of a tension at its heart. He speaks of 'internal' and 'external' pluralism, the first being the requirement that individuals have knowledge and understanding of a range of lifestyle and value options while the second identifies their continued existence as embodied social realities. When the importance of this tension is not realised by educationalists planning for the personal development of their pupils and too great an emphasis is placed on the need for *internal* pluralism, then the *external* pluralism upon which the liberal commitment to autonomy is, at least, instrumentally based, will be threatened. This danger is particularly apparent when common values are given too high a profile and the procedural values of the liberal state are seen as overriding those of parents since those intending to pass on their particular value system to their children would be likely to have that intention overridden by a multicultural educational programme that would undermine the effectiveness of the transmission process.[68]

Raz has effectively developed a form of *communitarian* liberalism, that counteracts very effectively the arguments of communitarians like MacIntyre and Sandel,[69] by suggesting that liberalism is itself a tradition,[70] requiring commitment and social embeddedness but usually on a larger scale and with more focus on the necessary rather than sufficient conditions of the good life, than is usual in communitarian thinking. It follows from this view that an individual's need for an education suitable for her attachment to the liberal political system can then become the basis for a common conception of personal education. However, liberal educationalists should be aware of the fact that such a viewpoint, when allied to a system of *common schooling* can, as has been suggested, have non-plural consequences. The maintenance of particular forms of life will be dependent upon the education of children into those forms of life and this will not be possible without appropriate particularistic, as opposed to common schooling. This tension between the educational commitment to 'internal' pluralism and a commitment to even limited 'external' pluralism, I will call the paradox of pluralist education. I will return to discussion of it in due course when we examine what I call the *'monising effects'* of a common conception of spiritual education that has pluralism as one of its central aims.

5.7 The development of autonomy, cultural attachment and autonomy driven schooling

The characterisations of autonomy offered by liberal political theorists and educationalists in the wake of communitarian criticisms of traditional counterparts has tended to emphasise the fact that optimally autonomous agents operate not from a perspective of complete critical detachment but from one that is situated personally, socially and culturally. This view of autonomy has been variously described as 'weak' (Halstead) 'complex' (Levinson) and 'normal' (Theissen) or 'situated' (Macedo) autonomy.[71] This complex, which makes up what liberal educationalists recommend as 'autonomy', has within in it two poles which, when seen as part of an overall *educational* aim, come into tension. Autonomy on the one hand embodies the notion of self-creation, self government (autarchy) or self direction. Raz, speaking of autonomy as a political rather than an educational ideal tends to emphasise this element, characterising it in the following way:

> The ruling idea behind the ideal of personal autonomy is that people should make their own lives. The autonomous person is a (part) author of his own life. The ideal of personal autonomy is the vision of people controlling, to some degree, their own destiny, fashioning it through successive decisions throughout their lives.[72]

This pole normally incorporates some notion that critical and rational assessments are being made from a point at some distance i.e. with knowledge and understanding of one's current commitments.

Much recent thinking on autonomy has attempted to combine a recognition of the fact that an individual's situatedness in a particular cultural context is an *essential* aspect of their being described as autonomous. Some liberal thinkers have gone further than this and argued that the self-creation pole *requires* that an individual has been personally developed into some particular tradition of value. Meira Levinson, in the course of her argument for the primacy of autonomy as a central component of a system of common education, puts the matter in the following way.

> Membership in a community and embeddedness within a cultural and normative framework is a primary need of individuals-and an essential

prerequisite for autonomy. One cannot act autonomously if one has no firm structure of beliefs on which to act.[73]

Without this *prior* development into a tradition of value an individual's personal decisions will be to an extent *arbitrary* and will therefore lack the *rationality* and unity which liberals take to be the distinguishing feature of the autonomous approach to life. These considerations suggest a set of paradoxical constraints that ought to be applied to any common conception of personal development, with autonomy as an aim. Firstly, it might not be wise to make the development of the internal pluralism mentioned, and advocated by Macedo, a central aim. Levinson, for example, argues that '*autonomy..demands that individuals have a plurality of commitments*'. This, she alleges will make them '*more receptive to other viewpoints*' and able to subject particular values to critical reassessment without '*..suffering a wholesale loss of identity*'.[74] The latter point raises the question of why such protection might be thought necessary if the prerequisite condition of cultural embeddedness has been satisfied. The point about 'receptiveness' appears not to be about autonomy as such but a requirement of something like *democratic civility*. We saw that a commitment of this kind to internal pluralism might undermine the nurturing of external pluralism, also required by the ideal of autonomy. But, in addition, and for the same reasons, its development will be in stark tension with the aim of providing children with the cultural embeddness *that itself underpins* the development of autonomy. Secondly, educationalists who work with and tacitly promote an unrealistic ideal of critical detachment, based upon the enlightenment ideal of rationality and associated with Kantian thinking, will also to that extent be undermining the development of the *situated* autonomy that was discussed above. And these negative effects would be felt not just by those who come from non-autonomous backgrounds but by pupils from *all* backgrounds. This suggests that liberals who wish to advocate autonomy as an *aim* of personal education should see the requirement for critical detachment, rather, in terms of '*critical openness*' contextualised in some specific tradition.[75] This will have implications in my view for the social democratic commitment to the common school and a common conception of education, since it suggests that committed schooling of the kind offered by religious schools could provide the *best* model for the kind of non-detached autonomous personal development advocated here.[76]

The quest for 'internal pluralism' and 'critical detachment' should not therefore be regarded as ends in themselves and, as is widely supposed, the very embodiment of an education for the development of autonomy. There are other reasons for caution when constructing a common educational programme emphasising these features which goes beyond the considerations of a liberal concern for autonomy and pluralism. If educationalists working for the state operate in a way that undermines the attempt by parents to pass on a particular form of life to their children then they must offer independent *political* justification for it. Important side issues are raised by the need for social embeddedness. This suggests that the primary emphasis of a common conception of personal development should be to inculcate *as a primary aim* the virtues of some particular tradition of value and practice. And this raises the question of who should decide the nature of *that* primary culture. For example both Raz and Macedo [77] suggest that the relevant primary culture is that of the nation. Here, social democratic liberals and others will, I suspect, divide over how much weight should be given to the views of parents in relation to that of the state in the resolution of this issue. I will return to detailed discussion of this at a later stage.[78]

5.8 Autonomy, transcendence and the language of spirituality

In the last part of this chapter I want to explore further the extent to which the idea of spiritual development might offer some appropriate notion of the character of a necessary and integral aspect of any programme of personal development with complex autonomy as its aim. In doing so I will make passing reference to the various self explanatory, organisational models for the national promotion of spiritual development set out in appendix 1.

The development of autonomy would seem to be connected necessarily to a commitment to the development of critical openness. And while this might not, for the reasons offered above, involve a full blown commitment to the promotion of values pluralism, it would seem to require a commitment to non-monism.[79] It might be argued that if a school adopts a rigidly monistic developmental ideal such that children are not actively presented with a sympathetic exposition of *at least* some alternatives to that favoured by the school, then it could not, *logically*, claim to be developing autonomy.[80]

The relationship between this notion of what is required of the liberal school, committed to the development of little more than personal autonomy, and the spiritual notion of transcendence may by now be obvious. A liberal educational institution as such should commit itself not just to pluralism but also expose pupils to systems of value other than (transcending) that which predominates in that particular institution. Thus, on the basis of a commitment purely to the educational value of developing personal autonomy, we might propose the following principle, constraining the promotion of *any* particular set of values in the liberal state school:

In actively developing pupils along the lines of value system x, some sympathetic exposure must be given by the same institution to value system/s non-x.

Even in the context of the civic pluralism of model 4,[81] a government committed to the view that any state funded education must, at the very least, be committed to the value of personal autonomy, would seek to lay down the above principle as a constraint. So while encouraging schools to actively promote particular spiritual and moral values in the name of pluralism, it might be insisted by a liberal government that some exposure be given to another viewpoint. For example, a school actively committed, within the framework of model 4, to the promotion of Christian values would have to have some transcendent commitment to the contestable nature of that viewpoint and to expose pupils to the values of secular humanism. By the same token, a school actively committed to the promotion of secular humanist values would have to have some transcendent commitment to the contestable nature of that value system and to expose pupils to the values of religion. In chapter six I will attempt to link this transcendent commitment to the epistemological doctrine of critical realism.

The upshot of this is that commitment to the development of personal autonomy alone, not to mention pluralism, requires some *metaphysical* commitment to a transcendent perspective to the effect that all traditions, including those favoured, embody a *contestable* claim to truth and value which relates to a reality independent of that tradition and its adherents and against which they may be judged. This does not mean that all state institutions should commit themselves to the view that there is some transcendent reality along the lines set out by religious adherents, but may be instantiated by such a view. The notion of transcendence, in use here, is a context dependent and relative one. What transcends 'x' can only be given a definite value once 'x' itself is given a specific value. This cannot be specified *in advance* since it will depend upon who exactly is given responsibility for the primary programme of personal development and its character. And that will depend on which of the various organisational models outlined in appendix 1 is adopted nationally.

Spiritual development with its built in reference to transcendence, plays a crucial part in ensuring that the above principle, based exclusively on the notion of personal autonomy, is adhered to within the state education system. It reminds those inclined towards an illiberal secular humanism that they must expose children to religious perspectives. This may be particularly difficult for secular humanists, who are inclined to regard their own perspective as intrinsically and incontrovertibly liberal, while taking it for granted that religious perspectives are intrinsically illiberal and controversial.[82] A liberal view of the state and a commitment to the educational value of personal autonomy does not, contrary to popular belief, commit the state or any of its institutions to the promotion of secular humanism or any other currently predominant and 'uncontroversial' world view; it does however, require the state and its institutions to be committed to the promotion of transcendence, conceived along the lines set out here. At the same time, the notion of spiritual development has an in-built even handedness, since it automatically reminds those otherwise inclined towards an illiberal *religious* monism that they must also expose the children in their care to non-religious world views. 'Spirituality', like 'transcendence' is a relative and context dependent concept. It is therefore a naturally and self regulating corrective within the life of a particular institution, requiring a combination of challenge and critique to supplement the active promotion of a specific primary value system.[83] In our present cultural climate where, arguably, secular humanism predominates, the requirement for schools to spiritually develop their pupils will take effect by protecting religious perspectives. But in another cultural climate, for example where an evangelical religious monism predominated, the self-same requirement would ensure that children are exposed to the values of secular humanism.

In the next chapter I will review the prospects for two widely held liberal attempts to put together a common conception of spiritual development. I will label these two views the experiential and non-realist approaches and I will argue that both are problematic especially within the liberal framework that is supposed to underpin them. Moving on from the criticism of the non-realist approach I will argue that a liberal approach to spiritual development has an intrinsic link with the metaphysical doctrine of critical realism.

Notes

1 This is the kind of justification of the liberal state offered by Joseph Raz (1986) and William Galston (1991). Perfectionism is the view that it is unnecessary for the liberal state to adopt a policy of neutral political concern or impartiality as anti-perfectionist liberals suggest. On the perfectionist view it is possible for liberal policymakers to favour particular substantive conceptions of the good life. However, perfectionist liberals do disagree about the kinds of values that the liberal state is justified in promoting. For example, Raz regards the promotion of autonomy as legitimate while Galston puts forward a more minimal perfectionist picture that rejects the promotion of autonomy.

2 Macedo (1995), p223-5.

3 Newby (1996).

[4] And, even where a constitutional commitment to liberal democracy did exist, there would still arise the question of which particular *conception* of 'democracy' its authors had in mind. This term, like that of 'liberalism' is open to an enormous range of interpretations. For a discussion of this see Held (1987), passim. That the term 'liberalism' is used in a number of quite different ways will be actively demonstrated in the course of this study but see also, Gray (1989).

[5] See, for example, Scruton (1984).

[6] See, for example Oakeshott (1962).

[7] See, for example, Hayek (1944), (1963).

[8] See, Berlin (1980), Gray (1995) and Rescher (1993).

[9] Rawls (1993), pp.3-4, cf.xvi, 3-4.

[10] Tamir expresses the relationship between political liberalism, which she, following Walzer (1992), calls 'Liberalism 1', as one of 'appropriateness' or compatibility between the two. I want to suggest that it is a logical relationship to the effect that unless Liberalism 1 is compatible with thick multiculturalism then it cannot get itself accepted except on a non-perfectionist rational basis. The argument that follows is intended in part to demonstrate this.

[11] Rawls (1993), p36.

[12] Ibid., p55f.

[13] This important aspect of the modernist worldview has been characterised and criticised extensively in recent times see, for example, MacIntyre (1981), chapters 4,5 and 6; Gray (1995), ch10; Dunne (1993), passim., Polanyi, M.(1958), (1969), passim., Taylor (1989), part 2; and for a discussion of the impact of this world view on educational issues, see Theisson (1993), p87-116.

[14] See Nagel (1986), p164ff.

[15] Some critics of Rawls' political programme note that his adherence to the burdens of judgement thesis reflects ultimately a skeptical thesis, about the impossibility of establishing a comprehensive conception of the good capable of underpinning public policy, and the tension that might exist between *that* commitment and his apparent optimism that a rational consensus could be established around a set of public values in the context of pluralism. This line of criticism, I think is aimed broadly at trying to prise Rawls away from his commitment to the 'burdens' in order to show that Rawls' views are really most coherently and consistently described as a 'thin liberal perfectionism' or even a 'thin communitarianism' rather than in terms of anti-perfectionism. This kind of critique, found on p220f of Mulhall and Swift (1992), reflects some elements of the argument developed here and provides independent support for the view expressed below that Rawls' anti-perfectionist liberalism must collapse either into a commitment to real pluralism or a thin perfectionist or comprehensive liberalism i.e. one that embodies a commitment to a liberal view of the personal sphere as well as the political domain.

[16] Op cit., p175.

[17] Ibid., p200.

[18] Strike (1993), p178f.

[19] See p106. On the issues around the extent to which state funded schools should restrain or promote non-public values, see the discussion of homosexuality in White,P.(1991) and the critical discussion of this social democratic position in McLaughlin (1995), p248-255.

[20] The ideal of the common school has been characterised by McLaughlin in the following terms as, '..a school which aspires not only to achieve a broad range of mix in its student body..but also one which is committed to a conception of common education'. Such a school should therefore be open to 'all students regardless of differentiating characteristics such as religious, ethnic, class or cultural background'. While he insists that it would be too much to expect a common school to actually contain such a broad mix, it is clear that the maximisation of diversity in these areas should remain something of an ideal for those who favour common schooling.

[21] Op cit., p175.

[22] Ibid., p24.

[23] See Rawls (1993), p200.

[24] Ibid., p58.

[25] This incorporates, from a logical viewpoint, circularity of argument in addition to the charge of political illegitimacy.

[26] Ibid., p60.

[27] Ibid., p61.

[28] This apparently counter-intuitive conclusion is reached on the grounds that such a group, seeing themselves as a minority in an otherwise liberal democratic culture, without any chance of ever exercising such power, would see such a stance as one of enlightened self interest. Since they themselves have no hope of exercising such power (and perhaps even if they did harbour such hopes) the consequences for their own cherished values would be far worse should some other group (i.e. the majority group) use political power to impose their own values on all. Supporting the liberal democratic conception of the use of political power would be the best modus vivendi even for those who would otherwise idealise its demise.

[29] It might be noted in passing that Rawls himself recognises that certain forms of life might die out in a democratic society and he quotes Berlin's view that this might regrettably be the case 'No society', he says 'can include within itself all forms of life. We may indeed lament the limited space, as it were, of social worlds, and of ours in particular; and we may regret some of the inevitable effects of our culture and social structure ...But these social necessities are not to be taken for arbitrary bias or injustice' (Rawls,1993, p197). I have been trying to show that far from being regrettable 'necessities', embedded in the programme of political liberalism, they are symptoms of social democratic assumptions that are unnecessary additions to it, aimed at justifying coercive political power precisely to deny political, cultural and educational ' space' to certain politically incorrect forms of life. Whether one speaks in terms of 'bias or injustice' it is hard to deny that this cannot claim to be a politics of *real* pluralism. It might be argued that certain politically incorrect modes of thought underpin actions which bring about harm to society itself or to members of

society. The attitudes associated with racism come immediately to mind. However such thoughts do not affect the thrust of my argument since such views and attitudes could quite easily be shown to fall foul of the second condition of legitimate partiality (S2CLP2) which makes reference to the harmful effects of such views. Such an approach could not in my view be taken of those who just happen to believe either that liberal democracy is an inherently wicked political system or that anyone with opposed views is absolutely wrong. But it is precisely views of this latter kind that may, according to Rawls and other SDLs, be legitimately eliminated using the state education system. My contention is that even Rawls' own principles of legitimate political action cannot support this.

30 Op cit., p200.

31 Ibid., p220.

32 It might be thought that the reasons for the difference relate to the fact that university students are adults who *choose* to associate with particular institutions and have an ability to exit from such association. Children, on the other hand, do not exercise such choice, nor do they have the same rights of exit. It is true that children themselves do not make choices regarding the institutions they are legally obliged to attend, but parents do exercise such powers on their behalf and they do so on the basis of non-public reason. On the other hand the state is regarded as having some legitimate interest in the well being of children and is charged with protecting children from the vagaries of whatever their parents' views are about their treatment and upbringing. But even this is insufficient to justify Rawls' assumption that questions about the education of children should be answered '*entirely* within the public domain'. Given the strength of the prima facie case that seems to exist for saying that parents should have a primary say in the nature of the education given to their children and even saying (in full account of the record of Fred and Rosemary West) that this is a matter for public *concern*, it is difficult to see why liberalism itself should support the view that the education of children must be an *exclusively* public matter, even if SDLs might, for political reasons, have it so. On the case for this primary right of parents, see Crittenden (1988) and chapters by Almond and MacLaughlin in Halstead (ed.) (1994). For the SDL viewpoint see the chapter by White, P in the same volume.

33 Macedo (1995), p226.

34 It is true that there are a range of possibilities regarding when abortion might be permitted to individuals, it remains the case that it is not possible to devise a law capable of satisfying all shades of opinion on the issue of whether abortion ought to be permitted at all. While this kind of analysis does apply to certain aspects of education policy, for example, the legal requirement that all children (5-16) must attend a school and the decision to fund state education, it does not apply to the nature of the education offered by a school since the state could provide funding for a diverse range of schools.

35 For a recent challenge to these political assumptions, see Tooley (1995).

36 Of the kind built into RWCS2.

37 Some social democratic liberals will, for political rather than educational reasons, be keen to make a logical link between the weaker requirement for civic education, and the stronger requirements set out in RWCS2, thereby with one move circumventing the inevitability condition (S2CLP1) that must be satisfied to license partiality under the ambit of what I called secularism 2. (see, p106). I hope that the remarks and distinctions outlined here will support those SDLs, like William Galston, who argue for a minimalist account of the scope and authority of public values in education (see, for example his critique of Gutmann's position in Galston (1989 and 1991), cf. Gutmann (1989).

38 Note the emphasis here. I am not suggesting that personal education itself is beyond the realm of public concern; this area is not *exclusively* non-public. The issue here is the extent to which it might be thought desirable, in the original position, for the *character* of the personal education to be publicly *determined*.

39 The likely effects of which are outlined in RWCS1.

40 See especially S2CLP1, p86.

41 Where only a 'thin' set of common values are available to support programmes of personal education and these are regarded as overriding where conflict arises with non-public values.

42 Galston (1991), p8.

43 Ibid., p9.

44 In parallel with the conclusions of my own detailed discussion above.

45 Ibid., p10. On a minimalist view of civic education and against Gutmann, cf. Galston (1989).

46 Ibid. p11, cf., p4.

47 Raz (1986), p133.

48 Op cit. p29ff.

49 cf., McLaughlin (1995) for some discussion of this debate.

50 Op cit., p252.

51 Macedo (1995).

52 Gutmann (1997), pp30-31, and see also D.Herzog, Happy Slaves: A Critique of Consent Theory, Chicago:Univ of Chicago Press (1989) and Macedo (1990), p269. It is of course arguable to what extent Gutmann's account represents a commitment to autonomy; certainly she does not frame her views in these terms. But she does, I think, argue that the state should promote the conditions of autonomy and that this should override the wishes of parents in cases of conflict. Any debate about whether or not this represents a perfectionist commitment to the promotion of autonomy or something rather more indirect(i.e whether Gutmann is closer to Raz than Rawls) is, for my current purposes, of little consequence.

53 Gutmann (1980), p350-351.

54 Levinson (1995), p56.

55 A view argued by Levinson (1995) passim.

56 See Raz (1986) p308. The fourth condition will be quoted and discussed below, the first three are as follows,

(1) All but the biologically determined aspects of a person's well-being consist of the successful pursuit of goals which he has or should have. Beyond its biologically determined component a person's well-being can be promoted only through his willing acceptance of goals and pusuits.

(2) People adopt and pursue goals because they believe in their independent value, that is their value is believed to be at least in part independent of the fact that they were chosen and are pursued.

(3) Barring a person's biologically determined needs and desires his well-being depends, at the deepest level, on his action reasons and his success in following them.

57 Raz (1986), p308.

58 Op cit., p369.

59 Op cit., p370.

60 Such a view would not lead one to advocate the perfectionist liberal commitment to autonomy as a necessary condition of *any* life that might be described as 'good'.

61 Op cit., p394.

62 Op cit., p412.

63 Op cit., p412ff.

64 Op cit., section 14.

65 Cf., comments and arguments on Haldane (1986) in chapter 4.

66 For example, Levinson (1995).

67 And, even the development of individuals into a pluralistic value system will require some constraints based upon the *narrowness* of the range of values to which a person could consistently be exposed. See, for example Macedo's argument against the narrow curriculum demanded by the Mozert parents in Macedo (1995).

68 At the very least such parents would be denied the assistance of schooling to aid them in the process of cultural transmission. For discussion of the two forms of pluralism cf. Macedo (1993).

69 MacIntyre (1981) and Sandel (1982).

70 Cf., MacIntyre (1988), chapter XVII; Mulhall and Swift (1992), ch8.

71 See, for example, Macedo (1995), p213ff; Theisson (1993), p118f ; Levinson (1995), p51 and also Kekes' notion of 'self direction', in Kekes (1989).

72 Op cit., p369.

73 Op cit., p54 and see also Ackerman's requirement for 'cultural coherence' in Ackerman (1980), p117.

74 Op cit., p55.

75 See Theissen (1993), p144; Hare (1979) and (1985) and McLaughlin (1984). These writers make out a case for the claim that such a contextualised conception of open schooling satisfies the requirements of autonomy as an educational aim. My own position is that such a conception *better* satisfies the requirements of complex autonomy than an education which is autonomy *driven*.

76 See also, McLaughlin (1984).

77 Raz (1986), p370 and Macedo (1990), p203f.

78 Levinson (1995), p50 and cf., Galston (1990), p254f.

79 I derive this terminology from Kekes (1993). A monistic approach to moral or political life is one which presumes that there is a single conception of the good life that could be applied to all individuals, either as human beings as such, or as a result of their cultural background. 'Non-monism' can be defined in contradistinction to this.

80 I am not suggesting that all schools should commit themselves to the development of autonomy but only to an exposition of the logical constraints of such a commitment.

81 See appendix 1.

82 For example, White (1995).

83 A similar analysis could be offer to demonstrate the language of spirituality and transcendence to contextualised educational programmes designed to develop 'critical openness' within a particularist educational setting (see the previous section).

6 Experience, Realism and Spiritual Development

Summary

In the first part of this chapter, I attempt to show that any educational approach to spiritual development will have to involve some particular evaluative developmental ideal. This will involve some adherence by policymakers to some notion of human well-being. In order to aid the process of policymaking, and to show the logical implications of taking up a range of policy positions, I put forward a framework for mapping developmental ideals. In the final section, I use the framework to discuss the prospects for two currently popular approaches to spiritual development. I show that, viewed from within a liberal political framework, the promise of these approaches is more apparent than real.

6.1 Spiritual development and the educational inevitability of evaluation

The definition of common spirituality, outlined in chapter three, is broadly conceived and could be instantiated in an infinite number of ways. Any given instance of such spirituality will be characterised, in part, by a cognitive framework which I will call a 'de facto' spiritual framework. Spirituality, in this sense, is not optional. Each individual has a framework of belief and value which informs, and is informed by, lived experience. For current purposes a de facto spirituality is the particular instantiation of the mechanism of common spirituality in the life of an individual. It is essential that we maintain a distinction between the de facto manifestations of common spirituality, held consciously or unconsciously by particular individuals, and the developmental spiritual frameworks used by those operating within contexts of nurture and education. This is recognised in a discussion paper issued by the Office for Standards in Education (Ofsted), the agency set up to oversee the inspection of schools in England and Wales.[1] In addition to a section on spiritual development there is another designed to clarify the concept of 'development' iself and how school practice in this area might be assessed. Here, three important things points are made. Firstly, it says that the school can't be judged on its ability to produce spiritual outcomes in the lives of its pupils since schools are not the only spiritual influence on them. Secondly, it says that there *are*, however, assessable *procedural* outcomes of a healthy spiritual development policy. Whatever a person's personal values, their ability to *express* them clearly or reflect on them *rationally* can be developed and constitute one aspect of school policy open to inspection and assessment. Finally, the document offers the horticultural notion of 'growth', with its associated ideas of 'nourishment' and 'soil', as a way of thinking of spiritual development in an open-ended way, appropriate for schools in modern Britain.

These comments may be satisfactory as a rationale for the *inspection* of schools but they may give out an authoritative but misleading signal to the effect that school policies do not require any substantive developmental thrust. The openness which was aimed for in the original definition of the 'spiritual' is not an option when we are operating with a notion of 'development'. Here a non-judgmental openness to an infinite range of possible spiritualities is not to be sought on grounds of pluralism or a misplaced desire to avoid passing judgement on the spiritual life of pupils since the notion of development *must* incorporate some particular view of human well-being, although that might be characterised negatively in terms of what is harmful. At an individual or communal level, we have to recognise that a de facto spiritual framework might be secular, materialist or even immoral. But it would be wrong to *assume* that because we might call this a 'spiritual' framework *in some sense* we are thereby compelled to accommodate it, *as an ideal*, in the policy for spiritual development. Schools should, for reasons set out above, promote a particular set of values which will, in turn, be grounded in some ideal view of human well-being. That cannot in turn be disassociated from a concern for the spiritual life of pupils which must, at the very least, regard some forms of common spirituality as harmful.

Developmental frameworks, such as those which might be incorporated within a school's policy on spiritual development, will have to include some evaluative element and will have to make implicit judgements regarding the spiritual state of the individuals under its jurisdiction. Even the most pluralist and liberal spiritual development policies will, at the very least, contain certain limits upon the range of allowable ideals of spirituality. Those limits will have built into them certain assumptions about human well-being. Monistic conceptions of spiritual development will embody a particular spiritual ideal, as well as a positive commitment to a range of values and beliefs.

There are a range of logical issues which can only be made clear and discussed adequately when a clear distinction is made between 'common spirituality' and spiritual development. It may be failure to recognise this distinction which makes several fashionable approaches to spiritual development seem attractive simply because they are, apparently, more accommodating of the secular world view so prevalent in the classroom and less judgmental of de-facto spiritualities.[2] Both OFSTED and NCC[3] guidance suggest that the values to be built into a policy will be the responsibility of the school, working in partnership. The danger of the approach taken by both the NCC and OFSTED is that, in recognition of the need for open-endedness, they are keen to emphasise the many and diverse de facto manifestations of the common spiritual mechanism while failing (NCC) or failing properly and clearly (OFSTED), to draw the kind of distinction which I am recommending here. The result of this may be to encourage school policy makers to adopt a wholly non-judgmental approach to the moral and spiritual development of their pupils.

6.2 A map of possible policy assumptions

In order to help policymakers get a clearer perspective on the logical implications of their working assumptions and to place both my following discussion (and hopefully, anyone else's) in a helpful context, I would like to put forward a theoretical framework for the mapping of *any* proposed model of spiritual *development*. It has been formulated as a series of dimensions of response to a number of questions which are laid out below each dimension, together with any further explanation. Each dimension is characterised by a title, given on the left, with the two extreme positions laid out on the right.

Eight Dimensions For Classifying Developmental Models of Spirituality

1. Source/s

Tradition------ Individual Experience

What are the creative sources of the process of spiritual development? Are traditional beliefs and practices seen as an enabling source or as a disabling hindrance to spiritual growth? One can imagine a series of answers here ranging from those who say that tradition is the creative source through to those who might claim that 'tradition' is part of problem, with an 'interactive' mid-position.

2. Location

Holistic----------Dualistic

Is the spiritual associated with the whole person or with some part/aspect (e.g. 'mind', 'soul', 'inner', 'outer')?

3. Context

Communal------Individual

Does the spiritual development necessarily require a communal context?

4. Developmental ideal

Specific----Non-Specific

Does the policy have specific developmental aims?

5. Conception of human well-being

Monist--Liberal--Pluralist

Does the policy incorporate a single set of values, reflecting a single conception of the good life (monism), does it incorporate a single set of values at the procedural level, while enabling individuals to develop one of a range of substantive good life conceptions (liberalism) or does it incorporate a plurality of good life conceptions even at the procedural level (Kekesian pluralism)?[4]

6. Approach to Truth

Objectivist--Instrumentalist--Subjectivist

Does the policy aim to facilitate discovery or self-expression ? If the notions of 'truth' and 'reality' are used to underpin spiritual development, how are they characterised?

7. Characterisation of Transcendence

Realist-------Non-Realist

Does the developmental ideal of the policy accommodate or rule out a metaphysically real approach to transcendence? How is the relationship between the immanent and transcendent characterised?

8. Assessment

Assessable-----Non-Assessable

Are the Can the level of spiritual development be assessed? criteria substantive or procedural?

This framework of dimensions should give a useful method of 'placing' any potential model of spiritual development, discussing its educational potential and its philosophical presuppositions. In the rest of this chapter I will canvass two currently influential models, the experiential and the non-realist, which might appeal to liberal policy makers, wishing to avoid the charge of indoctrination and recognising the plural and secular nature of modern Britain.

6.3 The experiential approach

The so called 'experiential' approach is already quite influential among teachers of religious education in Britain as a supplement to the phenomenological approach which had prevailed since the early 1970s. Its leading exponents argued that the new approach was needed because the theory and practice of religious education, in a bid to gain academic respectability, had lost sight of one of its essential dimensions. As presented by Hammond, Hay et al.,[5] the new approach is said to offer a methodology for recovering that *experiential* dimension in religious education lessons *and* for developing spirituality across the curriculum.[6] This can be done by using a series of activities, like meditation and guided fantasy, which allow pupils to reflect upon their own life experience within the context of what appear to be a set of therapeutic and neutral, set of procedures.

The experiential approach seems to embody values and assumptions which have their origins in the Romantic movement[7] and an attempt to nourish a child's spirituality through a focus on the allegedly natural and pure realm of her experience. The experientialist model, in identifying the *source* of spiritual growth in a reflection on personal experience, is clearly located at the right-hand pole of the first dimension of the grid outlined above, and as such embodies a commitment to the importance of the individual as the domain of spiritual inspiration. This individualism might be thought advantageous when considered in relation to dimensions 4 and 5. One of the disadvantages of the attempt to locate the source of inspiration in a traditional or community based viewpoint is that such a particular substantive conception of the good appears to be incompatible with the *impartiality* required by a liberal approach, particularly in the context of the common school in a plural society. The location of the source of spiritual growth in personal reflection on individual experience *appears* to enable liberal policy makers to avoid such problems and also to locate a source of spiritual inspiration in that which is most immanent and, therefore, least controversial. In relation to dimension 4, this emphasis makes the experientialist model compatible with an open-ended approach in which the de facto spiritual outcomes of implementation are not specifiable in advance since they will depend upon the personal experience of each pupil.

In a recent discussion of the work of Hammond, Hay et al., Adrian Thatcher[8] says that the emphasis upon 'inwardness' that characterises the experiential approach disqualifies it as a suitable candidate for the development of spirituality. Such an approach, he says, is dangerously dualistic and leads to a radical and unacceptable individualism. In terms of the framework of dimensions, the allegation is that the experiential approach must be mapped at the right-hand pole of *both* dimensions 1 and 2. However, while this may be true with respect to dimension 1, there does not appear to be any necessary connection between the experientialist approach and mind-body dualism. Thatcher's attempt to find evidence for the existence of philosophical dualism in a recent and influential exposition of the 'experiential' approach[9] demonstrates the need to recognise the distinction between, the attempt to locate the spiritual *exclusively* with the private and the inner aspects of human life and, the use of the notion of 'inner' experience and looking inwards as an *aspect* of spirituality.

These two views are importantly different. The first *does* associate the experiential logically with the dualist pole of dimension 2 and with an exclusively individualistic contextualisation of spirituality on dimension 3. Adopting an experiential approach that embodied these assumptions would to that extent also embody Cartesian dualism. The second, however, appears to be logically compatible with a more holistic approach to dimension 2 and a communal contextualisation of spirituality on dimension 3. Once the correct distinctions are made, we can no longer assume that *just* because a teacher employs talk about reflection on inner experience they are logically and automatically committed to Cartesian dualism.[10] Having elsewhere attempted to defend experientialists against this aspect of Thatcher's attack, I am not concerned to rehearse the detailed arguments.[11] However, Thatcher believes that the anti-empiricist philosophical tradition and, particularly, the writings of Wittgenstein provide a case for linking *any* talk of inner life or inner experience with radical dualism. It is worth spending some time here to discuss Thatcher's arguments since they would appear to remove the logical space for the kind of distinction that was set out above and this would seriously affect the logic of policy making in the area of spiritual development.

Thatcher identifies a range of philosophically dubious assumptions in the book. He locates these assumptions within the Cartesian tradition of metaphysical dualism which came to fruition during the Enlightenment but which has, he says, been largely discredited by recent philosophers. His evidence for the existence of philosophical dualism (the view that reality is composed of at least two kinds of stuff, the mental and the physical) in the experiential approach is the use of the notion of 'inner' experience as well as the talk of journeying, and looking, inwards to describe the aim of the activities outlined in New Methods in R.E. He quotes the following section from p.17,

> The subject matter of religious education ...is deeply connected with the inner experience of the pupils themselves.

and adds,

> References abound to 'inner intentions', 'inner experience', 'inner aspects', 'the inside world', 'going inwards', 'the inner self', 'inner space' and so on. The lack of criticism of this inner outer dualism is astonishing.[12]

Elsewhere, Thatcher[13] explains why philosophical dualism is unhealthy. It leads, he says, to a devaluation of the physical and material and an asocial individualism, which suggests that religion is essentially a private matter. Thatcher says that one of Wittgenstein's most 'profound achievements' was to show that this kind of dualism was a 'grave mistake'. He moves on to outline Wittgenstein's communitarian approach to the meaning of any language used to express '..my own mental states or feeling states' and to affirm that this kind of language isn't founded on a private language developed through the practice of inner pointing.

This argument,[14] which takes as its starting point the fact that we do have a mental life, is not directly about dualism but about the origins of sensation *language* and is directed against the notion that individuals have privileged access to their own mental states, a view which fuels the kind of scepticism about other people's minds which troubled many of Wittgenstein's contemporaries. In paragraph 243 of the Philosophical Investigations, Wittgenstein sets out the context for his argument by asking,

> Could we... imagine a language in which a person could write down or give vocal expression to his inner experiences- his feelings, moods, and the rest- for his private use?

Clearly neither the *existence* of inner experiences nor the value of speaking about them are at issue here, rather the question is whether or not the individual concerned has some epistemologically privileged access to them.

The private language argument which follows is *not* designed to show *either* that inner experience does not exist or cannot be spoken of, but rather that the criteria used for making inner judgements are fundamentally *public*. Aimed at the philosophical tradition known as 'phenomenalism' (an attempt to use the inner language of sensation and appearance to build an individualist foundation for all knowledge claims), these remarks do not relate directly to the language of the Experientialists. In order to show that their language or practice contravenes these Wittgensteinian arguments, Thatcher would have to show that their methods might lead children to believe that the language they use to describe their own experience derives its meaning *exclusively* from a private act of ostensive definition. But Thatcher provides no evidence to show that the authors of the New Methods book hold, or attempt to propagate, this view, beyond the fact that they use 'inner talk'. Nor do his remarks constitute a general argument to the effect that any attempt by educationalists to get children to focus on their experience will inevitably be flawed by dualism. One can quite legitimately use such language and be fully aware of the fact that '..expressing my own mental states or feeling states is impossible without a shared publicly owned language and considerable induction into its use'.[15] Also contrary to Thatcher's remarks, one could also presumably find an educational use for saying 'I describe my state of mind' *without necessarily* thereby affirming that it is in all respects like describing my room. As Wittgenstein remarks, 'You need to call to mind the differences between the language-games'.[16]

Ironically, it is clear from this that Wittgenstein's private language argument *presupposes* the credibility of inner talk. Perhaps the reference to 'loose talk' suggests that Thatcher will allow the possibility that used metaphorically, inner talk does not necessarily imply an ontological commitment to the existence of an inner entity composed of mental stuff.

Later on in his paper, Thatcher is unhappy about the use of ocular metaphors in the New Methods book and, while recognising that much truth-conveying talk uses metaphor, he suggests that some metaphors are inappropriate. Presumably the metaphors used by the Experientialists fail the test of appropriateness. At the very least, it might be noted in passing that this approach would be very uncongenial to Wittgenstein, who is famous for the view that language users, and not philosophers, are the best judges of linguistic 'appropriateness'. Wittgenstein's writings do not show that he disallowed all talk of the inner life as intrinsically dualistic. What they show is that such inner talk only finds its place within language games with essentially public and social criteria. If there is a Wittgensteinian conclusion to be applied in this area it is not, as Thatcher supposes, that we must stop speaking of inwardness or of inner reflection and concentrate *only* on public language and behaviour, moved in doing so by the very dualism that we explicitly set out to avoid, but rather that we recognise that the notion of 'experience' cannot be *confined* to some ephemeral stuff, somehow distinguishable from, but located within, our bodies.

The fact that the experiential approach to spiritual development can be mapped at the right hand pole of dimension 1, in individual experience, might be thought attractive to those liberal educationalists wishing to operate with a non-monist conception of human well-being, with non-specific developmental ideals (dimensions 4 and 5). And these advantages would be all the more pertinent where policy makers are constructing a common conception of spiritual development to be implemented *nationally*. Mystical writers often speak of a direct experience of God and it might be supposed that such experiences are unmediated by any particular tradition and, in fact, might be foundational for the various religious traditions that have grown up. Certain types of experience might be thought to be the epistemological basis for personal spiritual growth. Some religious education specialists, in particular, might think that the approach of mystics could open up a way of adding an important experiential dimension to the study of religion in schools and also provide the basis for a purely procedural and educationally valid approach to spiritual growth, precisely because it is, as it were, uncontaminated by any particular tradition. Clearly, however, this view rests on assumptions about the relationship between religious experience and religious tradition and it is a view which has been challenged and rejected by a number of writers working in the field of philosophy of religion, most notably Stephen Katz and John Hick.[17] These writers argue that the framework of values and beliefs which the individual has inherited from her community will *determine rather than reflect* her experience. If correct, this analysis has serious implications for the would be exponents of liberal experiential spiritual development since it undermines the promising link, noted earlier, between individual experience and non-monism since that experience will effectively prove to be a *reflection* of their own *current* values rather than a critical source through which new and better ones are developed. According to the anti-empiricist view of perception, each person would just have their current views reinforced by reflecting on their own experience. If all experience is tradition mediated, if not tradition determined, there is just no logical space, it is alleged, for the foundational purity which constitutes the educational promise of the experiential approach. Forces quite distinct from experience, and quite beyond the control of the teacher, would be the *real* agents of any change or 'development' if the experiential approach were to be combined with a disavowal of specific developmental aims. I do not intend to enter into the difficult and murky waters of this debate. But writers on spirituality who advocate an experiential approach cannot ignore such criticism or *assume* that it is wrong. My own view is that a more interactive and objectivist approach is possible which recognises both the experiential *and* traditional poles of spiritual development.

The problems remain, however, for liberals who look to the experiential approach for an impartial method of spiritual development that might underpin a nationally common approach. This is because the advantages of the approach for liberal policy makers rest upon the belief that experiences of the kind that this methodology engenders in the classroom are free from any contamination by any substantive tradition and might be compatible with all of them. If the experiences which children are given by means of this methodology reflect and reinforce their current values then it would appear that, *unless it is supplemented* by further substantial developmental aims, it could not be regarded as developmental in any real sense. Further to this my analysis elsewhere[18] of the theological presuppositions that underpin the particular experiential methods discussed above suggests that classroom activities designed by well intentioned educationalists may *themselves* embody the values of a *particular* tradition.[19] Methods and procedures sincerely regarded by their proponents as neutral or impartial may in fact be partial and controversial. Those who wish to use experiential methods alone to promote spiritual development must address the arguments of anti-empiricist philosophers, outlined above, which throw serious doubt upon the claim that individuals can have access to uncontaminated experience capable of promoting such growth. Until such criticisms are *addressed and countered* the experiential method cannot be *assumed* to be compatible with a liberal approach to spiritual development.[20]

6.4 The non-realist approach

In chapter 4 I noted that Mike Newby employed a non-realist approach to religious truth claims. It was alleged that by employing non-realism, in genuine pursuit of a secular approach based on impartiality, his approach actually embodied a secularism hostile to some rational and acceptable forms of religious belief, making it distinctly partial. It therefore violated the limits of liberalism itself. I want now to explore the non-realist approach further, first, to show why liberal policy makers might be attracted to it and, second, to problematise it *from within* the liberal political framework. I will then move on to explore the logical relationship that might exist between a liberal approach to spiritual development, whether focused on an individual school or as the context for a nationally common conception, and a *realist* approach to truth embodying a metaphysically significant commitment to the existence of a transcendent dimension. I am not concerned here to claim that non-realist spiritualities are wrong. My comments are exploratory and are designed to ensure that certain important philosophical presuppositions, which may animate the thinking of school policy makers working within the liberal framework, are brought out into the open and reflected upon in a critical light.

Non-realism is favoured by several moral theorists and radical theologians[21] to provide a non-metaphysical basis for moral and religious values. Ideas, like 'God', which were traditionally believed to have a metaphysical reference are reinterpreted in such a way as to have no metaphysical implications. As the name suggests such statements as 'God is Good' or 'Killing is wrong' can be believed as true, but truth, for such value statements, is defined either in terms of coherence within a wider socially constructed web of belief, based upon a particular form of life, or on the basis of purely subjective criteria.[22] It might be tempting, given the pluralist context, to incorporate this view at some fundamental level into a school spiritual development policy. Analogous to the 'bracketing' of truths into 'truth claims' in the phenomenological approach to religious studies, it might be thought possible and altogether more appropriate, to eliminate any metaphysically significant notion of transcendence from a school's policy. If metaphysically realist claims about spirituality are associated with religious fundamentalism and religious conflict then many will think it highly appropriate, especially in the state school, to abandon full blooded realism in favour of a privatised view of spiritual truth based upon the notion of what works for any given individual. It might be assumed, in addition, that any alternative realist conception would be necessarily authoritarian and closed. The most prevalent form of non-realism to be found in the literature on spiritual development is that of *instrumentalism or pragmatism*. It can be found, for example, built into the analogy of the spiritual journey, used by Hammond et al and also by Erricker.[23] Instrumentalism is a deceptively subtle form of non-realism because it can utilise the words 'truth' and 'reality', while disavowing any reference to a reality which *transcends* human rationality or purpose. Basically instrumentalism says that something is to be regarded as true if it serves the purposes of a human individual or community.

Liberal policy makers may feel that there is an inevitable link between a realist position on dimensions 6 and 7 and monism on dimension 5. This impression is compounded by the fact that it is shared by Christian communitarians writing in this area who favour both monism and realism.[24] I will attempt to show later that the link between realism and monism is purely contingent and rests upon a prevalent but false characterisation of realism. In order to show that realism *is* compatible with pluralism, I will attempt to offer an alternative characterisation.

The framework of dimensions shows the non-realist position on the right extreme of dimension 7, the characterisation of transcendence. Policy makers wishing to accommodate pluralism on dimension 5, may see the kind of non-realism outlined above as a way of avoiding aligning themselves with particular, challengeable and controversial metaphysical claims. The approach of non-realist theologians and philosophers, who translate traditional metaphysical religious claims into useful life guiding ideals with no metaphysical reference, would appear to offer a way of doing *that* while holding on to the idea of spiritual *development*. For similar reasons, the non-realist approach, with its disavowal of objective truth claims and its emphasis on the expressive, subjective and instrumental nature of truth claims, will appear attractive to those operating with liberal principles, since the notion of *objectivity* might, on the other hand, be thought to imply an agreed notion of spiritual truth most unlikely on a national scale and possibly not available even to a single school community, given a pluralist context. An adherence to pluralism on dimension 5 is clearly compatible with, and might be thought logically inseparable from, a commitment to non-realism, on dimension 7, and instrumentalism/ subjectivism, on dimension 6.

Having outlined the nature and attractiveness of non-realist strategies, I will now attempt to show that the apparent logical ties between them and liberalism are, in fact, non-existent. Firstly, I will show that instrumentalism requires a particular substantive conception of the human good, in order to prove itself coherent. This means that any instrumentalist approach to truth will *itself* embody certain presuppositions that must be made explicit and which may prove to be controversial. Secondly, I will similarly aim to show that theological non-realism, in particular, and all forms of non-realism in general, *must* embody some specific metaphysically significant claims about the nature of *reality*. Finally, in this section I will introduce an alternative characterisation of realism, critical realism, and show that a commitment to *it*, rather than non-realism, is a fundamental logical requirement of any nationally common conception of spiritual development that is to be compatible with liberalism and pluralism.

6.5 Instrumentalism and spiritual development

Any policy involving the notion of *development* must take up a position, implicitly or explicitly, on what constitutes human well-being for *all* the pupils coming under its jurisdiction. It would be impossible to speak *meaningfully* of development merely in procedural terms, by attempting, for the purposes of educational policy, to regard as good anything which 'helps' individuals, thereby converting the notion of truth into one of 'helpful belief'. This strategy seeks to avoid the unavoidable question as to what precisely it is that children are being helped towards and *that* must be open to further questions about whether *it is in fact* in the child's best interests. Thus we come, by a less direct route, to the kinds of controversial question which individuals and communities often disagree about and which the non-realist strategy *appeared* to avoid. These inevitable questions cannot be *avoided* by using the instrumentalist strategy but it may save policy makers from acknowledging and taking responsiblity for the answers that their policy *will* embody at some level. In order to satisfy the requirements of liberal accountability each and every school policy in the area of spiritual development will have to embody, as critically and explicitly as possible, a consistent and legitimate set of values based around a notion of what constitutes the well being of all the pupils who fall within its ambit.[25]

Instrumentalism will have, for the reasons set out above, to be aligned, explicitly or implicitly, with *either* an objectivist or a subjectivist conception of human well-being, if it is to satisfy the requirements of coherence and liberal accountability. The prevalent tendency is for those who favour an instrumentalist approach to align it with subjectivism. This is because that would enable the questions about the conception of well-being that underpin the policy to be shifted from the domain of educational policy, where such potentially controversial judgements would require justification in a pluralist context-especially where it were used to underpin a nationally common conception- into the *private* domain, where no such justification would be required, since it would affect only individuals. This I think, will be seen as inadequate, especially from the liberal political perspective, when it is remembered that the *individuals*, who will be required to decide what is or is not in their own best interests, according to this model, are *children*. If a spiritual development policy embodies instrumentalism, aligned with subjectivism in this way, then it will effectively embody an implicit commitment to a characterisation of human well-being in terms purely of each individual child's beliefs and decisions about her own best interests. It would constitute the promotion of a set of values and a view of what constitutes human well-being, that is, the view that *it is in a child's best interests that they be allowed to decide for themselves what is in their own best interests on the basis of their current beliefs and values.* This is a very particular and highly controversial view. One only has to think of some of the more outlandish de facto manifestations of what I have called common spirituality and, at the same time, consider some of the powerful influences on the beliefs and opinions of children, to see that the instrumentalist approach is not 'impartial'. That view would appear both naive and irresponsible in the light of these observations since it would give up all educational concern for the spiritual welfare of children.

If the kind of view just set out were used to underpin a nationally common approach to spiritual development, then it would amount to *promotion* by the state education system of a version of communitarian monism, by default and paradoxically, by means of a *non-interventionist* educational strategy. The outcomes of such a system are represented diagramatically in models 2 and 3 of appendix 1. It would be, *in effect*, equivalent to the state promoting the values of a subjectivist ideology as outlined in italics above and as represented by model 3. Viewed from a different perspective, and reflecting the fact that the view of human well-being represented at the individual level by the number '2' in model 3 is importantly procedural, the outcome might differ for each individual pupil. Each of the different numbers used at the individual level in model 2 will represent, the *differing* influences on the current beliefs and values of each child. The purpose of the foregoing discussion and the two models is to show that where instrumentalist strategies are used and aligned, implicitly, with subjectivism, to underpin policies for spiritual development, these will exhibit the characteristics of individualism and monism and will run against the requirements of liberalism and pluralism.

It is clear from this that where it is appropriate an instrumentalist view of spiritual development must itself rest upon *some* substantive notion of what constitutes human well-being, which cannot be both instrumentalist by nature, educationally appropriate and able to fulfil the requirements of pluralism and liberalism, since it will effectively promote a single set of values or enable the most powerful external agencies in a child's life to dictate the direction and character of spiritual growth.

Nonetheless, this approach does, in fact, embody a full blooded claim about the nature of human well-being. This amounts to an objectivist claim but, ironically, an *objectivist* claim about the validity of *subjectivism*. This demonstrates that dimension 6 of the framework set out above for mapping policy assumptions may be misleading if we take it to show that subjectivism and instrumentalism do not themselves rest logically on objectivist claims about human well-being (dimension 5) of the kind that have been set out above.

6.6 The presuppositions of theological non-realism and the notion of transcendence

If liberal policy makers were to follow Newby's lead and attempt to work with a view of spiritual growth underpinned by a non-realist approach to the question of the existence of a transcendent dimension, inspired by non-realist theologians like Cupitt and Phillips, then they would also be adopting quite specific and substantive claims about the nature of reality. I have neither time nor space here to argue this point in detail but it is clear that non-realism embodies a negative response to the metaphysical claims of traditional religion. The theological non-realists state that whereas traditional believers rested their religious practice upon such metaphysical claims, modern believers should be inclined to act with faith and give up such claims, including the view that God exists, since they can no longer be held as true by a rational person, in the light of the advances of modern science. In view of this, it is argued that the traditional beliefs should be reinterpreted rather than just discarded and this reinterpretation inevitably involves a move in the direction of subjectivism and instrumentalism that were examined earlier. For example, the notion of God is seen as the embodiment of all one's highest personal ideals, which guide spiritual growth.

This much I hope will be uncontroversial but it should be noted that even this brief sketch is enough to show that just because one regards oneself as a theological *non-realist*, that does not mean that the position involves no claims of a *realist* nature. Non-realism embodies the claim that certain traditional religious claims about the existence of a transcendent realm in general and of God in particular, can no longer be regarded as claims about the nature of a supra-human reality. This judgement clearly requires, however, some criteria by which the real and the non-real are to be distinguished. Non-realists are inclined to argue that only those religious claims which are compatible with the view of reality laid out by scientists can be regarded as valid. The *realist* claims that non-realists implicitly make are the claims of positivism or scientism.[26] This is the view that science is the only rational path to the true and the real and must be preferred to the paths of tradition and revelation. Where orthodox religious believers are inclined to regard science, tradition and revelation as valid and *compatible* sources of truth, the positivist approach of the non-realist theologian is to share the positivist's conflict model and its resulting dilemma: either, the latter two sources must prove themselves in terms acceptable to the criteria of the scientific tradtion, or they must surrender their claims to be truth altogether.[27]

While I personally find non-realist forms of theological and philosophical reflection unconvincing and impoverished, I think it would be wrong for educational policymakers to *exclude* non-realist approaches to the existence of a transcendent dimension for the same reasons that it would be wrong to exclude atheistic approaches to the spiritual. However, we saw that when non-realism is used to *underpin* a notion of spiritual development by Newby, it led to a policy with an inbuilt hostility towards traditional religious life that might be counted as unacceptable and I refer the reader back to chapter 4 for a reminder of that discussion. It seems counter-intuitive to suggest, as a non-realist model of development *logically* would, that spiritual development could be truly 'spiritual' while operating in such a way as to *rule out* the notion of divine transcendence as a potential source of spiritual inspiration.

The most important conclusion to be drawn, however, from this discussion of non-realism parallels, unsurprisingly, our discussion of instrumentalism in the previous section. We saw there that an adherence to subjectivism actually embodies an adherence to a particular objectivist perspective. In the case of non-realism we have noted also that there will inevitably be an implicit adherence to particular criteria regarded as capable of separating the real from the non-real. I have suggested that this almost always amounts, in the case of non-realist theologians, to a positive claim that science is the final arbiter between the real and the unreal. But this is no sooner stated than it is seen to be, at the very least, controversial and requiring further justification. Non-realism does not, as some are tempted to think, get us away from the problems of having to justify the basic policy assumptions in a pluralistic public setting.

6.7 Critical realism, transcendence and liberalism

Non-realism is less promising and more exclusive than might have been at first thought by liberal policy makers largely because, as we have shown, realist claims of some sort or another are actually unavoidable. I want now to ask whether we can find a version of realism capable of accommodating the full range of de facto spiritual outcomes, *including* those recommended by non-realist theologians and, at the same time, not linked to a single view of the good or the true, that might contravene the requirements of liberalism and pluralism.

In seeking to circumvent a monistic doctrine that embodied the view that there could only be one way of describing reality, liberal policy makers will want to avoid any form of realism which states that all attempts to encapsulate the truth are *equally* valid. In order to give the full breadth of pluralist options, our notion of realism has to be a form of metaphysical realism, capable of sustaining the transcendental claims that religious good life conceptions incorporate. Critical realism is the name of one version of metaphysical realism which claims that true statements do depict reality. It is based upon the view that our web of belief is grounded in communal experience, that our experience has its origins in a metaphysical reality of which we are a part and which remains even when it is unperceived by anyone. It includes and transcends human language and rationality. It can be characterised in a number of ways and it sets limits on what can be truly said and rightly done. It is not limited to the physical and is interwoven by values, which continue to exist irrespective of our acknowledgement of them. At some level, on this view, truth must be defined in terms of a 'fit' (not necessarily isomorphic) between this reality and what is said about it. At the very least, our ability to construct truth, meaning and purpose is limited by a sense of reality which transcends any given individual or community. This form of realism is not however tied to a single conception of reality because, in a way that mirrors many mystical religious traditions, it says that our language will never allow us to encapsulate it completely.[28] The charge of authoritarianism cannot be levelled at this view in the way that it could towards a realist view which claimed some uncontestable relationship between certain statements about the world and the world itself. As such, critical realism can accommodate a range of views about the world, from the fundamentalist through to the non-realist. It is a better basis for a non-monist policy than any based upon non-realism since that would self evidently lack the ability to accommodate any full bloodedly realist view of the transcendent. Critical realism recognises the non-realist approach as one contestable claim about the nature of reality and is therefore capable of accommodating it. The non-realist perspective is not, however, capable of accommodating the realist perspectives in the same way since it is logically bound to exclude them.

A policy based upon a critical realism of this kind which explicitly affirms a notion of truth built upon a metaphysical commitment to a reality which sets limits, but is itself not limited (or exhaustively characterised) by any particular view of it, looks to me like the best basis for encapsulating a broad range of lifestyle options on their own terms. Clearly, neither of the versions of non-realism that have been discussed in this chapter, despite their superficial attractions, ultimately seems capable of setting out the necessary limits, making its own presuppositions clear or dealing with the broadest range of life options impartially. It is arguable that a commitment to a significantly hidden transcendent dimension follows directly from the conception of common spirituality set out in chapter 3 and I would like, in the next section, to show how a commitment to such a dimension is accommodated by critical realism and is a fundamental aspect of any educational commitment to spiritual development.

6.8 Realism, transcendence and virtue

What should be largely uncontroversial is the fact that there *is* a reality which stands independent of each one of us and of all human beings collectively. We are independent of that reality not in the sense that we are separate from it; we are, in fact, constituent parts of it. But it stretches out over and above us in many 'directions'. No one individual, nor all individuals acting collectively, could control or determine its nature. This is a fundamental existential fact for all human beings. We neither completely understand nor do we have control over the reality of which we are a constituent part. The view that we do not understand it and that all particular answers to life's important questions are ultimately *contestable*, fits very well with both pluralism[29] and liberalism. Since, on these grounds no one understands it completely so no one, not even the state has the right to try to impose a particular answer on anyone else without their consent. This reality adds the transcendent dimension to our experience since it was around before us, we are both constituted as part of it, and it will inevitably extend beyond us into the future in a way that could not be guaranteed for any of its constituent parts, even the material things, so beloved of secular humanists.

There is a significant and culturally supported tendency in Britain to assume that a spirituality, of the kind that John White appears to favour, having as its focus undeniable aspects of our present experience, like the contemplation of physical objects, does not *itself* possess a hidden dimension. White rightly points out that the mental apparatus that we bring to our present experiences is non-material, and that this is the case even if the object of the experience is material. But the way in which *even* our most mundane experience of material objects transcends the realm of the material is arguably much more extensive than this picture suggests. The character and meaning which a basic physical object has for any given individual will itself reflect a framework of belief, understanding and evaluation which in some very real sense *transcends* both the object and the individual who perceives it. The question of what we see the object *as*, perhaps the most mundane question of all, will itself, according to the most persuasive and popularly held theory of perception,[30] be answered, in part, at this transcendent level. Both the experience of any individual, as well as the language in which ideas are expressed, contain elements which are irreducibly social and traditional. And this is as true of the radical critic as it is of the most temperamentally conservative person. This is not to say that individuals are socially *constructed*, but rather that the social elements form an irreducible and ineradicable part of our individual experience. A physical analogy might help here. We each have a physical body which is irreducibly and ineradicably an *individual* body, but its character is very strongly influenced by the bodies of our parents. They are the source of our individual body and determine its character. Both our personal experience and our bodies have their character conditioned by something outside themselves. In the case of our bodies that character is almost wholly determined by the bodies of our parents, our personal experience contains an irreducibly social and traditional element but is open to the possibility of change.

Our individual experience can therefore be thought of as constructed around a spiritual framework, which transcends any given experience, is non-material and contains elements that are hidden in a range of ways. This is connected, in my characterisation of common spirituality, with the cognitive aspects of common spirituality as '...a framework of ideals, beliefs and values about oneself, one's relations with others and reality/the world. Logically intrinsic to this framework, and rooted in a notion of what is real and ultimately significant, is some conception of the good life..' It is this framework that provides the basis for the discussion of the educational importance of transcendence that follows.

If what I have said is true then the development of self-knowledge and reflecting upon who we are is going to involve a growing acknowledgement of a dependence upon transcendent elements that are currently hidden from view. It will involve a growing acknowledgement that the way in which we see things is affected by hidden forces. Indeed our experience itself of the most mundane thing could be recognised as dependent upon our framework which is in turn one of many alternative frameworks (all of which are both non-material and very real). This aspect of self-knowledge, in itself an uncontroversial educational virtue, should give pupils a growing sense of a transcendent reality. This aspect of self-knowledge gives some indication of a transcendence which looks so to speak outwards (to a wider society) and backwards (towards the past and one's origins).

The growth of self- knowledge is also intimately connected with a forward looking perspective which might be characterised as self-direction. This might be described, in line with the Ofsted discussion paper, as 'a sense of meaning and purpose'. This too is a transcendent dimension of experience. This is not because it presupposes that there is some single and God-given meaning and purpose to human life which is right for all, though such a perspective is obviously (and quite correctly) not ruled out. It is transcendent, rather, because human life is, in a very significant sense, oriented towards a future both social and individual, which is currently and importantly *hidden*. Our goals and ideals are aspects of our current experience, they are born out of the values which ultimately depend upon our capacity to imagine yet unrealised states of affairs. Even the heroin addict is oriented towards the future in just this kind of way. The goals and values embodied even in this perspective are both spiritual and importantly rooted in a transcendent dimension. John White's reaction to the suggestion that spiritual development contains a commitment to help pupils to 'search for meaning and purpose' and 'to seek answers to life's great questions' is interesting. He says,

> ...talk of 'helping pupils to seek answers to life's great questions' suggests that there might be answers to be had...educators should jettison a question

> and answer approach to life and the universe and encourage pupils to dwell instead in the wonder of it all. We should want them..to be seized by the cosmic frisson...as far as attitude shaping goes, our main responsibility lies with the goal of contemplation and wonder.[31]

One might ask why a question and answer approach to these issues should be jettisoned by educators. Presumably because there is no *one* answer that all could agree to and so it would be wrong for representatives of the liberal state to suggest that there is. The recommendation to instigate contemplation and wonder therefore suggests that such activities are, for White, somehow value neutral. Alongside this, and underlying his analysis, is the assumption that there are *no* answers to be had. If this view is not held to be *neutral* then the case must presumably rest upon the view that it is, at least, *significantly non-contestable or uncontroversial.*

Firstly, if the preceding analysis of the transcendent nature of all human experience is correct, *no* experience is value free. If that is the case then every child who walks into a state school classroom comes bearing her own, perhaps quite unique, spiritual framework influenced by social and traditional factors. A programme of contemplation on, and wondering at, items of experience is therefore quite obviously value full. The question of what items might be used to instigate the cosmic frisson quite obviously presupposes, at some level, an answer to the question *'what is ultimately of value?'*. If a non-interventionist attitude is taken by the school then factors quite other than the school will determine the answers that children take from the classroom.[32] The kind of approach that is being recommended by John White is therefore non-neutral, contestable and *controversial*. It would require further justification, at the very least, before it could be considered as the basis for a common educational policy appertaining to personal development.

Secondly, John White's analysis rests on the assumption that there are no answers to life's ultimate questions. This in itself is a particular and far from uncontroversial point of view. It is a substantive viewpoint, otherwise known as non-realism[33] which, when deployed in the name of liberalism and pluralism, trades upon an apparent rather than real neutrality, together with a dash of equalitarianism (since in the land of no-answers all answers are equal). It is this 'neutrality' which, in my opinion, ought to be jettisoned by liberal educationalists. The notion that all children bring answers as well as questions with them into the classroom and that they ought to be helped, in a publicly accountable way, to seek the right answers, for themselves, seems to me *both* to require a commitment that right answers exist and to be a most uncontroversial stance for educationalists to adopt. Unlike John White's approach (involving as it does the answer of 'no answers'), it certainly doesn't involve any illicit assumption that there is only one rather controversial answer, itself dismissive of certain rival possibilities.[34]

The development of the capacity for self direction enables an individual to discern the possibilities inherent in the present moment. It is fundamentally related to the capacity to imaginatively construct a range of possible alternatives and is connected to the ability to sense a hidden dimension located beyond the present. It is not inherently self-oriented since a person is better equipped to play a role in the decision making of the *communities* of which they are a part if they are developed in this way. Neither is such a conception of the capacity for self-direction itself a recipe for pathological radicalism, encouraging children to be addicted to change and criticism for its own sake. In fact the capacity to transcend the present in the way suggested *might* lead one to appreciate the present all the more and to seek ways of conserving its valued aspects in the face of changing circumstances.

Also connected with the ability to imaginatively construct alternative possibilities and to empathise successfully with the thoughts and feelings of others, is good practical judgement or wisdom. This capacity is wholeheartedly dependent upon one's capacity to accurately discern what possibilities lie hidden within the present. In fact wisdom might be defined as the ability to see accurately what real possibilities lie hidden in the present and to judge, act or advise appropriately.

Returning to the individual's relationship with society, it is worth noting that self-control is both a virtue of many religious traditions and, arguably, a fundamentally important aspect of life in a liberal democracy, especially one where individual freedom is actively promoted. Its development in future citizens is therefore a task which the state education system should undertake. It is a task that suggests aspects of spiritual development and transcendence. In as much as a school attempts to develop a person's capacity to appreciate a transcendent dimension to their experience and to reflect upon the likely effects of their actions, it has given them the ability to appreciate the needs of others and to place their own needs in a larger perspective. It is the requirement to transcend or go beyond the self and to see the separation of self and others, which underpins selfish and anti-social behaviour, as something of an illusion. The development of a child's appreciation of this transcendent perspective is likely to lead them to exercise self-control and to act co-operatively for the common good, something which the liberal state has a legitimate interest in promoting.

In attempting to characterise above a set of personal characteristics that might be legitimately regarded by liberal educators as the developmental ideals of a common educational programme, I have in effect adopted and recommended a virtues based approach.[35] This approach to spiritual development has a number of significant advantages. Firstly it emphasises personal judgement and personal development rather than particular behaviour or a specific set of beliefs. It is therefore inherently open ended. However, since virtues cross the boundaries between the body-mind, rational-emotional and individual-social divides, they ensure that spirituality remains importantly rooted in aspects of experience from which the popular imagination might otherwise be inclined to disassociate it. The notion of 'virtue' itself rather like those of 'spirituality' and 'transcendence' acts as a kind of self-regulating corrective, working against a range of cultural biases. In appendix 2 the reader will find a characterisation of eight spiritual virtues, the development of which might form a *basis* for a nationally common approach to spiritual development and accommodates the arguments set out so far.

Up to this point I have attempted to work within the liberal political framework and have tried to set out the forms and limits of a legitimate nationally common approach. In the remainder of this study I ask whether a nationally common approach to personal development is either possible or desirable.

Notes

1 Ofsted (1994).
2 Newby (1996).
3 NCC (1993).
4 Kekes (1993).
5 Hammond, Hay et al. (1990).
6 See also for a similar approach, Marjon (1990), Mackley (1993), Stone (1992), FARE Project (1992).
7 See Taylor (1989), part 4.
8 Thatcher (1991).
9 Hammond, Hay et al. (1990).
10 The view that human beings are made up of two fundamental substances, the mental and the physical.
11 For a more detailed discussion of Thatcher's critique of the experiential approach, see Mott-Thornton (1996b).
12 Op cit., p23.

[13] Thatcher (1992), p2f.
[14] Wittgenstein (1953), sections 202, 256-281.
[15] Thatcher (1991), p23.
[16] Op cit.(1953), section 290.
[17] Katz (1978); Hick (1967/8).
[18] Mott-Thornton (1996b).
[19] Ibid., p160f, on the theological presuppositions embodied in the approach of Hammond, Hay, et al.
[20] See also, Wright (1996) for further criticism of the experiential approach to religious education.
[21] Phillips (1976), Cupitt (1980).
[22] As was noted earlier, it is possible to have a non-realist view of theological assertions and of moral claims, while holding a realist position on the assertions of science. In fact this is probably the most common combination of positions since non-realism emerged as one response to the atheistic claims of positivists, like Ayer and Flew. Some non-realist theologians, like Cupitt, have in recent writings and under the influence of French post-modernist writing extended their approach to all assertions. including those of science. The problem with this is that, when this move is made the very notion of the 'real' loses its meaning and so the position of 'non-realism' also loses all point. This form of non-realism cannot operate with any distinction between reality and fiction, except one based dangerously on social hegemony.
[23] Erricker (1993), p138-9.
[24] Hardy (1981), Haldane (1986).
[25] I would regard this as a logical requirement of the liberal approach, especially in a context where it is a acknowledged that parents have a right to exit their child from the school or any particular aspects of its curriculum. Once *that* right of exit is acknowledged, as it currently is in the English system, then clearly there is a concomitant right to information about any particular school's policies.
[26] Ward (1982), passim.
[27] For the positivist attack on theological assertions, see Ayer (1932) and Flew (1971).
[28] There is no sceptical claim being made here to the effect that a complete and correct account is an *impossibility* but only the view that any given account is *contestable*. Note the contrast with other stances, thought to be compatible with the liberal approach to public policy i.e. the view that all evaluative beliefs are either equally true (Macedo, 1995) or equally false (White,J.,1994).
[29] Rescher (1993), ch4.
[30] See, for example, Mulhall (1990) and McDowell (1994).
[31] White (1994), p373.
[32] See also models 2 and 3 in appendix 1, discussed earlier in this chapter.

[33] The relationship between theological non-realism and classical atheism is an interesting one. I am inclined to say that no distinction exists here at the level of metaphysical perspective. Some theological non-realists might deny this but I think the arguments put forward, for example by Ward (1982) are sufficient to support my refusal to accept any distinction between the two positions. The real difference between classical atheists and theological non-realists is that, despite its lack of reference to a metaphysical reality, the latter group still regard talk of 'God' as meaningful and useful while the former think that Godtalk should be jettisoned, along with the practices that are associated with it.

[34] White (1995).

[35] For a similar approach to moral and civic education, respectively, see Carr (1992) and White, P.(1996).

7 Pluralism and the Limits of Common Schooling

Summary

This chapter begins with a brief discussion of the incompatibility between a commitment to common schooling and the development of autonomy, on the grounds that the latter requires, as a primary educational aim, the formation of persons into a particular cultural tradition. From there I go on to explore Kekes' criticism of liberalism from a pluralist perspective. Kekes' commitment to an educational programme, which has as its central aim the development of pluralism, is exposed as somewhat inconsistent. This discussion leads on to the proposal of three normative models of pluralism, the third of which, 'civic pluralism', is then, in the following section, related to the approach of the conservative political tradition. In the final section an alternative model of the organisation of personal development within the state system is proposed, and linked to the conservative or civic pluralist political perspective. It involves, significantly, the rejection of the ideal of common state schooling and is therefore compatible also with the liberal commitment to the development of autonomy.

7.1 Introduction

In chapter five we saw how social democratic liberal thinking on the nature of autonomy emphasises the fact that it is important for individuals to be *both* critically open and culturally embedded in a particular values tradition. This community based, formative process must be established *before* a person can truly be described as 'autonomous'. I noted at the time some of the problems which adherence to this characterisation might cause for those advocating the development of autonomy as the *primary* aim of the common school. I also said that this communitarian liberal approach, while underpinned by a clear doctrine of human well-being, had no rationally justifiable way of answering the questions about which culture should be regarded as predominant in the educational context.

In order to understand why cultural embeddedness is an essential part of any coherent liberalism based upon autonomy we need to explore the intricate relationship, noted earlier, between autonomy and rationality. *Autonomous* choosing can only be adequately characterised in contradistinction to *arbitrary* choosing. However, rational choices can only be made from within some *given* framework of value which embodies a particular, substantive conception of the good. It is not therefore possible to develop a universally applicable notion of autonomy without at the same time making reference to some particular system of value which endorses a particular substantive picture of the good. But while this is the only basis upon which the development of autonomy can be justified as one of the aims of a common conception of education, it is the very thing which when allied to a commitment to a *nationally* common approach, contravenes the liberal commitment to impartiality and commits it to a subtle kind of cultural imperialism.[1]

The charge laid against the liberal approach here is not simply the usual one that its methodology, especially when translated into educational approaches to personal development, represents a subtle promotion of a particular ideology that betrays its alleged impartiality. More importantly, I have shown that, even where perfectionist liberals like Raz own up to, and offer justification for, this imperialist tendency, further problems emerge when such an approach is applied to *educational* policy. The liberal commitment to complex autonomy requires *either* some supplementation by a particular conception of the good *or* some justification for the view that our national culture *is*, as Raz alleges, a 'culture of autonomy'. In addition, and in order to underpin the second of these options, some reasoning will be required to show that the liberal state has an interest in conserving the national culture in its present form. Furthermore, it needs to be established that the common values of the national society are *adequate* enough to meet the requirements of complex autonomy. Arguments also need to be put forward to show that the common value of autonomy ought to predominate over those of parents when there is conflict between them.

Where liberals do recognise the need for some supplementation of common values in order to facilitate the requirements of the development of complex autonomy, it appears that their commitment to a nationally common conception of personal education, delivered by means of the common school, effectively prevents that supplementation from taking place in the setting of the child's formal education. Responsibility for any supplementation is effectively allocated to the parents, despite the fact that, on this view, this should be regarded as a *primary* educational aim. The fact that schools are not able to accommodate this educational aim is due to their commitment to the ideals of commonality and presumably the notion of equal entitlement for all. However the *net effect* of this is that the required supplementation may not take place since families are often ill qualified or equipped to undertake the work that this form of liberal theory requires of them. Ironically then the degree to which the necessary conditions for complex autonomy can be provided will depend upon the ability of *parents* to provide it[2] and many children will be disadvantaged in this respect as an indirect result of an educational commitment to common schooling.[3]

The upshot of this discussion of autonomy based liberalism, however, is that it *requires* that schools be more responsive to the values of the home and regard formation in these values as an educational *entitlement.* Ironically, it would appear to be incompatible with the ideal of the detached common school that some liberal thinkers recommend to promote it.[4] Some liberals will resist this conclusion and argue that common national values do exist and that they should be legitimately regarded as forming the *primary* culture of all children. This will require the kinds of arguments that were discussed in chapter 3. However, such arguments are likely to require a denial of the fact that Britain is a genuinely *plural* society.

Pluralism will emerge in this chapter not just as a de facto empirical claim about the nature of Britain, and perhaps all modern Western societies, but as a *normative* claim that is characterisable in at least three different ways. Philosophers are used to speaking of the 'varieties' of liberalism and it is my contention that philosophers must also now begin to speak of pluralism in the same terms. Here I claim to have discerned at least three very different possible varieties lurking behind much political and educational thinking. Up to now, focusing purely on the commitment to pluralism as an empirical claim, I have shown that while liberal thinkers regard it as the starting point for the appeal of their political ideas, their claims to nurture that pluralism are somewhat limited, especially and ironically when it plays a major part in determining the character of personal education programmes in the common school. I will argue that two normative versions of pluralism are available to educational policy makers which, on the surface at least, provide a powerful rival to that of social democratic liberalism. They challenge many of the basic political and epistemological assumptions which underpin much current educational thinking.

In the last part of this chapter, having attempted to show, using general arguments derived from John Kekes,[5] why all forms of liberalism will be prone to the kind of procedural imperialism that will make it incompatible with the promotion of pluralism, I will attempt briefly to canvas the various rival non-liberal political frameworks and examine their educational implications.

7.2 Liberalism, universalism and procedural imperialism

As part of their very claims to fairness and plurality, all forms of liberalism, both perfectionist and anti-perfectionist, will have an apriori attachment to a narrow set of procedural values. This means that while liberalism has an apparent compatibility with pluralism at the level of substantive values, it requires the state to operate monistically towards a narrow range of procedural values, regarding these as overriding in the public domain.

The most notable modern liberals, recognising the possibility of conflict at the procedural level, have attempted to offer a reductive analysis of traditionally important procedural values showing that *one single* procedural value ought to predominate, arguing that its procedural superiority is crucial for political decision making in a liberal society. For Rawls, Dworkin, Raz and Berlin the preferred candidates are social justice, equality, freedom and human rights, respectively. It is against the subtle, but inevitable monism of liberalism that John Kekes sets out an alternative pluralist approach to politics in the last chapter of his recent book, *The Morality of Pluralism.*[6] He claims that the essential difference between pluralists and liberals is that while liberals claim that some values should always override others where conflict occurs, pluralists say that *all* our values, moral and political, should be seen as conditional. Pluralists assert that to regard any value or range of values as overriding (with the capacity, in Dworkin's words, to 'trump' any other value) is to adopt an excessively rationalistic attitude towards the complexities of concrete moral and political decision making. It represents an ideological straitjacket by which policy makers in any society, let alone a radically plural one, should not be constrained. According to Kekes the liberal approach neither reflects actual political practice, nor would its implementation improve it.

Not only does Kekes regard the possibility of producing a successful reductive analysis of all the major liberal procedural values into a single value as extremely slim, he thinks that they (and other non-liberal procedural values) are

> equally important for exactly the same reason: their claims must be recognised by all conceptions of a good life if they are to yield the substantive values they promise.[7]

If, in the face of the failure of any reductive analysis, liberals were to agree that overridingness should be conferred onto some combination of procedural values then it would not help to solve conflicts between them, making the liberal thesis vacuous. If, on the other side, overridingness were conferred irrespective of this to a single value, then clearly such liberalism would sacrifice its compatibility with pluralism. Joseph Raz[8] explicitly recognises this and states that the liberal state's commitment to pluralism is purely instrumental and therefore limited. Where liberal policy makers combine a commitment to universality and procedural imperialism with social democratic liberal views about the nature and role of the state education system it is at least arguable that, due to the formative function of education and the difficulty of preventing the *effective* substantive transmission of procedural values, the outcome will be implementation through the education system of a programme of cultural imperialism.

The anti-perfectionist liberal justification for the impartiality of the state is a fear of state power being used in order to treat one value or several values as overriding. The pluralist argues that the best way to deal with this fear is to ensure that the state has no *overriding* commitment to any value, procedural or substantive-*even* liberal ones. Kekes rejects the notion that taking up this position against the liberal involves the acceptance of full blown relativism. Just because certain primary values are regarded as objective, universally applicable minimal requirements for good lives it does not commit one to the view that in all cases of conflict rational people are committed apriori to the *overridingness* of primary values, as liberals suppose. It is the commitment to the objectivity of certain primary values that provides a bulwark between pluralism and relativism, according to Kekes. The basis for the pluralist denial of overridingness even for primary values is that reasonable conflict resolution will not only require some empirical political judgement of the context within which the conflict arises but also a *balance* between the various values which have a claim on us.

7.3 The politics of pluralism and the ideology of pluralism

As well as characterising the pluralist view of the state in terms of its openness to the context and the non-ideological nature of its approach to

policy, Kekes summarises the pluralist view of the state in terms of the following principles:
The state should,
a) use its power to protect all the procedural and substantive values necessary for all good lives and
b) make it possible for citizens to pursue, within appropriate limits, such secondary values as they may require beyond the primary values to make a good life for themselves.

Kekes contrasts the political programme of pluralism with that of liberalism and declares that the pluralist will be even more interventionist. This is the case because the pluralist will be prepared to intervene both to encourage and limit certain substantive values. In the name of pluralism the state will go beyond neutrality, but, he says, the state should be guided by a conception of its function; namely '*to guarantee the conditions in which its citizens could make a good life for themselves*'. Kekes' discussion shows that the character of this intervention will be governed by a *particular* conception of the nature of the society in which it operates. That society will be regarded by the pluralist policy maker as a *pluralist* society. This does not look like an empirical claim about any particular society but rather a generalisation of the pluralistic theory of good that Kekes argues for; it therefore embodies assumptions about the nature of the construction of good lives. Later on, in the same discussion, Kekes makes the normative and substantive view that he wishes the state to sustain and nourish quite clear:

> ..the reason for organising the state so as to protect the plurality of values is the conjunction of the belief this book aims to defend, namely, that the best way in which individuals can make a good life for themselves is to have a plurality of values at their disposal, and the belief ...that the state's function is to protect the conditions necessary for the general availability of a plurality of values.[9]

In order that citizens in a pluralist society can be enabled to make good lives for themselves, it is the state's responsibility to make them familiar with a 'sufficient range of values'. Good lives on this pluralistic conception of the matter are *made* and involve a selection from the range of values available in a pluralist society.

There appears to be a conflict however between these aspects of the pluralist programme and the broad principles used to characterise it. If the state is to take a view as to the 'best way' in which good lives can be constructed, then it is difficult to see how this fits with its role of

'..*protecting all the procedural and substantive values necessary for all good lives'* since some conceptions of the good life may be at odds with the state's normative assumptions about the *best way of constructing* a good life. For example, to some groups the idea that good lives are 'constructed' by individuals for themselves would be regarded not just as wrong but spiritually dangerous.

It looks as if the attempt by the Kekesian pluralist state to 'guarantee the conditions in which its citizens can try and make good lives for themselves',and which will include an education system that teaches pupils about the plurality of values, will come into conflict with a least one group of people; those parents who are *required*, by a combination of financial and legal factors, to have their children educated by the state but who regard an education in the plurality of values as undermining rather than supporting their ability to make a good life for themselves and for their children. Parents with strong and traditional religious views are likely to fall into this category. Such parents might see it as an important aspect of their conception of a good life to *restrict* the range of values and the consequent amount of moral conflict that their children experience. They would also reject the axiom of Kekes' moral pluralism that a range of conflicting values have an equal hold on individuals. It is not clear how Kekes would advise the pluralist policy maker to resolve this conflict between the 'pluralism' of the state and a significant minority community, partly constitutive of the pluralist nature of society. But the situation presents him with a dilemma. Support for the parent would contravene the state's commitment to its own conception of pluralism while rejection of the parent's view must surely, in some sense, be an expression of non-pluralism.

Kekes does not discuss the educational implications of his political pluralism but I will, however, attempt to extrapolate his remarks in that direction in order to bring to light some possible inconsistencies within the kind of pluralist political framework that he proposes. I will show how a commitment to a programme of common education designed to promote pluralism would contravene the claim of the Kekesian state to avoid the charge of cultural imperialism. The individualism implied in Kekes' account of the *normative* pluralism operating behind the state's commitment to enable citizens to make good lives for themselves implies that pluralists, like liberals, would regard children as citizens in their own right. This might predispose the pluralist in the case of the kind of conflict outlined above to attempt to 'protect' the child from the non-pluralist wishes of the parents. It is difficult to see how, if that were the case, we could avoid the conclusion that the pluralist state should override the wishes of the parent in cases like this. Since the role of the state is couched in terms as strong as 'guaranteeing the conditions' and the laying down of 'limits', then it is not clear how the pluralism of the state can avoid overriding the non-pluralism of the parent in such cases. In which case Kekes' political programme looks just as overbearing in its advocacy of 'pluralism' as the various forms of liberalism are in their advocacy of liberal values. If that were the case, then Kekes would I think be guilty of an ideological attachment to a *single* value, ironically, that of pluralism itself.

7.4 The paradox of pluralist education

Considerations of cases like this suggest that, paradoxically, the state can best guarantee the conditions that will enable citizens to make good lives for themselves if it ensures that it is not, in implementing the politics of pluralism, operating with an ideological attachment to pluralism itself. The educational conflict exposed in the last section could be avoided by dispensing with a certain social democratic liberal assumption, which I take to be embodied in Kekes' educational programme. Central to this tension is the assumption that the pluralist state should make *itself* responsible for *determining* aspects of the personal development of its child-citizens through a common conception of pluralistic personal education.[10] The problem here, as has already been indicated, is that where the state uses its powers to determine the personal development of its citizens, along lines which it centrally determines then it will by that process tend *inevitably* to reduce rather than enhance the diversity and de facto pluralism of the civic society over which it presides.

Where Kekesian pluralism shares important political assumptions with the social democratic brand of liberalism, particularly its commitment to the ideal of the common school and its presumption that, at some level, the state should use its powers to ensure that an education of a particular character is given to all children within a particular polity, then the only real difference between the two programmes is that, for Kekes, pluralism itself should be promoted in the common school. This discussion shows that a commitment to the promotion of pluralism may mean different things to different theorists. Macedo, helpfully developed two *empirical* models of pluralism (internal and external pluralism) that enabled me to pick out important tensions within educational programmes designed to promote pluralism.[11] I think it would be helpful to develop a set of *normative* models of pluralism, combining a brief characterisation of basic aims and methods for its promotion. In each case I have tried to link each one to a broad political perspective and have tried to spell out its educational implications.

Pluralism 1.

Determinative or Ideological Pluralism (Kekesian model):

- all values (including moral and political values) are conditional

- since pluralism can be shown to be correct on rational grounds, it is in everyone's interests to live in a society where the widest variety of values are promoted

- the best society is one of maximum plurality of lifestyle

- the government should use its powers to ensure that children are introduced to the widest possible range of values since that can be shown, on rational grounds, to be in their best interest.

- the pluralist state may, on the above grounds, intervene in the education of children to prevent parents from setting limits upon the range of values to which their children are introduced i.e. commonality of schooling is required to ensure that children are enabled to make good lives for themselves.

Pluralism 2

De Facto or Democratic Pluralism:

- as a matter of empirical fact we live in a pluralist society i.e. a society of great value and lifestyle diversity.

- a certain level of agreement or consensus is required for a benign social and political order

- commonality of education is required to ensure a certain degree of agreement and personal commonality among citizenry in order to facilitate the conflict free operation of a pluralist society.

We have, in the course of this study, demonstrated that these first two types of pluralism will, when combined with a commitment to a common programme of personal education and delivered in the common school, have the inevitable effect of restricting the actual extent of value and lifestyle diversity in society. Their commitment is to ensuring that all pupils are exposed to a plurality of values (internal pluralism or multiculturalism) and so, on *pluralistic* grounds, they will restrict the degree to which parents within the state system can determine the values which come to be held by their own children. To that extent, the commitment to a genuine 'external' pluralism of those who support these first two models is questionable.

Considerations of this kind suggest a third and more radical approach the aim of which would be to nurture external pluralism. Ironically, and because of the examination of Kekesian pluralism in the last section, its approach might be characterised as non-monist rather than pluralist since the state would effectively avoid all attempts to *determine* the nature of the society over which it presides and merely set the conditions within which pluralism could develop, as it were, naturally.

Pluralism 3

Civic or Natural Pluralism

-the state should not attempt to use its powers to determine the nature of civil society

-the state should not commit itself to the promotion of a 'pluralist' or any other ideological notion about the nature of society.

-Constraint and determinative intervention by the state should be regulative or legislative and minimal.

-Civic communities (based upon the free and natural association) of individuals should be enabled to develop their own values.

-While the state might have a duty to ensure that all are educated i.e. to provide funding for education it has no consequent right to determine the nature of the values promoted by its schools, as a general rule.

7.5 The politics of civic pluralism

I have up to now been content to cast doubt upon the ability of anyone to construct a national consensus on values that might govern personal development.[12] But the political framework that forms the backdrop to the normative conception of pluralism 3, is one which goes further and challenges not just the possibility of forming such a consensus but also its *desirability*. The idea that such a consensus is not just desirable but essential is a fundamental axiom of social democratic political and educational thinking. It is the possibility of consensus which offers the social democrat a means of establishing on a polity wide basis a notion of what is good, that may underpin and justify the actions of an interventionist state. Such a consensus is both desirable and essential for the social democratic liberal educationalist because without it any nationally common approach to education is open to serious challenge.

Nicholas Rescher identifies John Rawls and Jurgen Habermas as the most influential advocates of the politics of consensus. He challenges the link that

Habermas draws between consensus, truth and the human good. That viewpoint is summarised in the following terms,

> As Habermas sees it, what is good for people, what human flourishing is all about, is what the members of a community come to agree on its being when they operate in conditions of unfettered deliberation and discussion-free from distortion and coercion. Properly founded social consensus is the definitive arbiter of the human good.[13]

Rescher locates the consensus seeking strand of political thinking with the philosophical tradition of Plato. It is he says, *'one which looks to systematic order through rational co-ordination under the aegis of universal principles'*. This tradition favours the *'rational uniformity of a harmonious consensus'*. He contrasts this with the political tradition of Aristotle that 'looks to organic balance and an equilibriation of diversity and division'. It is geared to '..pluralism of countervailing checks and balances'.[14] Rescher identifies the former tradition with that of socialism and social democracy, while the latter is clearly identified with the market oriented non-interventionism that is best characterised by the conservative tradition. He contrasts what he calls 'the polity of consensus' and 'the polity of pluralism' in the following way,

> The polity of consensus proceeds from a fundamentally socialistic commitment to the co-ordination and alignment of individual action into the uniform social order of 'rationalised' central planning... By contrast, the polity of pluralism abandons the goal of monolithically unified 'rational order' for the 'creative diversity' of a situation of variegated rivalry and competition. Its political paradigm is not that of a command economy with its ideal of rationalisation and uniformising co-ordination, but that of a free market with its competitive rivalry of conflicting interests.[15]

Rescher offers detailed arguments to suggest that it is wrong to assume that consensus is an essential prerequisite of a benign social order, a view which underpins much educational thinking about the need for a common conception of personal education. He cites a number of successful social institutions that work effectively through a process of conflict and acquiescence rather than consensus, including the Anglo-American legal system, few party electoral systems and binding arbitration.[16] While he recognises the dangers of conflict within society between those who have sharply conflicting values, he does not regard the attempt to get everyone to agree as a worthwhile solution, since it would reduce the creative diversity within society. In addition, we have seen that where attempts to generate a consensus are worked into a nationally common conception of education there might arguably be a reduction of personal liberty, that would certainly offend classic liberals and ought to be unacceptable to social democratic liberals.

If we relate Rescher's arguments to social democratic demand for a common civic education and common schooling, then we can say that it is no longer viable to assume without further justification that either of these are an essential prerequisite of a benign social order.[17] It cannot *automatically* be assumed that where schools are allowed to promote particular values that might conflict sharply with others it will lead to social fragmentation and political chaos, since a negative scenario of that kind rests upon just the assumption that Rescher and other pluralists challenge. Thus, one important reason to support a common approach to personal education is now in serious question.

In the next section, and in line with suggestions made by Rescher, I want to attempt to show that the British Conservative tradition, particularly as it is exemplified in the writings of Edmund Burke and Michael Oakeshott[18] is the political tradition that can in the British context be described as the politics of pluralism. This is because it is a tradition that is pledged to nurture and protect the naturally developing and independent life of civil society.[19]

7.6 Conservatism and the conservation of civil society

Several things should be noted about the work of conservationists. There are important structural, but entirely analogical, similarities between their work and the conservative approach to policy. These will first be outlined and then used to underpin my brief characterisation of that tradition.

The object of conservationist policies is try to 'preserve in being, to keep alive' a species of animal or a rain forest. If we consider the work of an organisation like Greenpeace or Friends of the Earth, then it is also clear that their work of conservation may be *radical* and involve a challenge to the status quo. The conservationist does not *determine* the character of that which she attempts to protect and keep alive. She respects it as it is in its independent and natural state, enabling it to live the kind of life that it is inclined to lead when freed from human interference. The conservative policy maker, likewise, sees her task as that of protecting and preserving the traditions and institutions which have grown up naturally through day to day human association. These, according to the conservative, have a rationality of their own. It would be an abuse to attempt to use the power of the state or the state education system, in particular, to ensure that future citizens are formed in order to match up to certain idealisations about how society *should or ought to be*. The work of the conservationist involves repairing the damage done by human beings, or preventing such damage. Conservative policy makers, likewise, may well regard the actions of previous *governments* as damaging to the social and political balance within civil society. The radicalism of Margaret Thatcher, often thought to be at odds with the traditional conservative approach, should be seen in this light as an attempt to restore a natural balance within civil society that had allegedly been disrupted by the intervention of previous governments. The aim of these radical conservative policies even when radical is always to be ideally characterised as *restorative* rather than *determinative*. Just as the conservationist works to restore the natural balance between a number of, often conflicting, forces within the environment, the conservative will attempt to ensure that the determinative forces within civil society are plural rather than single. The non-determinative approach of the conservationist reflects the fact that the objects of her environmental concern are already regarded as intrinsically good. It is not regarded as material for human creativity. The conservative has an analogous attitude to the independent life of British civil society; it is constituted in such a way as to maximise the opportunities for all to make good lives for themselves. This does not mean that life within that society is currently or ever was perfect. Nor does it mean that all change should be resisted since change itself is both a certainty and a necessity, requiring careful management.[20] The present state of society represents the historically rooted process of a free people working out their lives together.

While recognising the self-determined character of the object of her concern, that is, while respecting the fact that each individual knows best how it should live, the conservationist, more than most, recognises that the individual is heavily dependent upon a whole interactive network of delicately balanced forces. Refusing to act upon idealisations about how the rain forest or the blue whale should be or should live, the conservationist will have very clear and rationally worked out ideas about how to *enable* the species or organism to flourish *in its own way*. Such factual information and a rational approach will underpin their work. Indeed, it is their knowledge of that network of dependence that will enable the conservationist, to identify dangers and enact policies which sustain the endangered life form. Conservatives, likewise, recognise the fact that individuals find themselves embedded within a network of delicately balanced forces and their well being depends upon the maintenance of those forces. These forces are as delicately balanced for human beings as they are for trees, plants and animals.

The conservationist will be very much aware of the particular dangers of a group or member of the species becoming too dependent upon human aid. Wherever possible the conservationist will try to ensure that the population with which she is concerned are self supporting; this will be an important objective of her work. In a similar way, conservative politicians will be very much aware of the positive dangers of a dependency upon the state and its professionals. Generally, they will prefer to encourage individuals and publicly funded institutions to become self regulating in a way that is as free *as possible* from bureaucratic interference.

7.7 Conservatism and civic pluralism

I will attempt to outline those aspects of the conservative tradition which underpin its claim to be the political framework which best fits the normative pluralist doctrine that I have called 'civic pluralism' (pluralism 3).

The conservative tradition is characterised by a rejection of rationalism. It will not operate on the basis of a hard and fast adherence to apriori and universally applicable rational principles or policy ideals, nor upon idealised political notions about the nature of British society. This is because of a scepticism towards the view that rationality alone can provide the basis for satisfactory civil and political association.[21] Arguably this strand of conservative thinking reflects the influence of David Hume.[22] There is a recognition that practical political judgement will embody a *contingent* rationality that may not be open to abstract defence and political judgements will require the exercise of practical wisdom. This will apply particularly to the discernment of the exact requirements in particular historical circumstances about what is to be 'conserved' and what constitutes the appropriate degree of state intervention. This aspect of conservative thinking may be misunderstood as a lack of principle by those rationalist critics who would judge a political tradition by its abstract principles.[23]

As part of its rejection of the universalism which characterises liberal thinking about human well-being and truth, the conservative tradition locates the human good within a particular social context. Rejection of liberal universalism and rationalism will lead the conservative to regard with scepticism attempts to construct positive characterisations of 'the interests of children' on a nation-wide scale of the kind that might be required to underpin accounts of a common conception of education. This will involve a commitment to the primacy of intermediate social institutions between the individual and the state and attempts to to nurture a partnership between the family and the school. A key element of this non-determinative strategy will be a desire to maximise the influence of parents over the kind of education which their children receive.[24] But the attempt to maximise parental influence is not the same as allowing that influence to go unrestrained, there will also be a recognition that the power of parents will have to be *balanced* by that of professionals and the state.

Conservatives have quite distinct and definite ideas about what constitutes the necessary *conditions* for the good life but will refrain from stipulating what constitutes the good life *itself*. The conservative approach to the good is a procedural one but this procedural affiliation is focused upon the maintenance of a set of *historically given* procedures and institutions rather than upon the attempt to mould social life to meet the idealised set of overriding procedural *values*. This will embody an appreciation of the value of particular social relationships and traditions fundamental, for example, to the *British way of life*.[25] For the conservative civil society is primarily made up of associations which are given, historical and filial; these include, primarily, the family and the nation. Each of these is something which is bequeathed to us by virtue of the fact that we were born in a particular place, at a particular time, to particular parents. The school lies between these two and should reflect the influence of both of them. The *voluntary* associations that we form are largely secondary, from this perspective. Our choices and the rationality that we articulate in some significant sense *follow* on from our life in a given community. *That* life has a rationality of its own that is embedded in a particular culture, in civic institutions and in family life.[26] The whole, the nation, has a particular character because of a long process of human interaction. The life that we have is enjoyed because of that history and it must be given due recognition in any decisions that we make and the way we live, since otherwise that which sustains the good life which we enjoy might be damaged beyond repair. From the conservative perspective democratically elected governments acting enterprisingly and with good intentions on behalf of society are likely to do more harm than good.[27]

Conservatives will reject anti-perfectionism. At the same time however they will have a respect for the integrity of the British way of life as a living historical process within which schools play an important part. There are dangers if governments act on the basis of particular and determinative ideas about what that way of life is or should be. From this perspective those with responsibility for government should reject any full blooded perfectionism but *will* regard it as having a duty to nourish those procedures which it sees as vital to the well being and growth of civic culture. This characteristically expresses itself in attempts to ensure that schools are self regulating communities that are maximally freed from state interference. Structures will be put into place which will enable critically accountable institutions to plan their own future largely free of direct government or bureaucratic interference. Planning then emerges piecemeal out of day to day practice and is maximally responsive to the needs of users.

It may be impossible to characterise the conservative view as either weak or strong perfectionism, for the above reasons. However, the conservative position may be expressed quite precisely and categorically in terms of '*minimal* perfectionism'. With regard to state schools, the attitude of conservative governments will be geared to ensuring that these vital independent players in the life of civil society are freed to determine their own nature as self regulating and self determining social institutions. The conservative will not, in line with what has been said above, try to make an absolute statement about the degree of state intervention. It is possible though to state that for a conservative the state and its coercive activity must be kept as small as possible in any given set of circumstances. The exact nature of this commitment to the minimal state is expressed in the following way by Michael Oakeshott,

> ...governing is a specific and limited activity, namely the provision and custody of general rules of conduct, which are understood not as plans for imposing substantive activities, but as instruments enabling people to pursue the activities of their own choice with the minimum frustration. [28]

It should be noted that this commitment to the minimal state itself constitutes a non-rationalistic commitment both to liberty and to pluralism, since the conservative believes that a plurality of power and influence within both British society and the British constitution are fundamental to the freedom that exists in British society. The notion of the minimal state is not just linked for the conservative to a rationalistic notion of individual rights[29] but emerges from its unique model of democracy. It is a conception of the democratic process that both incorporates the formal democracy favoured by social democrats, but limits that solely to the legislative and executive aspects of government. In the wider conservative sense, the democratic process *is* the very process by which civil society obtains its character. It is a characterisation of democracy that is open to the influence of forces from

the past as well as those of the present, as well as a concern for the future. In order to characterise the conservative notion of democracy, it is necessary to distinguish between two forms of democratic expression:
a) representative or electoral democracy- the outcome of which is seen as regulative and legislative rather than determinative in its effect on civil society, as social democratic liberals would wish.
b) natural/ moral or civic democracy- which is the result of individual liberty and which in effect is macrocosmically determinative of the nature of national society.
As well as being based upon a diffusion of power between past, present and future, the democratic process conceived in this way may involve the democratic expression flowing from, for example, participation by the citizenry in the life of schools, local councils, hospitals, as well as the use of one's own resources, the ownership of property and the general free conduct of day to day life.[30]

The net effect of the conservative commitment to anti-rationalism, minimal perfectionism in the disposal of state power, aimed exclusively at the nurture of the independent life of civil society will inevitably lead to a non-ideological form of government which is most conducive to the development of what I have called civic pluralism (pluralism 3). This connection between conservatism and pluralism often goes unrecognised precisely because it is a non-ideological commitment; the conservative will have no interest in *promoting* a society constituted by a wide variety of viewpoints. Neither will she be concerned to prevent a consensus from developing as long as its development is a *natural* one that doesn't just reflect the fact that too much power has fallen into the hands of one group, individual or institution.

The exact nature of the conservative commitment to pluralism and to the true purpose of government is summarised in the following quotation from the writings of Michael Oakeshott,

> I and my neighbours, my associates, my compatriots, my friends, my enemies and those I am indifferent about are people engaged in a great variety of activities, We are apt to entertain a multiplicity of opinions on every conceivable subject and are disposed to change these beliefs as we grow tired of them...Why all this should be so does not matter. It is not necsessarily so. A different condition of human circumstances can easily be imagined, and we know that elsewhere and at other times activity is, or has been, far less multifarious and changeful and opinion far less diverse and far less likely to provoke collisions; but, by and large we recognise this to be

our condition, though nobody designed or specifically chose it in preference to all others. It is the product of ...human beings impelled by an acquired love of making choices for themselves.[31]

The acceptance of the natural and plural flow of civil society is the spring of the conservative approach to government. However, the conservative

..does not suppose that the office of government is to do nothing...the office which he attributes to government is to resolve some of the collisions which this variety of beliefs and activities generates; to preserve peace, not by placing an interdict upon the diversity, which springs from the exercise of preference, not by imposing substantive uniformity, but by enforcing general rules of procedure upon all subjects alike.[32]

7.8 Conservatism and commonality

Terry McLaughlin defines the common school as

..a school which aspires not only to achieve a broad range of mix in its student body, and to offer a form of common schooling but also one which is committed to a conception of common education.[33]

This notion of the common school has two distinct elements, that have been noted already; firstly, a commitment to a conception of common education and secondly, a commitment to certain ideals regarding the composition of the student population. Broadly speaking, the school population should ideally reflect the *diversity* of culture and ability to be found in the wider society. In the next section I want to try to show why this conception of common schooling is unacceptable from the perspectives of conservatism and Civic Pluralism.

We had cause, earlier to note the following principle which Amy Gutmann sets out to judge the acceptability of any common conception, from within the liberal political framework.

Any conception of common education based on liberal principles must be alert to the dangers of basing educational influence on a form of communitarian solidarity which requires that children be educated to accept the singularly correct and comprehensive conception of the good life.[34]

This will be acceptable from the conservative and pluralist perspective, *only if* it applies to the state education system *as a whole*, that is, upon the conception of a common education, imposed by the *state* upon all state schools. Adherence to this constraining principle will have implications for the way in which policies on personal or spiritual education might be organised on a national basis. Clearly, the first organisational model featured in appendix 1, which I have labelled 'Determinative Communitarian Monism', would be ruled out.

But when applied to the work of an individual school, whether it be run by the state or not, conservatives and communitarian critics of liberalism[35] generally will want to say that it represents, at the very least, a disavowal of the school's responsibility to operate an adequate *community based* system of personal development. Schools will transmit values and will affect the personal development of their pupils either by accident or design. Even if a school intends to restrain itself to a 'thin' set of procedural values, perhaps based upon the development of the ability to appreciate a range of different values and perspectives, this *will* have a positive formative effect that is 'thicker' than intended. This 'thicker' value set of more comprehensive values *will* creep into the hidden curriculum. Values will be expressed through the selection of issues for discussion. A *positive* model of evaluation will be effectively promoted by the restraint of the school since it will put into place a programme where teachers facilitate the discussion of a wide range of values, opinions and beliefs without offering specific guidance as to which one is to be regarded as correct. School teachers are important formative models for school children. In the school with 'thin' values, their professional procedural restraint will inevitably recommend itself in a comprehensive way to their pupils. Where the school policy advocates such restraint it is actually unlikely that individual teachers will be capable of restraining themselves from, or disguising their own personal response and this will lead to a degree of inconsistency on the part of the school, since the teaching staff are likely to hold a wide range of possibly contrasting views on important issues; such a regime will effectively form children in the quite specific view that good lives are best constructed by *individuals* on the basis of *rational* deliberation.

A 'thin' approach to school values of the kind that might follow from the application of Gutmann's principle, will lead to a 'silence'[36] on certain key issues. This will leave a formative vacuum, since any policy for personal *development* will *require* the school to base its educational influence on some '*...form of communitarian solidarity which requires that children be educated to accept the singularly correct and comprehensive conception of* *the good life'*. And, this will be a vacuum which parents may have neither the ability or means to fill but it *will inevitably be filled* by influences from beyond the school and the family. The likely effects of such non-interventionist policies are mapped out in the organisational models 2 and 3, discussed in chapter 6.[37]

In response to a widely recognised need to fill this vacuum at the level of the primary formative culture, many are inclined to look with renewed vigour for the construction of a national consensus.[38] There may be some scope for constructing a national consensus on specific kinds of behaviour that it would be in everyone's interests to discourage, based upon some shared notion of what behaviour and attitudes are harmful to others and the fabric of society. In addition there may be some scope for agreement about the need for the development of qualities like 'responsibility' and perhaps some of the personal characteristics outlined at the end of the last chapter.[39]

However, it is clear that in a plural and free society there will be scope for widespread disagreement even about the causes of social harm. Some will see any attempt to encourage a tolerant discussion of lifestyle options like, for example, homosexuality, as in itself harmful to family life and therefore constitutive of social harm. Those who view homosexual lifestyles more positively will see the attitude of those who promote traditional family life as itself harmful since it encourages intolerance and prejudice. And even if universal agreement were to be established around a set of positively characterised virtues and personal qualities, at least two considerations militate against our being able to conclude from this that they might form anything other than *a mere basis* for an adequate policy on personal development. It is a feature of such virtues and characteristics that they are non-specific and therefore open to instantiation in a wide number of ways that will be affected by the context of any particular action. It is *this* feature of such personal qualities that underpins the possibility that a national consensus could be built around them. However, when one begins to attempt to construct positive models of what 'being responsible' means in concrete moral situations- and this is a fundamental requirement of any policy that is to be adequately *formative*- then any agreement that might exist at the level of abstract terminology will, in all probability, begin to break down with some people regarding the models of responsible behaviour held by others as highly irresponsible. One has only to think of the discussion that might ensue if the question were raised as to how *responsible* it might be for nurses to strike in protest at alleged health service 'cuts', or to have an abortion, to see the problems that are raised for anyone wishing to suggest that such values could form the basis of a satisfactory common policy on personal development.

From these observations it is possible to develop the first stage of a complex argument against any national strategy to develop a common conception of personal education. Given the pluralist nature of society, the chances of producing a national consensus on such issues *thin* enough to gain the acknowledgement of all and *thick* enough to support an adequate programme of personal development are just non-existent.[40] The second stage to this argument refers back to Gutmann's principle. Since what is required from a national consensus is a set of values to fill the formative vacuum left by the restraint that a procedural approach engenders, it will inevitably, if it were deemed *adequate,* constitute a violation of that principle. This is because, as suggested earlier, such a policy of *non-individualistic, formative* personal development would *have* to be based upon

> ..a form of communitarian solidarity which requires that children be educated to accept the singularly correct and comprehensive conception of the good life.[41]

But I have argued that it will in fact be impossible for individual schools to *avoid* having some formative effect upon the children in its care, *even if* they decide either not to promote any values or if they decide to promote only a thin set of common values.[42] It has been shown that even where the school's restrained attitude to the promotion of values, does not itself manifest adherence to a specific tradition of values, then it amounts to an abnegation of responsibility which effectively, but not perhaps intentionally hands over control of children's spiritual development to the most powerful outside influences. Which ever of these alternative scenarios proves to be the case, the approach of the school does have an effect, albeit indirectly, upon the personal formation of the children for which it is responsible.

Given that it is inevitable that schools will have a role in the personal formation of children and will therefore have to break the limits laid down by Gutmann's principle, and given that a national strategy on this matter, in the context of a pluralist society,[43] is capable only of producing something which is either unacceptable or inadequate, the only question which remains to be asked is *who* should be responsible for *deciding* which positive community based value system should be adopted by any particular school. Conservatives and civic pluralists will, for political reasons, want to say that the state's involvement in the design of the values policies of individual schools should be minimal. In part this will be because they share the commitment to non-monism and liberty which underpins Amy Gutmann's axiom.

It will be difficult from that perspective to see who is *better placed* than parents, to make the kinds of decision that will have to be made if adequate formative personal development policies are to be constructed. And while it may be admitted that there are circumstances in which the state might be justified in dissolving this parental role, there will be a prima facie case for saying that parents ought to be enabled to determine, as far as possible, what constitutes the best interests of their own children. It follows from this that mechanisms should be put in place to ensure that the views of the school are not inconsistent with parental views and ideally that parents be maximally enabled to *determine* the nature of the singularly correct and comprehensive conception of the good life that will underpin the educational policies used to underpin their child's schooling.[44] If the primary duty of the pluralist state is, as Kekes suggests, to enable its citizens to make good lives for themselves and if parents may legitimately see the formation of their children as an important aspect of *their own* good life, then the state[45] has a duty to maximise parental control over the work of state schools in this area. Whereas liberals will be prepared to override parental wishes where these come into conflict with those cherished by the state, Conservatives will see parents as the primary determinative influence upon the values promoted by the school and will attempt to put in place procedures where parental wishes can prevail. The values promoted by state schools, from this political perspective, should be largely parent-driven, unless a good reason can be found to show that, in particular cases, this will lead to the harm of individuals or society. On this conception state intervention in the values promoted by a particular school is a possibility but ought not to be the order of the day.[46]

This situation is best facilitated by ensuring that policies in the area of personal development are determined at the lowest possible level. If such policies are made at national level then there is virtually no opportunity for groups of parents to influence the process. However, at the level of the individual school community this is possible, giving them the opportunity to adapt to parental requirements and producing as much diversity of school provision as is desired within society, ironically through the adoption by significantly monistic policies on personal development. The nature of school policies would then reflect the degree of pluralism and diversity within existing society and would not constitute an ideological attempt to promote it. Fundamental to the success of this strategy will be an attempt to put in place regulations that remove *as far as possible* the limitations on parental choice of school.

This will not mean that the power of either individual parents or the parental community will have absolute control over the policies of the school. Individual parents will only be able to exercise what power they have through their choice of schools with pre-existing policies and, once part of the parental community of a particular school, they will have just a single voice among many others; it will be the consensus view emergent within that parental community that will prevail over the determination of policy. Even the parents as a body will constitute but one of three powerful influences on the determination of policy for a particular school. Any policy will have to be worked out in relation to the views and expertise of educational professionals working in the school and will have to take account of the views of central government, which might intervene in extremis.[47]

7.9 Pluralism, conservatism and the common school

The above considerations also suggest a good reason for rejecting the other aspect of common schooling set out by Terry McLaughlin, that it should '*..aspire to achieve a broad range of mix in its student body..*' The arguments set out above favour the view that policies for the primary personal development of pupils ought to be worked out at the level of individual schools, on the grounds that this enables the key players (parents-in-community) to influence decision making.[48] The resultant policy will be regarded as most adequate (by parents themselves, as well as by civic pluralists) if its developmental aims reflect, *as strongly as possible, the values of the home.* It is likely that the closer schools come to meeting the common ideal, of maximum cultural diversity within the student population, the smaller will be the chances of achieving the kind of consensus on values that might enable a school policy to be constructed that all with a legitimate interest in the school community would find *acceptable*. This is because, if the school community is a microcosm of the national community, reflecting, in particular, its pluralism, then the *same* problems which plagued the attempt to find an adequate and acceptable basis for a nationally common conception of personal development will also, and inevitably, plague the construction of such a school policy. In pursuing, in such a diverse context, the ideal of *acceptability* to all one would most likely, perhaps necessarily, undermine the chances of achieving a policy that would be deemed *adequate* by all.

Neither, though, should the results of such a school based commitment to maximum diversity amongst the school population be regarded as adequate by educationalists since it will necessarily be so 'thin' as to amount to a failure of the school's duty, as an agent of the community, to fulfil its formative responsibilities. Interestingly, if parents are empowered to arbitrate on the adequacy of the school's personal development policies, it is likely that they will be operating with criteria that match those of conservatives, civic pluralists and, arguably, those liberals who argue in favour of the development of complex autonomy.

Monist policies would no doubt emerge from these arrangements which in themselves failed to reflect or promote the pluralism and diversity of British society. But conservatives and civic pluralists will not see here 'dangers' but obvious virtues and benefits. Arguments could be put forward, as we have seen, to challenge the social democratic assumption that some common conception of civic education is required for a benign social order. The result of allowing school communities a free rein over the construction of the primary component of their personal development policies need not lead to a situation where *no* common elements unite all school policies. It would be possible for the state to facilitate the construction and compulsory implementation of a common conception of civic education but only as a *supplement* to the core element, laid down by the school.[49] The organisational implications of this kind of approach are set out diagramatically in model 4 of appendix 1. This organisational approach would require further clarification, however, since it does not show who will arbitrate finally in situations of *conflict* between the school's policy and the supplementary civic element laid down by the state. I argued earlier that where the policy elements representing the national consensus are allowed to override those that represent those of the family, then there will be an unjustifiable constraint on liberty and pluralism.[50]

In addition, it could be argued that it is only right and just that a system is put in place which enables as many people as possible to give their children the kind of regime of personal development which maximally and positively promotes the values of the home. Such considerations seem particularly pertinent given the current situation whereby financial resources are sequestered, by means of taxation, to provide schools and where parents are *compelled* to relinquish their control over the personal development of their children for large amounts of time to the agents of the state. This can *only* be justified if there is a realistic chance of providing a school whose values meet the criteria of adequacy and acceptability set out above.

Civic pluralists and conservatives will, for these reasons, want any common civic element developed at a national level to be implemented on a voluntary basis. Any common conception developed by the state and distributed to schools will ideally have the status of advice and be designed to ensure that schools take the perceived national needs into account when they construct their own policies. This would not be to give unrestrained power to parents, either as individuals or as a community, since their views will have to be balanced at school level with those of the professionals working in the school. The situation just described is represented by organisational model 5.[51]

Despite the fact that they reject the assumption that all citizens must share the same basic values in order to maintain good social order, conservatives will recognise the need for *some* state veto upon the kinds of values that can be promoted by a school. However, this will be based upon a requirement that the state make out a case to show that a particular school's proposed policy is, in fact, harmful to the social fabric that might have to be tested before an independent body, e.g. a court of law. The resulting framework for the centralised prevention of the implementation of socially divisive or harmful policies would itself be subject to a plurality of influence and would not be based upon a rationalistic, and potentially oppressive, ideal about the conditions of a good society. Conservatives will point, in addition, to the fact that we have a system of law and punishment, as well as the disbenefits of excessive conflict, to suggest that everyone, irrespective of personality or belief, has an interest in *getting along* even with those with whom they fervently disagree. This constitutes a further dimension to the arguments set out above against the need for consensus values to be promoted via the state education system.[52]

The kinds of organisational relationship which conservatives and civic pluralists will favour, set out in models 4 and 5, is currently enjoyed within the state funded system only by three groups. Practising followers of Christianity and Judaism can send their children to state funded schools which provide a personal development regime based primarily upon a particular view of human good. In addition, those parents whose preference is for their children to be developed along the lines of the very thin liberal and ideologically pluralist values which are, arguably, currently prevalent in most other common state schools up and down the country, are also in this position. Conservatives will hope that recent reforms of admissions policy will actually have the effect of *reducing* rather than increasing the diversity amongst the student body of state schools, as a means in turn of improving the chances of building both acceptable and adequate personal development policies within the state sector.[53] I have little doubt that a fair degree of commonality will *emerge* naturally through these mechanisms, and *that* commonality would be, from the conservative perspective, all the better since it would be, in some important sense, natural and free of rationalistic political ideals that might inadvertently stifle real pluralism. The consensus that emerged from this kind of situation would do so not from the deliberations of a group of experts but from the actual practical life of each school community.

Notes

---

1 Mendus (1989), p88f, esp., p92.

2 That is, solely on the quality of a child's informal education beyond the school.

3 Later on in this chapter I will rehearse some arguments to show that parents ought to be able to rely on state funded schools to help them in the task of educating their children into the values of the home, but these will be based in a non-liberal political framework.

4 Levinson (1995) and contra., Taylor, J. (1996).

5 Kekes (1993).

6 Kekes (1993).

7 Ibid., p206.

8 Raz (1986).

9 Op cit., p216.

10 This would mirror the commitment by Macedo to a educational programme designed to develop what he called 'internal' pluralism.

11 See page 158 and the discusion of autonomy in Macedo (1993), where the distinction is presented.

12 This refers of course only to the arguments presented so far in this chapter. Earlier in the study, and attempting to work within the parameters of liberalism, I put forward a list of common virtues which, I suggested, might form the basis of a minimalist common conception of personal development (see appendix 2). The reader should not conclude on the basis of this that I am being inconsistent. My aim is to outline the parameters set by different political models. The liberal framework set out earlier tends to favour a minimalist common conception and it *is within that context* that appendix 2 should be read. The fact that I make the suggestions set out in appendix 2 should not be seen as support for a common conception. The political perspective being set out in the present chapter tends towards a disavowal of any centrally determined common conception.

13 Rescher (1993), p188. The best account in Habermas' own words of his views on the importance of consensus is to be found in, Habermas (1990). A full and sympathetic English discussion is to be found in McCarthy (1978), p291-333.

[14] Ibid., p186.

[15] Ibid., p187.

[16] Ibid., p159. Arguably the market mechanism itself, with its ability to minimise price and maximise quality in direct proportion to the amount of competitive 'conflict' between producers, constitutes perhaps the best example of a social institution benefiting from a lack of agreement.

[17] This kind of assumption was made explicitly by both Haldane and Macedo and used to underpin arguments for a compulsory, nationally common approach to education.

[18] Burke (1790); Oakeshott (1962).

[19] In support of the kind of characterisation of the conservative political tradition offered here I would refer to Norton, P.(ed)(1996),The Conservative Party, p68ff; Evans, B., and Taylor, A.(1996) From Salisbury to Major, p4f and p219ff; and Willetts, D. (1992 and 1994), passim.

[20] 'A state without the means of some change is without the means of its own conservation.', Burke (1789).

[21] A view associated with the leading philosophers of the French and German Enlightenment, Rousseau and Kant.

[22] Hume (1978), especially Bk.III.

[23] See, for example, Honderich (1991), passim.

[24] The influence of parents will be most sought in the areas of personal, moral and cultural development, where a national rational consensus as to the 'best interests' of children is judged to be largely unavailable and largely undesirable. The influence of parents is perhaps less likely to be sought on questions regarding the intellectual and academic development of children since, in that area, a rational professional consensus is judged to be available.

[25] This is quite distinct from some idealised, perhaps nostalgic, view of how things could be or once were, to be used as a model upon which determinative political action can be based. The commitment here is largely to the fact that, due to historical contingencies Britain does have a distinctive culture, but this is an empirical claim which involves no particular substantive characterisation of that culture. There is no inconsistency between saying that, on the one hand, there is a British way of life and, on the other, making the empirical judgement that it is one characterised by liberty and diversity. In view of this policies wrought from a commitment to 'the British way of life' could still be designed to nurture pluralism. I offer this reference to Britain merely as an example, of particular relevant to readers with an interest in the British conservative tradition and I don't intend to suggest that the conservative approach to policy is exclusive to Britain. For further discussion of conservatism in other national settings, see O'Sullivan (1976) pp 32-81.

[26] This perspective is characterised well with reference to the moral life by Oakeshott in an essay called 'The Tower of Babel', in Oakeshott (1962) p46f.

[27] Oakeshott gives an account of two contrasting models of the nature of political association which he calls 'enterprise' and 'civil' association, in Oakeshott (1975), part 2.

[28] Oakeshott (1962), p183-4.

[29] As found, for example in the writings of libertarian liberals like Nozick, where it is used to underpin a rationalistic conception of the 'minimal state'.

[30] For a discussion of this kind of view about the nature of democracy, see also Held (1987), chapter 6. This book should be read by those educationalists who, in the Deweyan tradition, wish to derive educational strategies from a commitment to 'democracy'. It demonstrates how fluid an idea democracy is and points to the need for clear specification and justification of the *model* that is being used/proposed before any educational implications are set out.

[31] Ibid., p185.

[32] Ibid., p188.

[33] McLaughlin (1995), p239.

[34] Gutmann (1993), p3.

[35] And, as has been argued, even those liberals who are committed to the development of complex autonomy.

[36] Strike (1993), p178.

[37] See appendix 1 and discussion of models 2 and 3 on p183.

[38] This is a strategy which is obviously favoured by social democratic liberals and communitarians.

[39] See also Appendix 2.

[40] A view shared by Galston (1989).

[41] Gutmann (1993), p3.

[42] This was demonstrated quite clearly in our examination of the experientialist and non-realist approaches to spiritual development in chapter six, where the attempt to devise strategies to embody liberal restraint, in an attempt to uphold an intuitive adherence to something like Gutmann's principle, led to an implicit adherence to a quite particular tradition of value, broadly characterisable as 'subjectivism'.

[43] Pluralism is used here merely as an empirical claim about the nature of modern Britain.

[44] For an example of this view, see Almond (1994) and discussion of it by McLaughlin (1994).

[45] At least on this conception of its role.

[46] This represents an important reversal of the model preferred by SDLs, where the values promoted by the school should be determined centrally by the state, professionals with guidance from educational philosophers. Parents are then given a right of exit or withdrawal, as it were, in extremis. On the ideal conservative model, it is parents-in-community and school based professional who are placed in the driving seat, and it is the state which is given the right to intervene if it sees problems with a particular school's values policy, and if it can justify its intervention to an

independent body, e.g. a court of law, success depending on whether it could justify its hostility to a particular policy by reference to something like either of the two S2CLPs discussed earlier (see page 86 and chapter 4, note 29).

47 The kinds of organisational arrangement set out here and linked to the conservative perspective, would not imply that state funding should automatically be granted to any set of parents who wished to set up their own school. This might imply a commitment to the existence of extremely small schools with significant dis-economies of scale. However, this doesn't follow from the conservative organisational model. Firstly, the levels of funding and the levels of dis-economy that might be tolerated by any government would have to be balanced against political and economic factors. Secondly, since conservatism has no ideological commitment to pluralism as such, it would not be constrained to enable small groups of parents to set schools up themselves.

48 Arguments which, it should be noted, did not make any *significant* use of libertarian liberal arguments about *parental rights*, but were rather based upon a demonstration of the *undesirability* of a common conception of personal education emerging from any adherence to either, the values of civic pluralism, the conservative distaste for centralised determination of the values of civic society or the liberal demand for the development of complex autonomy.

49 As suggested by Halstead (1995).

50 In chapter 5 I argued that this would seem to be the view most consistent with Rawls' political liberalism, but which would be violated by his own SDL proposals for civic education. So while conservatives might favour such an approach, I have shown that it could be shown to be a requirement of anti-perfectionist liberalism also.

51 See Appendix 1.

52 William Galston, for example, calls for a minimal common conception of civic education suitable for the continuation of liberal democracy. Galston's call will be rejected by conservatives on the grounds that it presumes that politicians or someone can discern objectively and legitimately what the character of this particular political unit is. Galston, speaking of the USA, speaks of 'liberal democracy' and challenges Amy Gutmann's more full blooded account based upon a rival conception of the nature of American society. Conservatives will prefer to set in motion mechanisms by which those with a legitimate interest in making determinative decisions which affect the nature of the character of British society can play their part in the on-going process which is civic society. This will be what it will be naturally, not the result of some rationalistic or ideologically based political plan.
Galston's call for common civic education also embodies the social democratic liberal assumption that if civic education is a good thing then the state should impose it and determine its character. Conservatives will be inclined towards the view that if civic education is important, as social democrats suggest, then its importance ought

to be recognised by parents and teachers, who will ensure that it is accommodated in the school's policies. See Galston (1989).

53 This perspective has been suggested also by writers who might not regard themselves as conservatives, recently, cf., Halstead (1996) and Hargreaves (1994). David Carr has also recently, Carr (1996), written interestingly in favour of what he calls a 'rival traditions approach' to spiritual development in education. This points, as he recognises, towards the kind of pluralist organisational arrangements that are suggested here.

8 Conclusions

In this study I have explored the extent to which a *common* approach to the spiritual development of pupils in state schools is desirable or possible. It has been shown that most writers on the subject assume that commonality of approach is somehow inevitable but they also recognise that special strategies have to be adopted in order to justify the legitimacy of a common approach in a society like Britain characterised by extensive cultural diversity.

Some writers attempt to make reference to the fundamental values of the prevailing culture and attempt to draw educational implications from what amounts to an empirical analysis. In chapter four I showed that further justification is required before empirical claims of this kind can be shown to have the kinds of educational implications that the writers featured there seem to assume.

I have shown that *even* where this kind of approach leads to the promotion of a very *thin* set of apparently unproblematic values, intended to contribute to the common good, the actual outcome of such a commitment, is unacceptable since it is likely to undermine the ability of certain cultural groups to provide an adequate education for their children and actively to promote values of which some do not approve. As a result an adherence to the promotion of common values will actively undermine the values system which some loyal citizens and those who value pluralism hold dear.

In order to establish a framework from which the political suitability of the common approach could be assessed, I set out in the first part of the study to establish a common *language* that might constitute the basis upon which the more controversial issues of development might be discussed. In chapter two, as preparation for this, I put forward a detailed critique of David Carr's attempt to extract an authoritative and distinctive conception of spiritual development from the logic of the word 'spiritual', as it is manifested in common English usage. Firstly, I questioned whether his account *did* accurately reflect the logic of our usage of the word 'spiritual' and, secondly, I showed that, *even if it did* , *that alone* would not be sufficient to justify its authoritive use in an educational context, as he appears to assume. Having argued against Carr, that it is both desirable and possible to attempt to produce a non-evaluative conception of the spiritual for the purposes of educational discussion, I set out in chapter three to develop a characterisation of what I call 'common spirituality'. This was underpinned by an extensive consideration of the logic of human agency and set out in contradistinction to various aspects of the rival accounts of Dewey, MacIntyre and Taylor.

Many thinkers committed to the common conception of spiritual development recognise that the common values that might be promoted are so 'thin' as to be educationally *inadequate*. They adopt strategies to get around this problem which, though well intentioned, actually embody and promote the views of a substantive values tradition. In chapter six I examined two such strategies, the experiential approach and the non-realist approach and demonstrated that neither could be regarded as suitable *even* from the liberal political perspective that inspired them. In order to facilitate that discussion I produced an eight dimensioned framework for mapping any set of *developmental* assumptions that might be used to underpin policy on spiritual education.

The remainder of the study consisted of an attempt to show just how the commitment to commonality of provision is both unnecessary and at the root of many of the problems concerning the development of spirituality in state schools. I linked the commitment to commonality of provision to a very particular political perspective which I dubbed 'social democratic liberalism' and, in chapters four, five and seven, I attempted to demonstrate that the common approach, far from being *required* by the two prominent forms of liberalism (associated with John Rawls and Joseph Raz) could not *even* be justified from those perspectives. The main bulk of chapter five consisted of an attempt to demonstrate that the justificatory mechanisms of Rawls' political liberalism are in fact incapable of sustaining the kind of commitment to a common civic education that he and other liberals regard as one of its primary educational implications. In particular, I showed that his justificatory procedures are incapable of sustaining his own unsubstantiated assertion that the education of children falls exclusively within the *public* domain. At the end of chapter five and at the beginning of chapter seven, I offered detailed arguments to the effect that the kind of educational commitment to the development of autonomy favoured by Joseph Raz appears to require a prior commitment to values *other* than that of autonomy itself. I argued that it required instead something like a commitment to the development of *critical openness* rooted in some *particular* tradition of values. This discussion of autonomy based liberalism brought into focus the issue of *which* set of values might legitimately be transmitted to children in state schools.

I then moved outside the liberal political framework in order to characterise political traditions that explicitly challenge any educational commitment to commonality of provision, preferring instead to empower intermediate institutions to develop values of their own. Having demonstrated that commonality of approach might be seen as problematic from a range of political perspectives, I attempted to set out what I take to be the organisational implications most likely to embody a commitment to pluralism.

I defended these parent-driven organisational arrangements using a range of arguments that complement, but did not rest upon, more familiar arguments based upon parental *rights*. Rather, they drew instead upon points made cumulatively throughout the body of the thesis to show that a common approach might firstly, have unacceptable effects *even* viewed from the liberal perspective and, secondly, would *undermine*, while often being thought to promote, the development of pluralism. Thirdly it would certainly violate the intuition of the conservative tradition that the offices of the state should not be used to *determine* the nature of civil society.

In the course of this I gave a novel characterisation of the non-ideological commitment to pluralism that I take to be built into the conservative tradition. This approach, which I dubbed 'civic pluralism', was contrasted with two other normative accounts of the pluralist political perspective derived from the writings of Kekes and Rawls. By reference to the writings of Kekes and Macedo, I demonstrated the paradoxical nature of any commitment to the development of pluralism through a common conception of personal education, by showing that it would effectively undermine, rather than promote, the external pluralism or thick multiculturalism existing already in society. On the other hand, it was shown that the civic pluralism, which I associate with the conservative approach to policy, *is* capable of nurturing just as much pluralism as will emerge naturally from the day to day life of civil society, *precisely because* it disavows any ideological attachment to *pluralism as such*. In passing I showed that while it might be thought that a multicultural or pluralist education *promotes* the virtue of tolerance, it in fact rules it out.

Appendix 1

Models for the national organisation of spiritual development

These models attempt to show the national effects of attempts by government to influence the personal development of pupils through its control of, or influence over, the nation's schools.

The numbers are used to indicate the differences and similarities between the aims of the professionals and policymakers at different levels within the national system of schooling and their likely outcomes in the lives of individual pupils. I have tried to indicate the exact nature of the intentions of government agencies and professionals in the text that accompanies each model.

Model 1: Determinative communitarian monism

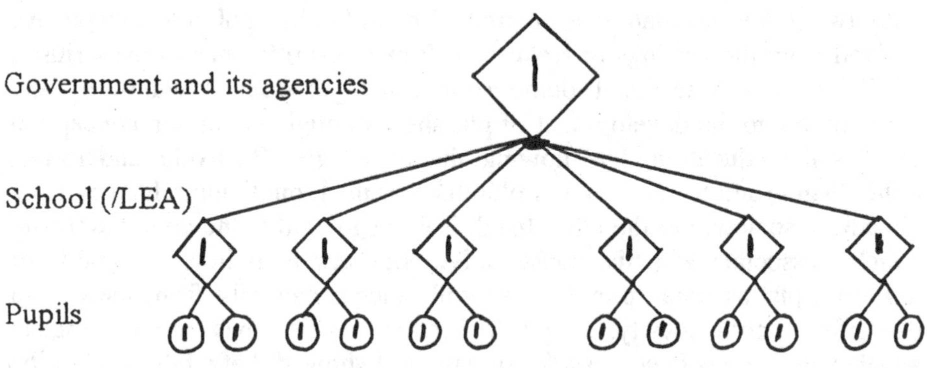

On this model both characterisation of the area of the spiritual and the developmental ideal are, to a significant extent, nationally determined or agreed. As the use of a similar number to represent both the substantive intentions of the policymakers and professionals together with the effects of their policies on the personal development of pupils suggests, the values recognised and promoted throughout the system will be homogenous.

Model 2: Non-interventionist micro(individualistic) pluralism

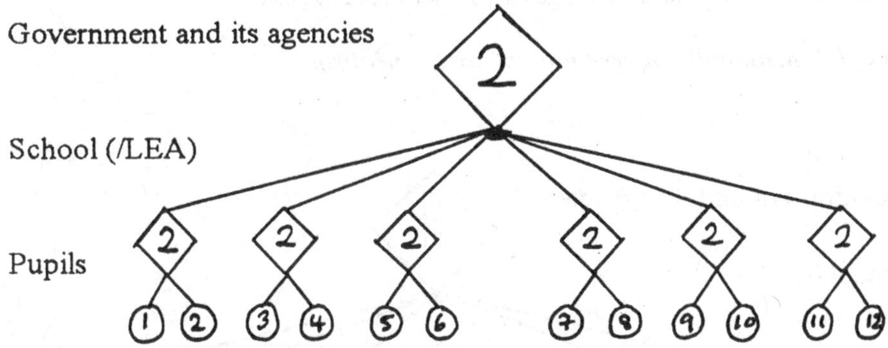

The organisational arrangements of this model are characterised by a broad non-exclusive characterisation of the area of 'spirituality' combined with a reluctance to build in any substantive developmental aims or goals, either at national, local or school level. Policies relate to a commitment to the value of certain procedural values (e.g rational personal reflection, autonomous decision making), themselves seen as 'non-substantive', rather than to a set of substantive values as such. Substantive outcomes will occur but, as the numbers indicate, professionals will take a similar and principled disinterest in the direction of the substantive personal development of individual pupils, who will then develop in a wide range of ways.

Model 3: Non-interventionist pluralist monism

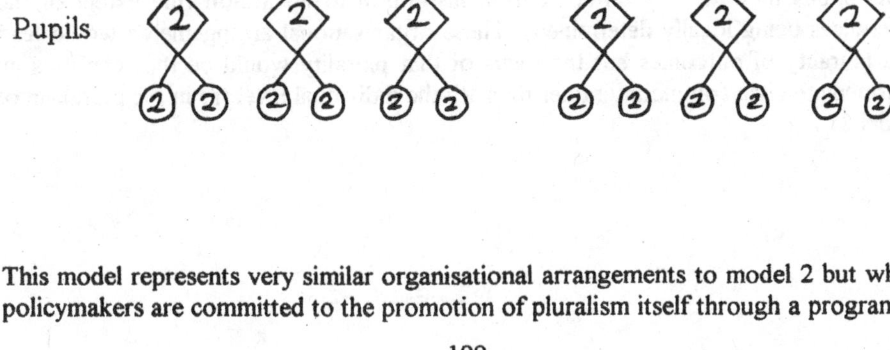

This model represents very similar organisational arrangements to model 2 but where policymakers are committed to the promotion of pluralism itself through a programme of multiculturalist spiritual development (and this could take place under the guise of personal, social or civic education). This model reflects ***explicit*** policy commitments similar to model 2, but the *implicit* situation, is much closer to model 1, with personal outcomes tending towards homogeneity rather than pluralism.

Model 4: Minimally interventionist civic pluralism

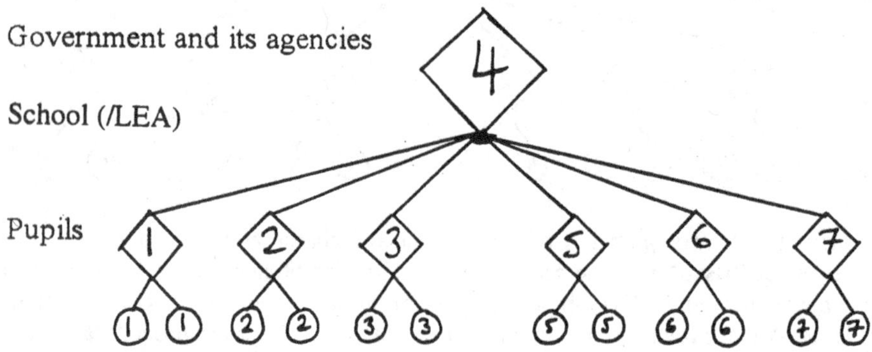

This model is based upon a recognition of the distinction between the area of the 'spiritual' and 'spiritual development'. The government is committed to intervene minimally in the determination of the direction of spiritual development after playing its part in developing a minimally exclusive characterisation of the area of the 'spiritual'. Under this model, government might lay down certain constraints upon schools so the developmental policies constructed at school level don't contravene a thin set of national values, relating perhaps to personal autonomy, democratic citizenship and pluralism. Schools would under this system be licensed to have specific aims of a substantive kind regarding the personal/ spiritual development of its pupils. Here the numbers show that there will be different set of policy intentions operating at national and school level but that the school values regarding the specific development of its pupils may be very different from institution to institution (the extent of the differences being locally determined). These organisational arrangements would lead to a plurality of outcomes but the locus of that plurality would be the school as an intermediate civic community rather than atb the individual level (as in the pluralism of model 2).

Model 5: Non-interventionist civic pluralism

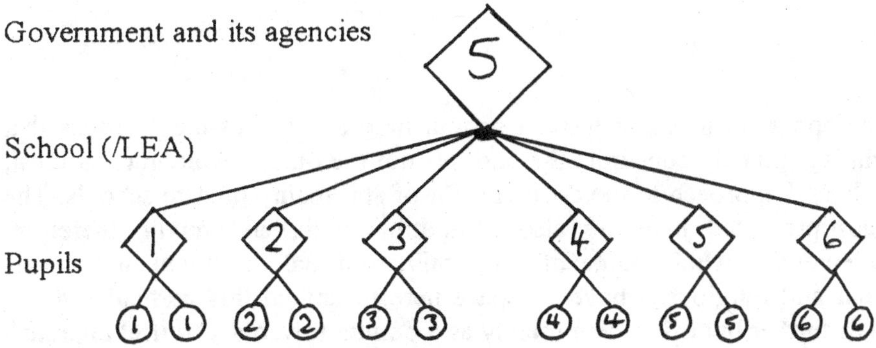

Under this model, the state would not attempt to regulate the conduct of schools in the area of personal development even where those schools were funded by the state. Adoption by a government of this approach would reflect extreme confidence in the ability of schools to be self-regulating communities of parents and professionals, working together in a socially responsible way.

Appendix 2

As an appendix to chapter six, I set out here a series of eight virtues that might legitimately constitute the basic, if not the only, developmental ideal, of a liberal approach to the development of spirituality in state schools. The virtues presented here are also compatible with, and might, therefore, supplement, a whole range of substantive spiritual development policies, secular and religious. I have no space here to defend this particular set of virtues further but offer them merely as a pointer towards a fruitful approach to policy and as a contribution to what I hope will be an on-going debate.

It should be noted that all of these virtues, no matter how apparently self-oriented they may seem, require a recognition of the individual as a part of a wider world and of a community. Each has a personal, social and civic dimension and they are interconnected, as the brief commentary to each one suggests. Given that these virtues are holistic and cut across a range of categories, it would be wrong to describe them using terms derived from one area of life. For example, to describe them collectively as 'civic virtues' would be to ignore their personal significance. Terms like 'personal' or 'moral' would also seem unnecessarily partial. However, to regard them as 'spiritual virtues' sets no limits to them in this way.

Eight spiritual virtues

1. Self-Understanding The ability to understand who one is and the various forces, physical, social and psychological, which have made each person what they are. Such knowledge is the basis of good judgement about one's own life and of others. Connected with this is respect and appreciation for the truth, legitimate authority and tradition (its inevitability, its enabling character and its authority).

2. Confidence and Courage This essential if one is to express one's own thoughts and ideas as a full member of the community and to live life to the full, coping in difficult times.

3. Self-control This is an essential prerequisite of moral, social and civic responsibility. In addition it is an essential part of spiritual development (related to good judgement, a respect for the truth and morality). It is linked to patience, active tolerance, respect for the sincerely held views of others and generosity.

4. Wisdom or Good Practical Judgement Exercised with a respect for the truth about oneself and others and tempered with a sense of justice, this capacity is an essential prerequisite of self directed decision making. It is resourced by knowledge and understanding of the world and one's place as a connected part of it.

5. A Sense of Justice Rooted in an understanding of the experience and needs of all other members of the community, this is connected with a sensitivity to the needs of others. It may be enhanced and expressed through the practice of self control.

6. Self Direction This might be characterised as the ability to direct one's own life, in relation to traditional, self-constructed or discovered goals and values, following a due process of reflection. In turn this will enable one to play a full part in helping to determine the direction of the civic communities of which one is a part. This requires a recognition of the need for a personal response to traditional values and institutions. This might also be characterised as having 'a sense of meaning and purpose'.

7. Imagination Imagination is connected with the ability to glimpse and respond to hidden possibilities which present themselves in experience. It is an essential feature of spiritual and moral development, enabling a person to transcend the present and the self in a range of ways. Imagination allows a person to envisage alternative possibilities, see the solutions to problems and to empathise with others. This capacity is the source of personal satisfaction, underpins the recognition that there is something more to life and to reality than the material and is often the first step in providing solutions and explanations. It also fuels the ability to cope (with, for example, failure, loss, suffering, challenge and success) and underpins the capacity for hope.

8. Generosity This is not just connected with material generosity but with a natural disposition (intimately connected, in turn, with the capacity for self control and justice) to give of oneself and of one's resources in order to make a contribution to the common good or that of another individual. It is linked to democratic virtues of tolerance and compromise.

Bibliography

Ackerman, B. (1980), *Social Justice and the Liberal State,* New Haven, Yale University Press.

Allen, R.T. (1982), 'Rational Autonomy: The Destruction of Freedom',*Journal of Philosophy of Education*, 16(2): pp.199-207.

Allen, R.T. (1990), *Polanyi,* London: Claridge Press.

Almond, B. (1994), 'In Defence of Choice in Education', in Halstead , J.M.(ed), *Parental Choice and Education*, p68-82. London: Kogan Page.

Alston, W. (1991), *Perceiving God*, Cornell: Cornell University Press.

Aristotle, (1980), *The Nicomachean Ethics,* Oxford: Oxford University Press.

Ayer, A.J. (1932), *Language, Truth and Logic,* London: Penguin.

Bailey, C.(1984), *Beyond the Present and the Particular: A Theory of Liberal Education*, London: RKP.

Banner, M. (1990), *The Justification of Science and the Rationality of Religious Belief,* Oxford: Oxford University Press.

Beehler, R. (1985), 'The Schools and Indoctrination', *Journal of Philosophy of Education,* 19:2, pp.261-72.

Beiner, R. (1995), *Theorising Citizenship,* New York: SUNY Press.

Bellah, R. et al. (1985), *The Habits of The Heart,* Berkeley: University of California Press.

Berger, P. and Neuhaus, R.J. (1987), *To Empower People: The Role of Mediating Structures in Public Policy,* Washington, DC: American Enterprise Institute.

Berger, P. (1969), *A Rumour of Angels,* London: Penguin.

Berlin, I. (1969), *Four Essays on Liberty,* Oxford: Oxford University Press.

Berlin, I. (1990), *The Crooked Timber of Humanity,* London: John Murray.

Berstein, R. (1983), *Beyond Objectivism and Relativism,* Oxford: Blackwell.

Best, R.(ed) (1996), *Education, Spirituality and the Whole Child,* London: Cassell.

Bird, G. (1986), *William James,* London: RKP.

Brent, A. (1978), *Philosophical Foundations of the Curriculum,* London: George Allen and Unwin.

Burke, E. (1993), *Reflections on the Revolution in France (1790),* Oxford: OUP.

Callan, E. (1985), 'McLaughlin on Parental Rights', *Journal of Philosophy of Education*, 19(1):pp.111-18.

Callan, E. (1988), *Autonomy and Schooling* , Montreal: McGill-Queen's University Press.

Carr, D. (1992), *Educating the Virtues*, London: RKP.

Carr, D. (1994), 'Spiritual Education: Towards a Distinctive Conception', *Oxford Review of Education* (Autumn).

Carr, D. (1993), 'Moral Values and the Teacher: beyond the paternal and the permissive', *Journal of Philosophy of Education*, 27:2., pp193-207.

Carr, D. (1996), 'Rival Conceptions of Spiritual Education', *Journal of Philosophy of Education*, 30:2, pp.159-178.

Carr,D., and Haldane, J. (1993), *Values and Values Education*, Fife: Centre for Philosophy and Public Affairs.

Carr, W. (1996), *Education and the Struggle for Democracy*, Buckingham: Open University Press.

Carter, S.T. (1993), *The Culture of Disbelief*, New York: Harper Collins.

Cavell, S. (1979), *The Claim of Reason*, Oxford: Oxford University Press.

Cooling, T. (1992), *The Epistemological Foundations of Contemporary Religious Education*, PhD Thesis: University of Birmingham.

Cooling, T. (1994), *A Christian Vision for State Education*, London: SPCK.

Cooper, D. E. (1993), 'Truth and Liberal Education', in White, P. and Barrow, R. (eds), *Beyond Liberal Education: Essays in Honour of Paul Hirst*, London: RKP.

Crittendon, B. (1988), *Parents,The State and the Right to Educate*, Carlton, Australia: Melbourne University Press.

Cupitt, D. (1980), *Taking Leave of God*, London: SCM.

Cupitt, D. (1991), *What is a Story?* London: SCM.

Dancy, J. (1993), *Moral Reasons*, Oxford: Blackwell.

Davis, E. (1993), *Schools and the State*, London: Social Market Foundation.

Devitt, M. (1991), *Realism and Truth*, Oxford, Blackwell.

Dewey, J. (1934), *A Common Faith*, Yale: Yale University Press.

Dewey, J. (1925), *Experience and Nature*, New York: Open Court.

Dewey, J. (1916), *Democracy and Education*, New York: Macmillan.

Dewey, J. (1915), *The School and Society*, Chicago: University of Chicago Press.

Dunne, J. (1993), *Back to the Rough Ground*, Notre Dame and London: Notre Dame University Press.

Elliot, R.K. (1982), 'Objectivity and Education', *Journal of Philosophy of Education*, 16(1): pp.49-62.

Felderhof, M.C.(ed.), (1985), *Religious Education in a Pluralistic Society*, London: Hodder and Stoughton.

Flew, A. (1971), 'Theology and Falsification' in Mitchell, B.,(ed), *The Philosophy of Religion*, Oxford: Oxford University Press.

Franco, P. (1990), *The Political Philosophy of Michael Oakeshott*, New Haven: USA and London.

Galston, W. (1991), *Liberal Purposes: Goods, Virtues and Diversity in the Liberal State*, Cambridge: Cambridge University Press.

Galston, W. (1989), 'Civic Education and the Liberal State', in Rosenblum, N., (ed), *Liberalism and the Moral Life*, Cambridge, Mass: Harvard University Press.

Gardner, P. (1988), 'Religious Upbringing and the Liberal Ideal of Religious Autonomy', *Journal of Philosophy of Education*, 22(1):pp.89-105.

Gardner, P. (1991), 'Personal Autonomy and Religious Upbringing', *Journal of Philosophy of Education*, 25(1):pp.69-81.

Gilliat, P. (1996), 'Spiritual Education and Public Policy', in Best, R.(ed) *Education, Spirituality, and the Whole Child*, London: Cassell.

Grant, R. (1990), *Oakeshott*, London: Claridge Press.

Gray, J. (1986), *Liberalism*, Minneapolis: University of Minnesota Press.

Gray, J. (1989), *Liberalisms*, London: Routledge.

Gray, J. (1993), *Post-Liberalism*, London: Routledge.

Gray, J. (1984), *Hayek on Liberty*, Oxford: Blackwell.

Gray, J. (1995), *Enlightenment's Wake*, London: Routledge.

Greenleaf, W.H. (1966), *Oakeshott's Philosophical Politics*, London.

Griffin, J. (1986), *Well-Being*, Oxford: Oxford University Press.

Grimmitt, M. (1987), *Religious Education and Human Development*, Great Wakering, Essex: McCrimmons.

Gutmann, A. (1987), *Democratic Education*, Princeton: Princeton University Press.

Gutmann, A. (1980), *Liberal Equality*, Cambridge: Cambridge University Press.

Gutmann, A. (1982), 'What's the Use of Going to School?', in Sen,A., and Williams, B.(eds), *Utilitarianism and Beyond*, Cambridge: Cambridge University Press.

Gutmann, A. (1985), 'Communitarian Critics of Liberalism', *Philosophy and Public Affairs*, Vol. 14.

Gutmann, A. (1989), 'Undemocratic Education', in Rosenblum, N.,(ed), *Liberalism and the Moral Life*, Cambridge, Mass: Harvard University Press.

Gutmann, A. (1993), 'Democracy and Democratic Education', in *Philosophy and Education*, 12:1, p.3.

Habermas, J. (1990), *Moral Consciousness and Communicative Action*, Cambridge, Mass: Cambridge University Press.

Hacker, P.M.S. (1975), *Insight and Illusion*, Oxford: Oxford University Press.

Haldane, J. (1992), 'Religious Education in a Pluralist Society: A Philosophical Examination', in Francis,L. and Thatcher, A.(ed), *Christian Perspectives on Education*, pp.181f. Leominster : Gracewing.

Halstead, J.M. (1995), 'Voluntary Apartheid?: Problems of Schooling for Religious and other Minorities in Democratic Societies', in *Journal of Philosophy of Education*, 29:2, p257-252.

Halstead, J.M. (ed), (1994), *Parental Choice and Education: Principles, Policy and Practice*, London: Kogan Page.

Hammond, J. (1992), 'Turning To Tradition', *Journal of Beliefs and Values (NATFHE)*, 13(2): pp.4f.

Hammond, J., and Hay, D. (1992), 'When You Pray Go to Your Private Room: A Reply to Adrian Thatcher', *British Journal of Religious Education*, Summer 1992: pp.145-150.

Hammond, J., Hay, D. et al. (1990), *New Methods in Religious Education Teaching- An Experiential Approach*, Harlow: Oliver and Boyd.

Hardy, D. (1982), 'Truth in Religious Education' , in Hull, J.,(ed), *New Directions in Religious Education*, pp.112f, Lewes: Falmer.

Hare, W. (1979), *Open-Mindedness and Education*, Kingston and Montreal: McGill-Queen's University Press.

Hare, W. (1985), *In Defence of Open-Mindedness*, Kingston and Montreal: McGill-Queen's University Press.

Haworth, L. (1986), *Autonomy: An Essay in Philosophical Psychology and Ethics*, New Haven and London: Yale University Press.

Hay, D. (1992), 'Religious Experience and Values', in Francis, L. and Thatcher, A. (eds), *Christian Perspectives on Education*, Leominster: Gracewing, pp.351ff.

Haydon, G. (1994), 'Conceptions of the Secular in Society, Polity and Schools', *Journal of Philosophy of Education*, 28:1 pp.65-75.

Haydon, G., (ed), (1987), *Education For a Pluralist Society: Philosophical Perspectives on the Swann Report*, London: Bedford Way Papers (30), Institute of Education.

Hayek, F.A. (1963), *The Constitution of Liberty*, London: Routledge.

Hegel, G. W.F. (1977), *Phenomenology of Spirit (1807)*, Oxford: OUP.

Held, D. (1987), *Models of Democracy*, Cambridge: Polity Press.

Hick, J. (1967/8), 'Religious Faith as Experiencing -as', in Vesey (ed), *Royal Institute of Philosophy Lectures: Talk of God*, Vol.2.

Hill, B. (1989), 'Spiritual Development in the Education Reform Act', *British Journal of Educational Studies*, 37: pp.169-182.

Hill, B. (1990), 'Will and Should the Religious Studies appropriate to Schools in a Pluralist Society Foster Religious Relativism?', *British Journal of Religious Education*, 12:3, pp126-136.

Hirst, P.H. (1972), 'Christian Education: A Contradiction in Terms', *Learning For Living*, 11:4, pp.6-10.

Hirst, P.H. (1974), *Moral Education in a Secular Society*, London: Hodder and Stoughton.

Hirst, P.H. (1985), 'Education and Diversity of Belief' in M.C.Felderhof (ed), *R.E. in a Pluralistic Society*, pp.5-17, London: Hodder and Stoughton.

Hirst, P.H. (1993), 'Education, Knowledge and Practices', in Barrow, R., and White, P. (eds), *Beyond Liberal Education: Essays in Honour of Paul Hirst*, London: Routledge.

Holmes, M.,(1992), *Education Policy for Pluralist Democracy: The Common School, Choice and Diversity,* London: Falmer.

Honderich, T. (1990), *Conservatism,* London: Hamish Hamilton.

Horton, J.(ed), (1993), *Liberalism, Multiculturalism and Toleration,* London:Macmillan.

Horton,J., and Mendus, S. (1994), *After MacIntyre,* Cambridge: Polity Press.

Houlgate, S. (1991), *Freedom, Truth and History: An Introduction to Hegel's Philosophy,* London Routledge.

Hudson, W.D. (1982), 'Educating, Socialising and Indoctrination: A Reply to Tazos Kazipedes', *Journal of Philosphy of Education,* 16(2): pp.167-72.

Hull, J.M.(ed), (1982), *New Directions in Religious Education,* Lewes: Falmer.

Hume, D. (1978), *A Treatise of Human Nature* (1888), Oxford: Oxford University Press.

Huxley, A. (1932), *Brave New World,* London: Chatto & Windus.

James, W. (1985), *The Varieties of Religious Experience,* Cambridge: Harvard University Press.

Jonathan, R. (1997), 'Illusory Freedoms: Liberalism, Education and the Market', *Journal of Philosophy of Education,* 31(1): pp.1-217 (Special Issue).

Kant, I. (1953), *Groundwork of the Metaphysic of Morals,* trans. H.J.Paton, London: Hutchinson.

Katz, S. (ed),(1978), *Mysticism and Philosophical Analysis,* London: Sheldon Press.

Kazipedes, T. (1982), 'Educating, Socialising and Indoctrinating', *Journal of Philosophy of Education,* 16(2):pp.155-66.

Kazipedes, T.,(1987), 'Indoctrination, Doctrines and the Foundations of Rationality', in *Philosophy of Education: Proceedings of the 43rd Annual Meeting of the Philosophy of Education Society,* Arnstine and Arnstine (eds), pp.229-49.

Kekes, J. (1988), *The Examined Life,* Cranbury, New Jersey: Associated University Presses.

Kekes, J. (1989), *Moral Tradition and Individuality,* Princeton: Princeton University Press.

Kekes, J. (1990), *Facing Evil,* Princeton: Princeton University Press.

Kekes, J. (1993), *The Morality of Pluralism,* Princeton: Princeton University Press.

Kekes, J. (1995), *Moral Wisdom and Good Lives,* Ithaca and London: Cornell University Press.

Kenny, A.J.P. (1973), *Wittgenstein,* London: Penguin.

Kerr, F. (1986), *Theology After Wittgenstein,* Oxford: Blackwell.

Kymlicka, W. (1989), *Liberalism, Community and Culture,* Oxford: Oxford University Press.

Laura, R.S. and Leahy, M. (1989), 'Religious Upbringing and Rational Autonomy', *Journal of Philosophy of Education*, 23(2): pp.253-65.

Levin, M.D. (ed), (1993), *Modernity and the Hegemony of Vision*, Berkeley: University of California Press.

Locke, J. (1983), *A Letter Concerning Toleration*, (ed) James H. Tully. Indianapolis: Hackett.

Loughran, T. (1994), *Freedom and Good in the Thomistic Tradition* Faith and Philosophy, 11:3 (July).

Macedo, S. (1990), *Liberal Virtues*, Oxford: Clarendon.

Macedo, S. (1996), 'Transformative Constitutionalism and the Case of Religion' in *Philosophy of Education Society of Great Britain, Conference Papers*, 1996, pp.6-17.

Macedo, S. (1995), 'Multiculturalism for the Religious Right? Defending Liberal Civic Education', *Journal of Philosophy*, 29:2, p.223-238.

Macedo, S. (1993), *Liberal Virtues*, Oxford: Oxford University Press.

MacIntyre, A. (1981), *After Virtue*, London: Duckworth.

MacIntyre, A. (1988), *Whose Justice, Which Rationality?* London Duckworth.

Martin-Soskice, J. (1985), *Metaphor and Religious Language*, Oxford: Oxford University Press.

Mc Carthy, T. (1978), *The Critical Theory of Jurgen Habermas*, Cambridge: Polity Press.

Mc Dowell, J. (1994), *Mind and World*, Cambridge, USA: Harvard University Press.

McLaughlin, T.H.(1994), 'The Scope of Parent's Educational Rights', in Halstead , J.M. (ed), *Parental Choice and Education*, London: Kogan Page, p94-107.

McLaughlin, T.H. (1984), 'Parental Rights and the Religious Upbringing of Children', *Journal of Philosophy of Education*, 18(1): pp.75-83.

McLaughlin, T.H. (1985), 'Religious Upbringing and Liberal Values', *Journal of Philosophy of Education*, 19(1): pp.119-26.

McLaughlin, T.H. (1995), 'Liberalism, Education and the Common School', in *Journal of Philosophy of Education*, 29:2. pp.239-255.

McLaughlin, T.H. (1996), 'Education of the Whole Child?', in Best (ed), *Education, Spirituality and the Whole Child*, London: Cassell.

McNaughton, D., (1988), *Moral Vision*, Oxford: Blackwell.

Mendus, S. (1989), *Toleration and the Limits of Liberalism*, London: Macmillan.

Mooney, F. (1990), *Law, Religion, Education and the Common Good: Boundaries Dimly Perceived*, Notre Dame, Indiana: University of Notre Dame Press.

Morgan, K. (1974), 'Socialisation, Social Models and the Open Education Movement', in Nyberg, D (ed), *The Philosophy of Open Education* London: RKP.

Mott-Thornton, K. (1996a), 'Experience, Critical Realism and the Schooling of Spirituality', in Best (ed), *Education, Spirituality and the Whole Child* London: Cassell.

Mott-Thornton, K. (1996b), 'Language, Dualism and Experiential Religious Education', *British Journal of Religious Education*, 18:3, pp155-165.

Mulhall, S. and Swift, A.,(1992), *Liberals and Communitarians*, Oxford: Blackwell.

Mulhall, S. (1990), *On Being in the World*, London: RKP.

Murdoch, I. (1970), *The Sovereignty of Good*, London: RKP.

Murdoch, I. (1992), *Metaphysics as a Guide to Morals*, London: Penguin.

Nagel, T. (1986), *The View From Nowhere*, Oxford: Oxford University Press.

National Curriculum Council (NCC), (1993), *Spiritual and Moral Development: A Discussion Paper*, York: NCC (Reissued by the School Curriculum and Assessment Authority, (1995), London: SCAA).

Nell (O'Neill), O. (1975) *Acting on Principle*, New York: Columbia University Press.

Newbigin, L. (1982), 'Teaching Religion in a Secular Plural Society', in *New Directions in Religious Education*, Hull, J.(ed), Lewes: Falmer.

Newbigin, L. (1995), *Proper Confidence*, SPCK: London.

Newby, M. (1996), 'Towards a secular concept of Spiritual Maturity', in Best (ed), *Education, Spirituality and the Whole Child*, London: Cassell.

Newton-Smith, W.,(1981), *The Rationality of Science*, London: RKP.

Nicholls, D., (1974), *Three Varieties of Pluralism*, New York: St. Martin's Press.

Nisbet, R. (1986), *Conservatism: Dream and Reality*, Milton Keynes: Open University Press.

Norman, E. (1992), 'Christian Politics in a Society of Plural Values', in Cohn-Sherbok, D., and McLallan, D. (eds), *Religion in Public Life*, New York: St. Martin's Press, pp.17-28.

Nouwen, H. (1975), *Reaching Out: The Three Movements of The Spiritual Life*, New York: Doubleday.

Nozick, R. (1974), *Anarchy, State and Utopia*, New York: Basic Books.

National Union of Teachers (NUT), Discussion Paper. (1984), *Religious Education in a Multi-Faith Society*, London: National Union of Teachers.

Nyberg, D. (1974), *The Philosophy of Open Education*, London: RKP.

Oakeshott, M. (1962), Rationalism in Politics and Other Essays, London: Methuen.

Oakeshott, M. (1933), *Experience and Its Modes*, Cambridge: Cambridge University Press.

Oakeshott, M. (1975), *On Human Conduct*, Oxford.

Office for Standards in Education (Ofsted). (1994), *Spiritual, Moral, Social and Cultural Development: An Ofsted Discussion Paper*, London: Ofsted.

Office for Standards in Education(Ofsted). (1993), *Handbook for the Inspection of Schools*, London: HMSO.

O'Keefe, B. (1988), *Schools For Tomorrow: Building Walls or Building Bridges* Lewes: Falmer.

O'Sullivan, N. (1976), *Conservatism,* London: J.M.Dent and Sons.

Peacocke, A. (1983), *Intimations of Reality* Notre Dame: Notre Dame Press.

Phenix, P.H. (1975), 'Transcendence and the Curriculum' in Pinar, W.F. (ed), *Curriculum Theorising: The Reconceptualists,* Berkeley: McCutchan Publishing Corporation.

Phillips, D.C. (1975), 'The Anatomy of Autonomy', *Educational Philosophy and Theory,* 7(2): pp.1-12.

Phillips, D.Z. (1976), *Religion Without Explanation,* Oxford: Blackwell.

Pippin. R. (1989), *Hegel's Idealism: The Satisfactions of Self-Consciousness,* Cambridge: CUP.

Plantinga, A. (1983), '*Reason and Belief in God*', in Plantinga ,A., and Wolsterhoff, N.,(eds), *Faith and Rationality,* Notre Dame, Indiana: Notre Dame University Press.

Polanyi, M. (1958), *Personal Knowledge,* London: Routledge.

Polanyi, M. (1946), *Science, Faith and Society,* Oxford: OUP.

Polanyi, M. (1966), *The Tacit Dimension,* London: Routledge.

Priestley, J. (1985), 'Towards Finding the Hidden Curriculum', *British Journal of Religious Education,* 16(3): pp.112-19.

Proudfoot, W. (1985), *Religious Experience,* Berkeley: University of California Press.

Rawls, J. (1980), 'Kantian Constructivism in Moral Theory', *Journal of Philosophy,* Vol. 77.

Rawls, J. (1993), *Political Liberalism,* New York,: Columbia University Press.

Raz, J. (1986), *The Morality of Freedom,* Oxford: Oxford University Press.

Rescher, N. (1993), *Pluralism: Against the Demand for Consensus,* Oxford: Clarendon Press.

Rockefeller, S. (1991), *John Dewey: Religious Faith and Democratic Humanism,* Columbia: Columbia University Press.

Rosenblum, N. (ed), (1989), *Liberalism and the Moral Life,* Cambridge, USA:Cambridge University Press.

Sandel, M. (1984), 'Morality and the Liberal Ideal', *New Republic,* Vol.190(May).

Sandel, M. (1984), 'The Procedural Republic and the Unencumbered Self', *Political Theory,* Vol.12.

Sandel, M. (1982), *Liberalism and the Limits of Justice,* Cambridge: Cambridge University Press.

Scruton, R. (1984), *The Meaning of Conservatism,* London: Macmillan.

Scruton, R., Ellis-Jones, A., O'Keefe,D. (1985), *Education and Indoctrination,* Harrow, Middx: Educational Research Centre.

Seligman, A.,(1993), *The Idea of Civil Society,* New York: Free Press.

Sherry, P. (1981), 'Von Hugel: Philosophy and Spirituality', *Religious Studies,* 17: pp.1-18.

Sherry, P. (1977), *Religion, Truth and Language Games,* London: Macmillan.
Smith, J.E. (1992), *America's Philosophical Vision,* Chicago: Chicago University Press.
Smith, J.W.D. (1974), *Religion and Secular Education,* St. Andrews: St.Andrews Press.
Spong, J. (1994), *Resurrection: Myth or Reality?* London: Harper Collins.
Standish, P. (1992), *Beyond the Self*, Aldershot, UK: Ashgate.
Standish, P. (1995), 'Post-modernism and the education of the whole child', in Journal of Philosophy of Education, 29:1, pp121-35.
Stanesby, D. (1985), *Science, Reason and Religion,* London: RKP.
Starkings, D. ed. (1993), *Religion and the Arts in Education: Dimensions of Spirituality,* London: Hodder and Stoughton.
Starkings, D. (1987), 'How Should R.E. Change People?', in Westminster Studies in Education, 10: pp.53-62.
Strike, K. (1993), 'Ethical Discourse and Pluralism', in Strike, K.A., and Ternasky, L.P.(eds), *Ethics for Professionals in Education,* New York: Teachers College Press.
Swann Report. (1985), *Education For All: The Report of the Committee of Equiry into the Education of Children from Ethnic Minority Groups.* London: HMSO.
Tamir, Y.,(1995), 'Two Concepts of Multiculturalism', in *Journal of Philosophy of Education,* 29:2, pp.161-172.
Tarcov, N. (1984), *Locke's Education for Liberty,* Chicago: Chicago University Press.
Taylor, C. (1989), *Sources of the Self,* Cambridge: Cambridge University Press.
Taylor, C. (1992), 'Multiculturalism and the Politics of Recognition', in Taylor, C. and Gutmann, A (ed), *Multiculturalism and the Politics of Recognition,* Princeton, USA: Princeton University Press, pp 25-73.
Taylor, J. (1996), 'A Plea for Parental Choice: A Classic Liberal Critique of the Detached School', *Philosophy of Education Society of Great Britain, Conference Papers,* pp.142-148.
Thatcher, A. (1992), 'The Recovery of Christian Education', in *Christian Perspectives on Education,* Francis, L. and Thatcher (eds), A., Leominster: Gracewing, pp.273-81.
Thatcher, A. (1991), 'A Critique of Inwardness in Religious Education', *British Journal Of Religious Education,* 14(1): pp.22-27.
Thatcher, A. (1992), 'Radical Christian Spirituality', *Journal of Beliefs and Values,* (NATFHE), 13(2): pp.2f.
Thiesson, E.J. (1993), *Teaching For Commitment,* Leominster: Gracewing.
Tiles, J.E. (1988), *Dewey,* London: Routledge.
Tooley, J. (1995), *Disestablishing the School,* Aldershot, UK: Ashgate.
Walker, R. C. (1980), *The Coherence Theory of Truth,* London: RKP.

Walzer, M. (1992), 'Comment', in Taylor, C. and Gutmann, A. (ed.), *Multiculturalism and the Politics of Recognition,* p 99-103, Princeton, USA: Princeton University Press.

Ward, K. (1983), 'Is Autonomy An Educational Ideal?', *Educational Analysis* 5(1): pp.47-55.

Ward, K. (1992), 'Is a Christian State a Contradiction in Terms?', in Cohn-Sherbok, D. and McLallan, D.,(eds), *Religion in Public Life*, New York: St. Martin's Press, pp.5-16.

Ward, K. (1982) *Holding Fast to God,* London: SPCK.

Webster, D. (1990), 'A Spiritual Dimension For Education?', in *Christian Perspectives For Education*, Francis, L. and Thatcher, A. (eds), Leominster: Gracewing, pp.356-364.

White, J. (1990), *Education and the Good Life,* London: Kogan Page.

White, J. (1994), 'Instead of Ofsted', *Cambridge Journal of Education,* 24:3, pp.372-374.

White, P. (1996), *Civic Virtues and Public Schooling: Educating Citizens for a Democratic Society,* New York: Teacher's College Press.

White, P. (1994), 'Parental Choice and Education for Citizenship', in Halstead , J.M.(ed), *Parental Choice and Education,* London: Kogan Page, pp.83-93.

White, P. (1991), 'Parent's Rights, Homosexuality and Education', *British Journal of Educational Studies*, 39:4, pp.398-408.

White, P., (ed), (1989), *Personal and Social Education: Philosophical Perspectives,* London: Kogan Page.

Willetts, D. (1992), *Modern Conservatism,* London: Penguin.

Willetts, D. and Gray, J. (1997), *Is Conservatism Dead?,* London: Social Market Foundation.

Williams, B. (1985), *Ethics and the Limits of Philosophy*, London: Fontana.

Williams, R. (1984), 'Theological Realism', *Modern Theology, 1.*

Wittgenstein, L. (1953), *Philosophical Investigations,* Oxford: Blackwell.

Wittgenstein, L. (1969), *On Certainty,* Oxford: Blackwell.

Wright, A. (1996), 'Language and Experience in the Hermeneutics of Religious Understanding', *British Journal of Religious Education*, 18:3, pp166-180.

Index

References from notes indicated by 'n' after page reference